Annie Brassey

Sunshine and Storm in the East

Annie Brassey

Sunshine and Storm in the East

ISBN/EAN: 9783743387829

Manufactured in Europe, USA, Canada, Australia, Japa

Cover: Foto ©Lupo / pixelio.de

Manufactured and distributed by brebook publishing software (www.brebook.com)

Annie Brassey

Sunshine and Storm in the East

SUNSHINE AND STORM IN THE EAST,

OR *CRUISES TO*

CYPRUS AND CONSTANTINOPLE.

BY

MRS BRASSEY,

AUTHOR OF 'A VOYAGE IN THE SUNBEAM.'

WITH UPWARDS OF 100 ILLUSTRATIONS
CHIEFLY FROM DRAWINGS BY THE HON. A. Y. BINGHAM.

Disembarkation of the Sultan at Mosque at Funduklı.

LONDON:
LONGMANS, GREEN, AND CO.
1880.

All rights reserved.

DEDICATION.

To the

BRAVE TRUE-HEARTED SAILORS OF ENGLAND,

OF ALL RANKS AND SERVICES,

These Pages are Dedicated.

I love the sailor: his eventful life,
His generous spirit—his contempt of danger—
His firmness in the gale, the wreck, the strife:
And though a wild and reckless ocean-ranger,
God grant he make that port, when life is o'er,
Where storms are hushed and billows break no more.

PREFACE.

My tables, my tables,—meet it is, I set it down.

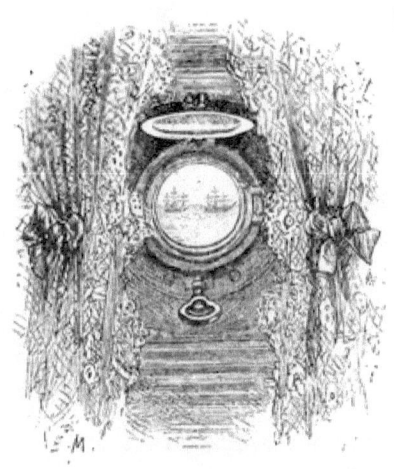

ON our return from a cruise to the Arctic Circle in 1874, after remaining but a few days in England, we started on a voyage to the East. It had always been a dream of my youth to visit Constantinople, the city of gilded palaces and mosques, of harems and romance—to skim the placid waters of the Bosphorus and the Golden Horn; and the present time seemed to furnish an excellent opportunity to do all this, and to revisit the Ionian Islands. I continued my old practice of writing long journal letters home to my father, to be afterwards circulated among other relatives and more intimate friends. The

'Voyage in the Sunbeam' has been so kindly received that I am encouraged to present these letters also to the public.

In 1878 we found ourselves once more in the Mediterranean. This cruise included a visit to Cyprus and a second visit to Constantinople. Melancholy indeed seemed the change in the Turkish capital during the four years since our last visit—a change from all that was bright and glittering to all that was dull and miserable and wretched. It may perhaps be interesting to the reader to compare impressions formed under circumstances so widely different, though the narrative must necessarily appear disjointed and disconnected on account of the intervening years. The title of the book is meant to indicate the change which had passed over Constantinople in the period between our two visits.

A journal kept while cruising in the Mediterranean, though less novel than the story of a family yachting voyage round the world, may yet present some points of interest to the many friendly readers of 'A Voyage in the Sunbeam.'

For the design on the cover I am indebted to M. Gustave Doré. The artist seeks to convey the idea that the good genii of the sea, pleased with the 'Sunbeam's' frequent and lengthened visits to their ocean home, are spreading out before her a panorama of all the countries of the world, to tempt her to start once more for 'fresh woods and pastures new,' Constantinople and Cyprus being faintly indicated on the scroll.

The illustrations are chiefly from drawings by the Hon. A. Y. Bingham; a few are from other artists and from photographs taken by myself. They have been all engraved on wood by Mr. Pearson.

ANNIE BRASSEY.

Errata.

Page 165, line 3, *for* Cecillo *read* Circello.
,, ,, 6, *for* Port d'Ango *read* Porto d'Anzio.
2, ,, 22, *for* paat *read* pal.
,, 369, ,, 22, *for* Allen *read* Allix.

CONTENTS.

PART I.

CONSTANTINOPLE, IONIAN ISLANDS. (1874.)

CHAPTER		PAGE
I.	Our Start—Ryde, Tangier, and Gibraltar	1
II.	Tetuan, Ceuta, and Sicily	16
III.	Athens, Greece, and the Archipelago	32
IV.	Constantinople	51
V.	The Bosphorus and its Palaces	63
VI.	The Black Sea, Skutari, Broussa, Harems	75
VII.	Visits from Turkish Ladies. Feast of Bairam. Walls and Palaces of Constantinople	101
VIII.	The Sea of Marmora, Dardanelles, Smyrna, Ephesus, Chios, and Milo	112
IX.	Zante, Ithaca, Cephalonia, Corfu, and Albania	131
X.	Paxos, Spartivento, Messina, and Naples	148
XI.	Bastia, Nice, Paris, and Home	165

PART II.

CYPRUS, CONSTANTINOPLE. (1878.)

CHAPTER		PAGE
I.	Portsmouth, Brest, and Vigo	175
II.	Cadiz, Seville, and Gibraltar	193
III.	Oran and Cagliari	212
IV.	Naples, Pompeii, Pæstum, Capri, Messina, and Cyprus	232
V.	Island of Cyprus.—Port Papho, Limasol, Larnaka	250
VI.	Nikosia, Mathiati, and Famagousta	264
VII.	Kyrenia, Morfu, Kikko, and Karavastasia	290
VIII.	Rhodes, Besika Bay, the Dardanelles	307
IX.	Artaki Bay, English Fleet, and Constantinople	324
X.	Adrianople	354
XI.	Constantinople again, Gallipoli, Syra, and Milo	367
XII.	Milo to Malea and Malta	387
XIII.	From Malta to Marseilles	396
XIV.	Home once more	405

APPENDIX.

1874.

	PAGE
LOG OF YACHT'S HOMEWARD JOURNEY FROM NICE	411
LIST OF OUR PARTY, CREW, AND SERVANTS	415
SUMMARY OF THE VOYAGE	417

1878.

LIST OF OUR PARTY, CREW, AND SERVANTS	420
PROGRAMME OF THE ORAN RACES	422
TEMPERATURE OF CYPRUS	426
NOTE A	430
NOTE B	431
NOTE C	432
SUMMARY OF THE VOYAGE	434
POSTSCRIPT	437
INDEX	439

LIST OF ILLUSTRATIONS.

[*Engraved by G. Pearson.*]

MAPS.

MAP SHOWING TRACKS OF THE 'SUNBEAM' IN 1874-5
AND 1878 . . *At commencement, before Frontispiece*
MAP OF THE ISLAND OF CYPRUS, SHOWING THE TRACK
OF THE 'SUNBEAM' *At end of Book, after Index*

FULL-PAGE ILLUSTRATIONS.

HEADQUARTERS, NIKOSIA .	*Bingham* .	*Frontispiece*	
DINING SALOON .	*Photograph*	*To face p.*	76
THE 'SUNBEAM' IN A GALE OFF MILO	*Bingham* .	,,	126
VIGO BAY	*. Bingham* .	,,	174
KYRENIA	*. Bingham* .	,,	290
CONVENT OF LA PAIS	*. Bingham* .	,,	292
MEETING SIR GARNET WOLSELEY	*. Bingham* .	,,	296
NAUMACHIA AT CYZICUS .	*. Bingham* .	,,	330
ADRIANOPLE — BRIDGE OVER THE TUNJA	*Bingham* .	,,	358

WOODCUTS IN TEXT.

		PAGE
Disembarkation of the Sultan at Mosque at Fundukli .	Photograph by Mrs. Brassey .	Title-page
A Peep through a Porthole .	Mott	vii
A Rough Night for Boating .	Bingham .	1
Cape St. Vincent .	Bingham	7
Tangier . .	Photograph	9
Bargaining in the Bazaar	Hodgson	11
Moorish Musician	Photograph	13
Woman of Tetuan .	Photograph	21
Gibraltar .	Bingham .	25
Deck View	Photograph .	33
Greek Costume .	Photograph	38
Athens .	Photograph by Mrs. Brassey .	40
Woman of Athens	Photograph	42
The Promenade at Euripo . .	Photograph by Mrs. Brassey .	45
Castle of Euripo	Photograph by Mrs. Brassey .	47
General View of Constantinople	Preziosi	51
Tower of Hero and Leander, in the Bosphorus	Photograph	55
Fountain St. Sophia	Photograph .	59
Turkish Waist Clasp .	Photograph	62
Palace of Dolmabagtcheh	Photograph .	66

LIST OF ILLUSTRATIONS.   xvii

		PAGE
YACHT'S DECKHOUSE	*Photograph*	70
TURKISH LADY	*Photograph*	74
DANCING DERVISHES	*Photograph*	77
TURKISH CEMETERY	*Photograph by Mrs. Brassey*	82
SOLDIERS' CEMETERY AT SKUTARI	*Photograph*	83
THE SULTAN'S CAÏQUE	*Mott*	85
BROUSSA FROM HÔTEL D'OLYMPE.[1]	*Preziosi*	90
THE SULTAN'S YOUNGEST SON	*Photograph*	111
ORIGINAL SKETCH BY THE SULTAN	*Abdul Aziz*	113
SMYRNA CAMEL	*Photograph*	117
AQUEDUCT NEAR EPHESUS	*Photograph by Mrs. Brassey*	119
A CAMP ON THE ROAD	*Photograph by Mrs. Brassey*	122
MUÑIE, MR. CRAKE, EVIE ROBINSON, AND FÉLISE	*Photograph by Mrs. Brassey*	125
RUINS OF AMPHITHEATRE AT MILO	*Photograph by Mrs. Brassey*	128
THE 'SUNBEAM' WHEN FIRST LAUNCHED	*Photograph*	130
A CHURCH AT ZANTE	*Photograph by Mrs. Brassey*	131
OLIVE-GATHERING IN CEPHALONIA	*Photograph by Mrs. Brassey*	134
AN EXTRA BATH	*Bingham*	141
SOME OF OUR CREW	*Photograph by Mrs. Brassey*	144
CITADEL OF CORFU	*Photograph*	145

[1] Incorrectly printed, in the inscription, 'Hôtel de l'Europe.'

LIST OF ILLUSTRATIONS.

		PAGE
An Unpleasant Demand for Ammunition	*Bingham*	147
The Smoking Room	*Photograph*	154
Amphitheatre at Taormina	*Photograph*	157
Harbour at Bastia	*Photograph*	165
Last of the 'Eurydice'	*Bingham*	175
The 'Assistance' running into us	*Bingham*	178
Dining under Difficulties	*Bingham*	180
A small Derelict	*Mott*	187
Off the Bayona Islands	*Bingham*	190
Tobacco Manufactory at Seville	*Bingham*	199
A Water Party	*Bingham*	206
Colliding nearly	*Bingham*	209
Spanish Market Boat	*Bingham*	211
Oran Harbour	*Photograph*	212
Moorish Girl	*Photograph*	215
Our State Room	*Photograph*	219
Amphitheatre at Cagliari	*Photograph*	229
Sardinian Clothes-dealer	*Photograph*	231
Bay of Naples	*Bingham*	233
'The Image of him!'	*Bingham*	240
Landing-place at Capri	*Bingham*	243
Woman of Capri	*Bingham*	244
Steps at Anacapri	*Barclay, R.A.*	246
Cape Spada	*Bingham*	248
Earring from Curium	*Mott*	249
Port Papho	*Bingham*	250
Mounting the 'Minotaur'	*Bingham*	252
Earring from Curium	*Mott*	256

LIST OF ILLUSTRATIONS.

		PAGE
LARNAKA	*Bingham*	261
GOLD EARRING	*Mott*	263
'WILL THEY EVER HEAR?'	*Bingham*	264
ASKING FOR A PILOT	*Bingham*	265
ARRIVAL IN CAMP	*Bingham*	267
RUINS OF FAMAGOUSTA	*Bingham*	284
ANCIENT GUNS	*Bingham*	287
'GET UP, YOU LAZY MAN!'	*Bingham*	289
A HEAVY LOAD	*Bingham*	294
KIND ATTENTIONS	*Bingham*	299
PRISON AT RHODES	*Harry Johnson*	306
RHODES	*Müller*	307
STREET OF THE KNIGHTS	*Photograph*	310
'MA'S DONKEY MAN'	*Bingham*	312
UPSIDE DOWN	*Bingham*	316
BONNER'S PIGEON	*Mott*	320
'SUNBEAM' AGROUND	*Bingham*	322
'WHY, HERE'S THE OWL!'	*Mott*	323
LUNCH WITH A TURK	*Bingham*	330
'YOU ARE NOT A TENNIS BALL!'	*Bingham*	333
MOSQUE OF SULTAN ACHMED	*Photograph*	335
REFUGEES AT PRINCESS NAZLI'S DOOR	*Bingham*	339
PIGEONS AT THE MOSQUE	*Bingham*	344
PICK-A-BACK	*Bingham*	346
PRINCESSES EMBARKING	*Bingham*	349
TURKISH BRACELET	*Mott*	351
BULGARIAN EARRING	*Mott*	353
BULGARIAN EARRING	*Mott*	359

		PAGE
REFUGEES ON TRAIN	*Mott*	364
EARRINGS AND NECKLET IN ONE .	*Mott* .	366
BULGARIAN CHILD'S BRACELET.	*Mott*	368
CHILDREN'S NURSERY .	*Photograph*	373
BRAVING THE ELEMENTS .	*Bingham*	378
SYRA .	*Photograph*	380
HERMIT OF MALEA .	*Bingham*	389
A QUIET TIME	*Mott*	395
THE MEET AT BATTLE ABBEY	*Bingham*	407

PART I.

CONSTANTINOPLE AND THE IONIAN ISLANDS.

1874.

Lying off Ryde.

SUNSHINE AND STORM IN THE EAST

(1874-1878).

CHAPTER I.

OUR START—RYDE, TANGIER, AND GIBRALTAR.

*One woe doth tread upon another's heels,
So fast they follow.*

ON *Friday, September 3rd*, 1869, we had started from Cowes in the 'Meteor' for the opening of the Suez Canal. In more ways than one that cruise turned out badly, as the equinoctial gales detained us three weeks at Brest, and the yacht had been driven back to Southampton, obliging us to make the first part of our voyage by the ordinary means of conveyance. I caught a bad fever while travelling in Syria, of which I nearly died in Malta, and still feel the ill effects sometimes. However, we were not influenced by the sailor's superstition, and arranged to start again on *Friday, September* 4, 1874, from Hastings in the 'Sunbeam.' On that morning it poured with rain, and blew with such force that the Fishermen's Regatta had to be postponed, with the exception of the Fishing Boats' Race. These boats are able to sail in any weather, but only ten started out of thirty-seven entered, and even these were under double-reefed sails.

Saturday, September 5th, was a lovely morning, without a breath of air, but by half-past ten the wind began to rise; by twelve it was high, and before two it was blowing a gale. When the yacht arrived and dropped her anchor, it was with great difficulty that the luggage could be got on board, soaking wet, by a sort of extemporised crane.

Monday, September 7th, was finer, but with a strong southerly wind still. We lunched with the Prince and Princess of Roumania in St. Leonards, saw some interesting rocket practice (for saving life at sea), and then drove to Court Lodge, in order to afford our guests an opportunity of seeing something of Sussex farming, hop-picking, and fat beasts, with which they were much interested. This was followed by a rough and homely tea, which we all enjoyed, and it was long after dark before we separated, with mutual regrets, and promises to meet again in Roumania, which country they gave us a hearty invitation to visit.

Tuesday, September 8th.—I had a telegram from Tom to meet him at Ryde; so we left Bexhill at half-past one, and arrived in due course at Portsmouth. A rough crossing to

Ryde pier, and a good tossing in the gig, took us on board the 'Sunbeam,' which we found all ready for sea; but there was apparently no hope of starting for some time.

Wednesday 9th and *Thursday 10th* were terribly rough. Most of the yachts slipped away to Portsmouth, Southampton, or to lay up, and I do not think a single yacht's boat tried to land except our own, which, being a powerful lifeboat cutter, was very safe and tolerably dry, though heavy to work under oars.

Friday, September 11th, was calmer, but very wet. Tom and I went over to Sandown with the children, to spend the day with some old friends. Sandown itself is wonderfully altered and improved since we were there last. Many pretty rows of villas with verandahs have sprung up, in gardens of their own, looking more like a German watering-place than one of our stiff 'parades by the sea.' After lunch, Tom and a friend decided to walk home. The children, being very wet after their dabble on the sands, were sent back by the first train, and I arranged to drive out to Bonchurch and return by the 6.30 train. We had a lovely drive in spite of the rain; but the pony was fat and slow, and we arrived at the station just in time to see the train going off. We drove on to Sandown, and my host kindly accompanied me to the pier-head at Ryde, where I found the cutter and six men had been waiting for me since seven. Our old captain, Bishop, who has retired, and is now a yacht-agent ashore instead of a yacht-captain afloat, tried hard to persuade me not to go off, as it was blowing so hard, pouring with rain, and pitch-dark. However, I knew the boat and the men, and how anxious those on board would be if I did not arrive. I therefore determined to start, with three reefs in the lugsail, two men holding on to the halyards, one to the sheet, all ready to let go. As soon as we got from under the lee of the pier we were nearly blown back. Then we narrowly escaped being run down by a steamer, which the wind would not allow us to weather. Being compelled to bear up, we had hard work beating to windward; but we persevered, although at every minute we shipped seas, which kept three men constantly baling. At last, just as I was beginning to despair, John, the coxswain, cried out, 'Down sail and pull for your lives, men, or we shan't get on board to-night.' We saw the yacht, a perfect blaze of light, the deck-house illuminated, and lights all along the bulwarks, which were lined with the anxious faces of all on board, passengers, servants, children, and crew, some holding lanterns, and some ropes. We bumped against the yacht, ropes were thrown over, and we were with great difficulty passed round under the stern, tossing about, sometimes far above and sometimes far below the yacht, till we were under the lee side. Then I was most thankful to be half thrown, half dragged on board. The men followed as best they could, clinging and swarming up the ropes like monkeys. Wet and terrified as I was, it was nothing to what they had suffered on board. For the last two trips the boat had been half full of water, and as the gale had been increasing for the last hour, they had almost given us up for lost. When one of the crew first saw our boat through the black darkness, Tom was just starting in the other cutter with ten men to look for us, and if possible to stop my trying to get on board that night. Had we missed the yacht the first time, it would have been impossible to pull up to her again. We should then have been obliged to run for Portsmouth Harbour, and probably to stay out all night, or till the tide turned or the wind moderated. It was really blowing a regular equinoctial gale. We had two anchors down, with sixty fathoms of chain on one and forty on the other anchor, and even then we dragged.

Saturday, September 12*th.*—After all the trouble and anxiety with the boats yesterday, Tom thought it better to go into Portsmouth Harbour, where we could land in peace in any weather. We steamed across, and took up our old quarters at the buoy belonging to the 'St. Vincent's' brig. In the afternoon we went to a pleasant dance on board the 'Excellent,' where we met many old Mediterranean and Canadian friends, some of whom adjourned to tea on board the 'Sunbeam.' The weather had quite taken up, the wind changed to N.E., and we wanted to be off at once. But some of our men were on shore; provisions and water also were wanted; so we determined to start at six the next morning.

Sunday, September 13*th.*—Sailors love to start on Sunday as much as they hate to start on Friday. Everyone, therefore, was in good spirits as on this most lovely morning we steamed slowly out of the harbour, past Ryde and Cowes, through the Solent to the Needles, which we passed at 10 a.m., and got into the swell outside just as we were having service at 11 a.m. By noon we were off St. Alban's Head. At 7.30 p.m. off the Start. Flat calm. Our party this time consists of Tom, myself, and the three children, Tab, Mabelle, and Baby, of which the two eldest are to return from Gibraltar with Fisher; Mr. Swift, with my cousin Miss Eva Robinson, and Mr. Bingham, completing our number.

Monday, September 14*th.*—Still calm. At 10 a.m. we were off Ushant, at noon off the Chaussée de Sein, having come from Portsmouth—278 miles—in twenty-eight hours. At 1 p.m. we ceased steaming, and with a light north-easterly breeze, and all fore and aft sail set, steered for Cape Ortegal.

Tuesday, September 15*th.*—In the Bay of Biscay, with pleasant weather, moderate sea, and wind from S.E. At noon we had sailed 113 miles since the same hour yesterday, and were 176 miles from Cape Ortegal.

Wednesday, September 16*th.*—We made the land near Cape Ortegal about 2 p.m., and at 10 p.m. were about 15 miles from Cape Finisterre, with the revolving light in view. In the morning it was so calm that when Muriel, in a fit of mischief, threw her shoe overboard, the dingy was lowered to pick it up. The weather was bright and sunny, with paltry winds. We tried sailing, but, after flopping about in a very heavy swell from noon till 11 p.m., we raised the funnel and proceeded under steam, to the great comfort of everybody on board. Distance, from noon yesterday till noon to-day, 197 miles.

Thursday, September 17*th.*—A strong wind, freshening to a moderate gale, all day. We ceased steaming at 11 a.m. At noon we were 50 miles off Cape Mondego, having run 190 miles since noon yesterday. At 10 p.m. we were off the rock of Lisbon. The swell all day from the north-west was very heavy. At night it blew so hard that the jaws of the main boom were carried away, and it was a terrible business securing it again. It swept the whole of the after-deck with the greatest violence, describing more than a semicircle, and nobody could get near it till the vessel's head was brought to the wind. Then they lowered the sail, and ultimately made all safe, fortunately without injury to life or limb, though the standard compass was upset, companion smashed in, and Tom's azimuth carried overboard. Several whales have been seen at different times, one blowing up so close to the yacht as to produce the appearance of an escape of steam from the engine-room. Shoals of porpoises played around us every day. The water

Cape St. Vincent.

has been full of jelly-fish of all kinds, each beautiful in colour and shape, but none more so than the lovely little Portuguese men-of-war, with their graceful delicate sails set to the breeze, sailing before the wind. At night the sea was splendidly illuminated with minute star-like zoophytes, making the water look like the reflection of the brilliantly star-studded sky above. Everything showed how much we had changed our latitude since starting from England.

Friday, September 18*th.*—The morning rose with a fresh

fair breeze, but very heavy swell from north-west, causing the 'Sunbeam' to roll deeply for some hours before rounding Cape St. Vincent at noon. We signalled our number, and after passing the cape, though the wind freshened, the sea was smooth, and we had a most delightful sail along the south coast of Portugal. In the evening we saw the light off Cape St. Mary; and we had a quiet night, which was a great treat.

Saturday, September 19*th.*—The morning was very hot, with a flat calm and a heavy swell. Fires were lighted and the funnel raised, ready to steam into Tangier, when a violent squall of wind came on suddenly, and continued for some hours, lashing the waves into foam, and raising so much sea in a short time, that we had more water on board than we wanted, and we all felt far more uncomfortable than during the whole passage thus far from England. We were under the shelter of Cape Spartel about 11 a.m., and as we coasted along had lovely views, especially as we rounded the last point and made Tangier, resembling, like most Oriental towns seen from a distance, a pearl rising from the ocean. Soon after noon we put off in the boat to land at Tangier, sending the yacht out to sea for a few hours. We took our passports, but were not allowed to land for want of the bill of health, which Tom had unfortunately left behind, thinking it would not be needed. We sent a message to the consul; but he said it was of no use. So we sent a second message, and after some delay were told we might land in half an hour. In the meantime Tom transferred us into an empty boat lying at anchor, and went off in the gig under sail, to try and intercept the yacht and procure the important document. This he succeeded in doing just as all the consuls and vice-consuls of every nation (whose name is Legion here) had consented to allow us to land.

During the three hours we were bobbing about in the broiling sun, we had been amused by watching Arabs

Tangier

riding races on the shore, and some washing their horses, swimming them right out to sea. When wet themselves, their shiny black and brown muscular bodies looked like bronze as they sat, firm as rocks, on their horses, which plunged and snorted with fear when out of their depth. No matter what they did, their riders stuck to them like wax.

On landing we went straight to the Royal Victoria Hotel, kept by a black steward of the Duke of Edinburgh, who had married a Scotch cook. It is very comfortable : good cuisine and wine, nice clean rooms with a lovely view looking north, and consequently much cooler than Gibraltar. We were greatly pleased with the picturesque look of the town and the people, and we settled to spend Sunday here. After lunch we went for a stroll through the market, which was crowded with Arabs in their white haiks, negroes in their striped abbats, Bedouins in their burnous, and Moors and Jews in their bright-coloured dresses of all hues. The women were even more gorgeously draped than the men. As it was their Sabbath, they were all in their best. The faces of the Jewesses were uncovered ; the Moorish women were muffled up to the eyes, and waddled along like animated bundles of dirty clothes. Outside the gate were strings of camels from the interior, mules and horses from neighbouring villages, with more wild and picturesque people encamped in little striped tents or small bamboo-covered huts, at work on their various trades, or cooking their frugal meal at the door. Large families of children, babies and all, in spite of the intense heat, were packed as close inside their tents here, at the very edge of the Great Desert, as we had found the Lapps, almost on the verge of the eternal snows, when we saw them not two months ago. This similarity of habit between two very different peoples, one living under a broiling sun the year through, the other existing with hardly any sun at all, is certainly curious and interesting. There were snake-charmers fascinating the slimy reptiles before the gaze of an admiring circle ; story-tellers telling and acting their romances to a crowd lolling about on rocks and stones at the side of the hill, extemporising a sort of theatre to listen to the Arab *improvvisatore*. At the *table d'hôte* we found a great influx of visitors, arrived by steamer from Gibraltar to spend Sunday.

On our way to the boat after dinner, we stopped at a very small Moorish *café* lighted by two little wicks floating in oil held in two tumblers, suspended by long chains from

Bargaining in the Bazaar.

the low ceiling till they were almost level with the floor. Here we all crouched down on our heels and partook of *café à la turque*—a large tea-spoonful of coffee, another of sugar, put into a small cup and boiling water poured on it, making it thick and sweet, but very high-flavoured and good. It was a curious, weird scene. Half a dozen men were playing cards in one corner, a man thrumming a sort of mandolin in another, and our guide trying to make music out of a large key, a pair of snuffers, and a knife, all produced from his pocket, which, rapped in a monotonous manner, formed an accompaniment to a still more monotonous song. The row off in the moonlight was lovely, and the sea-breeze most refreshing after the stuffy town.

Sunday, September 20*th.*—We went ashore quite early, this being market-day, to see much the same sights as yesterday, only more of them, and more crowd. Tom read service at 11.30 a.m. We had a visit from the captain of the Spanish man-of-war, 'Nave de Tolosa,' which has now been lying in the bay more than two months since the time when, in common with many ships of other nations, she was sent to assist in quelling the disturbances among the Khabyles. She has remained ever since, the officers and crew stopping their full pay from the Moorish war indemnity, as it passes through their hands towards Spain, while most of the other ships of their country get nothing in the present disturbed state of affairs; so they are wise to stay where they are, dull as they say they find the place. We asked the captain how the war was going on, but he did not know anything about it, and seemed to care less.

After lunch we went on shore to the Caasba at the top of the city, from which we had a charming view over the whole place, which, like most African cities, is built of mud, either just plastered up with straw or made into bricks, for the most part whitewashed, but sometimes painted red and yellow, or occasionally left to their original colour. The mosques are the same, but the minarets are of green, red, and yellow tiles, with generally a palm-tree growing near, giving a most beautiful effect. After dinner a Moorish wedding procession passed at the end of the street. We pursued it through the narrow pathways all over the town, guided by the firing of guns and the anything but sweet sounds of the musical instruments that accompanied it. Ultimately we reached the bride's house, and saw her in a square box (covered with muslin and decorated with coloured tassels) let down from the roof and put on the back of a mule. The cumbersome structure took four men all their

Moorish Musician

time to hold it, and even then it went shaking and wobbling about in a way eminently calculated to make the unfortunate bride miserably ill before she reached the end of her journey; for though her husband's house was not very far off, they took her all round the town, and up and down all the streets. We followed the procession some little way; but the music was very monotonous, the constant firing of guns in one's ears unpleasant, and the accompanying crowd odoriferous, though most picturesque in the bright moonlight. So we wended our way to the gates, which, after some little delay and fuss, were opened for us. A crowd accompanied us to the beach, and we had another delightful moonlight row.

Monday, September 21*st.*—We started for Gibraltar at 11 a.m., and arrived about 2.30 p.m., after a pleasant sail through the splendid Straits under our square sail and studding-sail only. Captain McCrae sent out a boat to take us to a sheltered berth inside the New Mole, and we had scarcely dropped our anchor before some naval friends came on board. Then another old friend arrived, who brought the unpleasant news that the English homeward-bound mail was due this evening, instead of not till Wednesday, as we expected. So we had a great bustle to get the children's things ready. It was indeed a terrible disappointment to us all, this sudden parting, and if the children had only asked, I do not think I could have had the heart to refuse them another week. But I am now very glad that they did not, as it was much better they should go home. We landed about 5 p.m., went up to the Signal Station on donkeys, an expedition which was much enjoyed, and dined at the Club-House Hotel. We had only just time to take the children to the yacht again, pack up some things, and go on board the 'Khedive.' There were only forty first-class and forty second-class passengers on board. The children, and Fisher, their maid, had two fine large berths to themselves. We none of us liked saying good-bye, but at last we thought it was all over, the parting bell had rung, and we were slowly and sadly descending the companion ladder. Suddenly two little heads and four little arms appeared through the portholes, waving a last farewell, and 'Good-bye, papa! good-bye, mamma!' came sobbingly from the lips of Tab and Mabelle. Captain Andoe, who has just completed his term of service in the 'Invincible,' was on board. He was rowed alongside by a crew of officers, and it was very inspiring, though rather melancholy, to hear their cheering as the 'Khedive' moved slowly off, the bands on the other ships playing 'Should auld acquaintance be forgot?' 'Home, sweet home,' 'Cheer, boys, cheer,' &c. It was altogether a sad moment; but, like other disagreeable things which have to be done, it was perhaps better to get it over quickly, without much time to think about it. When the ship's lights disappeared round the rock beyond Algeciras, it made us feel how completely our little ones were separated from us, for a time at all events.

> I never spoke the word farewell
> But with an utterance faint and broken,
> A heart-sick yearning for the time
> When it should never more be spoken.

CHAPTER II.

TETUAN, CEUTA, AND SICILY.

The weary Arabs roam from plain to plain,
Guiding the languid herd in quest of food;
And shift their little homes' uncertain scene
With frequent farewell: strangers, pilgrims all,
As were their fathers.

GIBRALTAR, Tuesday, September 22nd, 1874.—We were in a great mess, scraping masts and coaling, with hulks alongside, when all the captains of the fleet arrived to visit us, one after another. Such a procession of gigs you never saw. They expressed themselves much pleased with the yacht, in spite of the state of dirt and confusion we were in. After taking lunch, and witnessing a review of the marines, we went on board the 'Swiftsure,' I think one of the most beautiful ships of this fleet.

Wednesday, September 23rd.—We left the yacht at 10.30 a.m., and started at 11 in the Messageries Nationales (late Impériales) boat 'Africaine' for Tangier. It was a glorious day; but the vessel, being very light in ballast, rolled a good deal, and lunch had to be eaten under considerable difficulty, with an accompaniment of disagreeable sights and sounds. We reached Tangier about 4 p.m., photographed, and strolled about till dinner, and afterwards had coffee on the roof of our hotel. The view was lovely —east over the bay to the Atlas Mountains, and west over the quaint old town with its picturesque battlements.

Thursday, September 24th.—We were called at 4.30 a.m., and started soon after 6 a.m. I rode 'Al Tail,' a beautiful thoroughbred Barb, charming in his paces and in every other respect except his fighting propensities, which compelled me to keep a respectful distance from everybody else. The road, or rather track, ran through a pretty undulating country, with hills covered by aloes, myrtles, wild olives, palmettos, and gum cistus; while on the plains we saw the stubble of Indian corn, millet, wheat, barley, and maize. We met crowds of Arabs, with women and children, camels, horses, ponies, mules, and donkeys, going into market, Thursday being almost as great a market day as Sunday. A great many large hawks were soaring overhead, and in one place at least a dozen were gathered together over the carcass of a sheep. After sundry delays we reached the encampment about 12.30 p.m., all very tired, and thankful to throw ourselves down in the shade, to pant and drink sherbet. Evie and I rested all the afternoon, whilst the gentlemen went out shooting, returning with a fair bag. The sunset and moonrise were lovely, and a blazing tree in the foreground accidentally set on fire by some Arabs added to the picturesque beauty of the scene. A most excellent French cook has been secured for the camp, so at 7 p.m. we sat down to a dinner that would have done no discredit to the most civilised cuisine in London or Paris. Nothing could exceed the comfort of our encampment, consisting of five tents, each well furnished, besides a dining tent, where eight could dine with ease. The gentlemen were put up in pairs, and Evie, I, and a Spanish maid (provided especially for our comfort) occupied another tent, while the French cook had the cooking tent to himself.

During the night it became very cold, and early in the morning a little rain fell, which made the temperature much pleasanter than yesterday.

Friday, September 25th.—The gentlemen went out shooting early, returning about 8 a.m. with nine brace of partridges, some hawks, rabbits, &c. At 10.30 a.m. we started for Tetuan. At first the road was not only very stony, but up and down hill. After riding four hours, we halted under the shade of a couple of large wild olive trees, on the banks of a stream fringed with oleanders in full bloom. Another three hours' ride brought us into Tetuan, a walled city, standing on a height commanding views of the lower range of the Atlas Mountains. The last few miles took us through lovely gardens, irrigated with tiny streams, each stream with a luxuriant line of maidenhair fern hanging over it, and the land producing its second crop of Indian corn, millet, wheat, melons, mulberries, figs, pomegranates, oranges, apples, or prickly pears, in the most abundant profusion. On the sides of the mountain the fields looked quite green and English, making a strong contrast to the burnt arid desert we had been passing through. It was almost dark when we reached the town, and pursued our way through the dirty tortuous streets, across the market-place, through several gates, until we reached the Jewish quarter (where the inhabitants are always locked up for the night), and found our inn. Such a funny little place! We had to bend almost double to pass beneath the entrance door. A narrow passage led us to the courtyard, open to the air, with a grating over it. Some very steep tiled steps took us to the first floor, where we found the dining-room, which had two beds in it, and two bedrooms opening on to the gallery. They all had the tiniest windows at one end, and were lighted by large folding doors giving access to the gallery, which naturally rendered them anything but private. Above, there were rooms not so pretentious, but more airy, opening on to the house-top. At dinner we were joined by some officers who had been unable to get their leave on Wednesday morning, and had started at night in a felucca, only to be becalmed, spend two days and a night on the road, and finally land at the mouth of the river and walk seven miles over the sand.

Saturday, September 26th.—It rained heavily during the night, but we were on horseback by 6 a.m., all in a state of wild excitement about the boar-hunt. We rode through gardens like those we saw yesterday for about two hours, till we arrived at the meet. The scene was singularly picturesque. On a little hill near an Arab village, about a dozen Arabs, in long burnous, with bright-coloured turbans and long silver- and brass-bound guns, were seated on the ground, eating prickly pears, whose inner skins lay in a purple, scarlet, and orange heap in front of them, making a lovely bit of colour in the foreground. A little farther off stood a group of men, holding in leash a dozen boar-hounds of all shapes, sizes, and colours; and again on the right another dozen men looking on, whilst the dead body of a shot fox lay at their feet. The country was undulating, and the view extended over sea, mountain, and plain. After another quarter of an hour's ride we dismounted, and were put in position, while the Arabs and dogs went round to draw. It was very hot, and as an hour and a half passed by without an incident, I think almost everybody fell asleep. About 10 a.m. the first beater came over the crest of the hill. Others soon joined him, making a great noise and hullabaloo; dogs barked, and there was great excitement. Presently we saw a large wild boar stealing up the ravine near us. Several shots were fired at him, but the brushwood was thick, and he escaped. Then came a tiny boar, which nobody took the trouble to fire at. Then came an enormous creature, at whom everybody fired, but whom nobody hit. This went on for about another hour and a half. Ten pigs were seen, but only one was killed, and two jackals. Then came breakfast, a most welcome meal after our early start and weary wait in the sun; for in this sport, as in deer-driving, no one may move or speak. After a hurried meal, Evie and I returned home to rest, while the gentlemen went on shooting. They had a long walk, saw more boars, but did not shoot any, and could not fire at the small game, their guns being loaded with bullets. Shooting in Morocco is rather a dangerous amusement on the whole, the Moors being so very casual with their guns. An English sportsman had been shot dead in the last expedition, a fact which forced itself unpleasantly on our minds when we heard a bullet whistle over our heads. Then, too, if you wound a boar and do not kill him, he is pretty certain to rush out of the brushwood and rip your leg up with his tusks.

Evie and I had a delightful ride home, but we were so tired that we were glad to rest all the afternoon, so we did not see much of the town. After dinner we had a very pleasant chat on the house-top. Finding it impossible to return to Gibraltar in time by Tangier, we determined to ride to Ceuta on the next day, and take the boat to

Algeciras and Gibraltar, so as to be back on Monday, as arranged. This being the Feast of Tabernacles, there were curious little tents or booths of green branches in the streets and on the house-tops of the Jewish quarter, and none of the Jews could touch a lamp after sundown, which was very inconvenient. A hanging lamp in our room was most quaint: an enormous tumbler, surrounded by nineteen smaller ones, all held up by charms against the evil eye. I made a bid for it, but as it was a feast the owner could not transact any business, but promised to write and let me know as soon as the feast was over.[1] They brought us the hotel book, to write our names in. It began in 1838, and contained only four or five English names in it each year, and six ladies' names during the whole period.

Woman of Tetuan

Sunday, September 27th.—All the officers remained behind for a shooting expedition, but came to their tent doors to see us off when we left at 6 a.m. The first part of our road was much the same as yesterday. In two hours we had our first view of the sea—blue as ultra-

---

[1] 1879.—I have never heard from the man himself, but have been informed by friends who have visited Tetuan that he always points it out as Mrs. Brassey's lamp. I wish he would send it to me.

marine, breaking on the shore of snow-white sand—from the top of a small hill. About 10.30 a.m. we stopped under the shade of some tamarisks, by the sea-shore, for breakfast, and when we started again at noon the heat was intense. At 2 p.m. we were obliged to dismount again and rest for a few minutes under the shadow of a rock. The road was most lovely; now along the beach composed of the whitest sands and shells, with a few larger ones sprinkled about, then along a path cut through the cliffs overhanging the sea, into whose blue depths you seemed to penetrate for miles, all the coralines, sponges, and waving seaweeds, and zoophytes being clearly visible at the bottom. A little farther off were hills with beautiful shrubberies, occasional large mulberry trees, and groves of myrtles in full bloom, under whose lowest branches you can ride without bending your head. Descending to lower ground, we rode along the shores of a lake literally teeming with rare wild fowl and fish of every description. If it had not been so hot, and if we could have allowed ourselves three days, and encamped every night, so as to have ridden only in the early morning and late evening, it would have been too delightful.

About 4 p.m. we reached the outposts of Ceuta, where our Moorish soldier had to give up his arms. He would reclaim them when he went back to the desert. We entered the city through gates, along ramparts, over drawbridges, and through fortifications of the strongest description. At last we reached the *fonda*; but it was full of soldiers, and the landlord had no rooms, much less beds. He gave us something to eat, and afterwards we strolled round the town, pursued by a crowd of small boys. The town is curiously like Gibraltar in shape and situation. The fortress is on a high rock communicating by a low spit of sandy shore with the mainland; but as the town is on the low ground at the foot of the rock, the inhabitants would have a very bad time of it in case of siege. The high ground on the mainland, too, commands the rock, so that altogether it could never be made so strong a place as Gibraltar. It swarms with soldiers. Not a creature spoke anything but Spanish, and as I had forgotten nearly all I used to know, it was with some difficulty we procured what we wanted and settled with our Arabs. We managed to get some dinner with the soldiers, and at last found a little man who spoke about twenty words of English and as many of French, and as he knew the hotel people, he persuaded them to procure us a sitting-room at a friend's house in which to pass the night. There we got through the dark hours as best we could, much eaten of mosquitoes and much disturbed by people running through our apartment, which was, after all, rather a passage than a sitting-room.

Monday, September 28th.—At 5 a.m. we roused ourselves, changed our riding habits for ordinary dresses, tried but failed to procure even a little coffee, and after great difficulty persuaded some people to carry our luggage to the quay Our polite little friend of last night turned up—Señor Luis Tareño y Rodriguez, Secretary to the Convict Establishment at the Iles Chafarrines, on a month's leave with his brother Señor Antonio Paus, Receveur des Douanes—and at the last moment the Arabs arrived with our saddles, boar-skins, &c. The steamer 'Dos Hermanos' did not start till 8 a.m. instead of at 6.30 a.m., so we need not have been in such a hurry. Nothing was provided to eat on board, and after a rough and rolling passage we reached Algeciras about 10 a.m. Without landing we got into a small boat, and, sailing and rowing, reached the yacht soon after noon; and you may imagine how delightful her cleanliness and comfort seemed after our recent experiences. Muñie was delighted to see us again, and as the felucca came alongside she kept shrieking over the bulwarks, 'So glad to see you back again! oh, so glad!'

Tuesday, September 29th, was another hot morning, with a cool breeze from the west. We went to bathe at the ladies' bathing-place, a most luxuriously arranged establishment, where you can bathe either out at sea or under cover. Anything so lovely as the sea anemones along the edges of the rock I never saw, particularly one as large as the palm of one's hand, waving its beautiful green feelers with exquisite mauve tips in every direction in search of its prey. His Excellency the Governor, our old friend Sir Fenwick Williams, arrived this morning at daybreak in the P. & O. steamer 'Australia' from England, but did not land till 8 a.m. at the Ragged Staff, where he was received with all the usual honours; so, while bathing, we had the benefit of many guns and much music. As some friends came on board to breakfast, it was late before we landed again for our expedition to the galleries, which are the great feature of the Rock. But I have been round them so many times, and have described them so often, that I will not say another word about them. Having gone through all the upper galleries and St. George's Hall, and admired the lovely views seen through the embrasures, each like a picture in its dark frame—a bright bit of sunlight, blue sky and sea, with distant country views, or the little boats dancing at anchor or shooting across the harbour —we returned to our car, and went through the dirty, crowded Waterport, to the market, which was full of people, the stalls covered with meat, fresh fish, fruit, and vegetables. Passing out at the gates, over the moat, we emerged on a sandy plain, and, traversing the English lines, crossed the neutral ground to the Spanish lines, where, after a cursory examination, we were allowed to

Gibraltar.

enter the village of Campimento. Here we tacked on a leader to drag us through the heavy sand, and had a delicious drive round the bay, just at the edge of the waves, till we turned off from the sea on the high road to Campo. This part was not so pleasant, for it was hot and dusty, and the road bad, and we were bumped and jolted about considerably. We soon reached the friendly house whither we were bound, a large, square, comfortable building, deliciously cool, and standing in a nice garden of its own, with hedges of plumbago and scarlet geranium, myrtle and rosemary. After passing several pleasant hours we were obliged to say good-bye at 4 p.m., to be back in time to receive Sir Fenwick Williams and his aides-de-camp on board to tea. Having dined at the Club-House, we made another attempt at the Circus, but there seemed a fate against us. This time it was shut because it was Tuesday.

Wednesday, September 30th.—Fires had been lighted before daybreak, and, while waiting for the steward with the fresh milk and provisions, we tried some steam manœuvres, then signalled our last adieux to the 'Helicon,' and steamed from under the shadow of the Rock, and out of the glassy bay, exactly at 8.30 a.m. Outside Europa Point a nice breeze sprang up from the westward, and we set all our running canvas, and proceeded at the rate of eight knots, soon increasing to ten.

Thursday, October 1st.—At noon we had run 250 miles from Gibraltar. Latitude 36° 39′ N., longitude 0° 30′ W. The wind increased to a moderate gale, with a heavy swell from the north-west, which rolled and tumbled us about most terribly, and prevented any of us sleeping at night. About 8 p.m. we made the light on Cape Tenez.

Friday, October 2nd.—At daybreak we were off Algiers, near enough to see the houses in the town and environs plainly. By noon we had run 206 miles since the corresponding hour yesterday. Latitude 37° 16′ N., longitude 3° 48′ E.

The breeze continued as before, the swell increasing till we rolled so much that it was almost impossible to sit, stand, or lie down. Our chairs were lashed, and everything made as snug as could be under the circumstances.

Saturday, October 3rd.—The north coast of Africa was in sight the whole day. We saw turtles floating on the sea and basking in the sun, and some flying-fish came on board. Distance at noon, 137 miles. Latitude 37° 40′ W., longitude 6° 38′ E. The wind continued to blow with considerable force from the westward, accompanied by a heavy side swell from the Gulf of Lyons.

Sunday, October 4th.—Rounded the island of Galita, at a distance of thirty miles, during the night. At noon the distance run was 198 miles, and we were twenty miles north of the Graham Shoals, and about seventy miles south of the island of Sardinia. The breeze was still fresh and fair, but the sea more moderate.

Monday, October 5th.—The breeze failing, we steamed ahead at 1.30 a.m. At daybreak we made the high mountains in the interior of Sicily, and shortly afterwards the islands of Sevanza and Maritimo, steered past Mount St. Julian towards Cape St. Vito, which we passed at a distance of three miles, and then crossed the Bay of Castellamare to Cape di Gallo. The scenery all along the coast was superb; splendid rocks and precipices, interspersed with sunny slopes and rich fertile plains, teeming with every kind of grain and fruit, now in rich luxuriance. About 11 a.m. we reached the bay of Palermo, and by noon were moored inside the Mole. Distance, 171 miles. Latitude 38° 8′ N., longitude 13° 15′ E.

The yacht was scarcely inside the Mole before we were surrounded by boats, whose proprietors were anxious to sell their various wares: coral, shell-boxes, canary birds, marble table-tops—wonderfully pretty and wonderfully cheap—hideous animals, and mermaids with long tails made of shells, piled-up baskets of most delicious grapes, figs, melons, pomegranates, prickly pears, and pears without prickles. We landed on the Marina, and walked straight to the comfortable Hôtel Trinacria, where the landlord received us with exactly the same irreproachable manner displayed twelve years ago, when we were here in the 'Albatross.' Early in the afternoon we started for Monreale, through the clean straight streets, full of excellent shops, then along a hot, dusty road, up a steep hill commanding beautiful views of the town and the *conca d'oro* (golden shell) in which it is situated. Every ten or twenty yards there were sentries, and at intervals of every mile guard-houses, or rather huts, with four or five soldiers in each, as a protection against the brigands, who have been very troublesome lately. All the way up the sides of the mountains were gardens, vines, oranges, prickly pears, pink oleanders, and purple ipomœas.

At the summit stands the town of Monreale, with its cathedral and monastery. The latter is now used for barracks; but the views from it, especially from the terrace in the garden, are very fine, looking over the entire city and the luxuriant plain in which it is situated. The cathedral itself is splendid and almost unique, lined with splendid mosaics on a gold ground, representing the whole history of the Old and New Testaments. Its architecture is a mixture of Norman, Byzantine, and Gothic. The drive back in the cool of the evening was quite delightful, though we could not stay out as long as we should have liked, having stupidly arranged to dine at the 5.30 *table d'hôte*, an insane hour for dinner in this climate at this time of year, wasting as it does the short but most delicious sunset and twilight hour. Afterwards we lounged about the Marina, enjoying the delicious sea-breeze, and had a delightful row on board.

Tuesday, October 6th.—We went ashore about 11 a.m. landing at the Mole, and driving first to the cathedral, and then to the Capella Reale, attached to, and in fact forming part of, the king's palace. It is an exact contrast to the large, light, airy, spacious, lofty cathedral, being very small, but perfectly encrusted with the richest mosaics on a gold ground, representing the history of the Old and New Testaments, something like Monreale, the columns being richly covered and inlaid. The floor is tesselated with gold and coloured marbles, the roof of carved wood, painted in grand designs, not a pin's point being left that is not covered with the richest decoration. The windows being small, and of coloured glass, made it look gloomy; but with brilliant sunlight, and full of priests in gala robes, it must be indeed a gorgeous sight. The apartments in the palace are numerous and lofty, and all the windows command splendid views in different directions over land and sea.

In the afternoon we drove to the base of the Monte Pellegrino, all through the older part of the city, and by the Mole. At the end of the road we left the carriage, mounted our donkeys, and started up the very steepest zigzag path, built on arches over a torrent, some hundred years ago, at an enormous expense, for the convenience of pilgrims to the shrine of St. Rosalie, whose bones were supposed to have delivered the city of Palermo from plague. The then archbishop told the people their souls would be saved if they made the road, and it was done. The views all the way up were very fine till we got to the shrine, in a grotto, where they wanted us to stop; but we declined, as it was late, and we wished to see the view from the summit by the statue. There seemed no possible way of proceeding; but a good lady opened the front door of her house, our donkeys stepped in, and we proceeded along a dark, very smelly passage, about a hundred yards long, from which we emerged on a stony plain, about a mile in extent, which we crossed, and then reached the statue, standing on an extreme point hanging over the sea, but much in ruins. The head is off, the hands are broken, and the arcade that had once surrounded it is also tumbling to pieces. The view ought to have been magnificent, along the coast to the island of Ustica, on the west to Alicudi and Filicudi, on the east to Stromboli and Lipari, while inland the massive peak of Etna, more than a hundred and twenty miles off, should have risen boldly up; but unfortunately it was misty, so we could only imagine these beauties, and then ride as fast as we could back to the shrine, by which time it was quite dark, and all the large flocks of goats and turkeys which we had passed on our way up had gone home to bed.

The ride down was dark, but pleasant, the lights of the town at our feet twinkling, whilst the whole landscape was illuminated from time to time by lightning, and the occasional rumble of thunder added grandeur to the scene. The donkeys were not of the best, and riding down the steep declivity was very tiring, as they were constantly stumbling. After some difficulty we found the carriage, and got on board the yacht about 7.30 p.m. The lightning was even more brilliant after dinner than before—almost continuous—lighting up all the ships in the harbour, and the town itself, like a most brilliant electric light. The

Marina was delicious—beautiful trees overhanging the sea—and the Flora Gardens, full of choice exotics, whose scent was almost overpowering, were brilliantly lighted up.

If one could only lie with safety in a yacht in the bay of Palermo, just off the Marina, it would be about the most agreeable winter quarters one could imagine; but the roads are not very safe or comfortable, the harbour is crowded, airless, and stagnant, and the incessant barking of dogs and other discordant shore noises make night hideous.

I was awakened in the night by hearing some one come downstairs. As there was then a noise in Evie's room, I got up to see what was the matter, and in the dark tumbled over a man's head. Evie then came from the nursery, where she had been to call nurse, and told me she had heard some one fall. On receiving no answer to her repeated questions, she lighted a match, and seeing a man lying down, trying to hide, as she imagined, she tried to escape into our room, but as he stopped up that door she went to wake nurse. We woke Tom and Mr. Bingham, and they found he was one of our men, who had not been well for some time. He had been on shore, and, the wine he had taken having affected his head, he had, come in his sleep to try and take out the boxes in his charge from the hatch which is under the floor of Evie's berth. It was alarming for the moment, and woke us all thoroughly, for of course we thought he was a thief who had crept across the other ships and come on board to rob.

CHAPTER III.

ATHENS, GREECE, AND THE ARCHIPELAGO.

*Athens, the eye of Greece, mother of arts
And eloquence.*

Wednesday, October 7th.—We were to have been off at 6 a.m.; but there was some delay about the bill of health, followed by countless aggravating hindrances, and it was 10.30 a.m. before we could start. The thunder-storm of last night had not entirely passed off, and it appeared to be raining heavily along the mountains on shore. We steamed out of the harbour, and then found a fair breeze, which lasted till 7 p.m., when it dropped completely.

Thursday, October 8th.—At 4 a.m. we got up steam, and, passing the islands of Lipari, Panaria, and Stromboli, were off the Faro of Messina, and entered the Straits about 11.30 a.m. The scene was exquisitely beautiful. The Straits at this point are not more than a mile wide. The rocks of Scylla, crowned with a ruined fortress, and the whole of the coast of southern Italy, are spread like a panorama before you, while the Sicilian coast is equally lovely. Messina was reached all too soon. We landed (this time armed with the bill of health) at the 'Sanità,' and after being detained about three-quarters of an hour, answering unimportant questions, and interviewing the British Consul, we were allowed to enter a carriage and proceed to the Hôtel Victoria to order lunch.

The old *proveidor* we had in the 'Meteor' met us, and conducted us with great pride about the town to the post-office, where we were detained another three-quarters of an hour, posting the letters, and vainly asking for some we never received. Thence we went to a coral shop, where, times being so bad, they were ready to dispose of their goods at unprecedentedly low prices, in order to obtain the

Deck View.

means of paying their house-rent. The accommodation at the hotel was fair, and the landlord remembered me, and brought me a lovely bouquet. After luncheon and a drive, we re-embarked. The 'Sunbeam' had not dropped her anchor, but had been cruising about in the Straits. The steward soon joined us with our fresh provisions, and about 4 p.m. we steamed easily down the Straits. As a fresh fair breeze was blowing, the fires were now allowed to burn themselves out, and the sails were hoisted. The ever lovely Straits were illumined by the light of the setting sun. This is now the fifth time we have been here, and each time we think them more beautiful even than before. About 7 p.m. the breeze began to drop with the sun; half an hour later it was a flat calm.

> Framing the mighty landscape to the west
> A purple range of mountain-caves, between
> Whose interspaces gush'd in blinding bursts
> The incorporate blaze of sun and sea.

Friday, October 9th.—At 1 a.m. the fires were lighted, and by 8 a.m. we were under steam, not having shifted our position two miles during the night. It was a glorious day, but a flat calm. With two fires only, we steamed easily nine knots. At sunset we saw Mount Etna—11,000 feet high—as though rising from the sea, a hundred and twenty miles off, the island of Sicily quite disappearing from sight. A cuckoo came on board and was caught, but we soon released him, hoping he would reach the land. The night was quite superb, myriads of stars being visible; and the multitudes of brilliant animalcules in the water seemed to reflect them, as the 'Sunbeam's' bows threw a wave of light from under her. The most beautiful phenomenon of this sort previously seen during this voyage was off Lisbon, on a rough night, when the sea was like molten gold, lit up to such a depth that hundreds of fish could be seen darting away like comets on all sides. On the present occasion there were a great many shooting stars and meteors of extraordinary brilliancy. The nights are so warm that one delights in sitting on deck to watch these erratic luminaries, and it is hardly possible to determine when to go to bed. The heat in the day is great—

75° in the shade in a thorough draught on board—but there is always such a pleasant breeze, that we have never felt it oppressive.

Saturday, October 10*th.*—At 1.30 a.m. I was awakened by a knock at our door, and heard a very frightened voice saying, 'Please, ma'am, is Mr. Brassey there? Edgar Jones is taken very bad with cramp, on deck, and I think he is dying.' I went on deck, and found the poor man lying in great agony, surrounded by a group of his shipmates; so I called Tom, and we compounded him two draughts and some embrocation, which in a couple of hours brought him round, and with a little more treatment he is nearly well to-day. It was a somewhat alarming incident for the middle of the night, and made us reflect that the presence of a doctor on board would sometimes be a comfort. We have had a good deal of illness of this sort among the men; but in this climate, with fruit so delicious and cheap as it is at every port we touch at, it is not much to be wondered at.

A fresh breeze had sprung up just before sunrise. By 6 a.m. all sails were set, and we were bowling away eleven knots before a fair wind, with a heavy swell on our quarter, coming down the Adriatic. About 11.30 a.m. we saw the Greek land and the island of Zante in the distance, and soon after we were under their shelter, and our speed had increased to thirteen knots. When Tom was taking his observation at noon, he noticed an eclipse of the sun commencing, which we had not previously thought about, and which we subsequently watched with great interest through one of my prepared dry plates for photography.

At 4 p.m. we could make out the bold outline of

the coast and the island of Navarino, which at sunset looked specially beautiful. The breeze fell light soon after, and from 8 to 12 p.m. we were completely becalmed. To-night, as usual, there were myriads of stars above, the jelly-fish in the sea apparently reflecting them below.

Sunday, October 11*th.*—At midnight we were under steam; about 1.30 a.m. we made Cape Matapan, and about 4 a.m., when we were off the island of Cerigo, a strong contrary breeze sprang up. The sun rose over a lovely scene, enlivened by crowds of ships, either profiting by the favourable breeze or beating against it, as their course lay. We steamed across the gulf of Nauplia and Argos, past the island of Bello Pulo, and then had to change our course slightly in order to make Cape Hydra. Though the thermometer was still 72° in the shade, the north-easterly breeze—almost a trade wind in these parts, so prevalent is it—made it feel quite cool. The blue of the sea is exquisite, broken up here and there by little white curly-crested waves, and the rich yellow, brown, and red tints of the rocks and islands which rise from it contrast beautifully with its vivid ultramarine. We expect to reach Athens between nine and ten to-night, and it is to be hoped we may, for we have no bread or fresh provisions on board, the hot weather having compelled us to throw all the latter away, and our last live chicken will be killed and consumed for lunch.

All the afternoon the wind continued to increase in force, much delaying our progress even when we were under shelter of the land and in comparatively smooth water. At 5.30 p.m. we had service, in spite of the howling of the wind, and by 8 p.m. we had passed the island of

Ægina and the bay near the isthmus of Corinth, and were off the island of Salamis. The harbour of the Piræus is difficult to enter at night, on account of its narrowness, there being hardly the width of two ships between the lighthouse and a great rock bearing a beacon but no light. However, Tom managed it successfully without a pilot, and by 10 p.m. we were safely anchored inside.

Monday, October 12th.—At 6 a.m. the health officers came on board and informed us that there were some cases of small-pox in the town, and that, although the Greek authorities would not be able to furnish us with a clean bill of health when we left, the Turkish consul might give us a *visa*, which would make matters right. After a little debate we decided to run the very slight risk of quarantine at Constantinople, and land. Soon after, the captain of the Russian armour-plated frigate 'Prince Pajowski,' and the captain of the French corvette lying here, came on board, to offer us any assistance we might require (our own gunboat, the 'Torch,' having gone away for a few days), and as neither of them had heard anything about small-pox we were much relieved. The yacht was soon surrounded by a crowd of boats, some with fruit, some with washerwomen, some with interpreters. Of the latter we selected one Angelo Mellissino, who turned out to be a very satisfactory choice.

Directly after breakfast we landed, and, hiring one of the numerous pair-horse barouches in waiting, were quickly driven through the streets of the Piræus, along the road towards Athens. The white-petticoated and large-trousered men, with bright sashes and braided jackets, struck us all much, as also did the great-coated women, many of whom wore a fez with long gold tassel, even when in European dress, which looked most incongruous. The road runs across a large plain covered with vines and olives, pomegranates and figs, and when we remember that there is no artificial irrigation, and that it has not rained for six months, it is wonderful how such splendid fruit can be

Greek Costume.

produced. There are no fences, and all along the road the wild-looking drivers of the quaint country carts were making excursions into the vineyards, and filling their aprons with grapes. Halfway to Athens there are two wells and a few huts, where drivers and horses usually stop to drink, a refreshment necessitated not so much by the length of the journey as by the dust which hangs over everything in thick white clouds. Soon after we emerged from the avenue of Bella Sombras, and came in sight of Athens and its Acropolis, the ruins standing out against the bright blue sky, the only bit of colour anywhere. Everything else is grey at this time of year. All the hills are burnt up. The plains are worse. The houses are drab, cream-colour, or white. The roofs are all grey, and the trees and the green shutters so coated with dust, that they are grey too. It is only towards evening, when the mountains are clothed in the purple colouring of sunset, that there is any relief from the monotonous aridity.

We drove first to the Temple of Theseus, the most perfectly preserved temple of the ancient world. The situation has sheltered it from shot and shell; but without doubt it owes its escape from destruction in part to the circumstance that in the middle ages it was consecrated as a church. It is a beautiful building, with its double row of columns, bas-reliefs, and roof, all perfect, and now contains an interesting collection of antiquities, gathered from its immediate neighbourhood. Thence we drove up the hill to the Acropolis, passing on our way the modern observatory on the Hill of the Nymphs. The Hill of Pnyx rose on our right, and the Areopagus, where St. Paul preached, on our left. We entered the gates, and passing among ruins of all kinds, statues, bas-reliefs, columns, capitals, and friezes, soon approached the propylæa. Then we went to the little Temple of Victory, closed with iron gates and full of most exquisite bits of statues and bas-reliefs, specially two dancing girls, graceful in attitude and full of life and action. After these preliminary peeps at loveliness and art we went up the long flight of steps past the Pinacotheca, and soon stood on the top of the Hill of the Acropolis, and in full view of all its glories.

On one side was the splendid Parthenon, on the other the Erectheum, with the Porch of Caryatides, called Beautiful; and right well it deserves its name. Six noble columns are still standing. We strolled about for a long

Athens

time, took some photographs, admired the lovely panoramic view from the top—over the town of Athens, to Eleusis, Salamis, and Corinth on one side, and from Mount Pentelicus and Mount Hymettus to the Elysian fields—till our eyes wandered round by the ancient harbours of Phalerum and Piræus, back again by the Street of Tombs to Athens, looking more dusty and more grey than ever as we gazed down on its grey-tiled roofs. Even the gardens and palm-trees hardly relieved it. It was nearly three o'clock before we could tear ourselves away, and, hungry and tired, we repaired to the comfortable Hôtel des Étrangers, where we found rest, refreshment, and piles of English papers to read. Both bedrooms and sitting-rooms were very clean and well furnished.

Having called on some friends at the English Embassy, we drove to the Arch of Hadrian and the Temple of Jupiter Olympius, or rather what remains of it—fifteen lovely columns standing, and one on the ground in pieces. A coffeehouse-keeper had established himself close by, and there were many little deal chairs and tables arranged under the shelter of the giant columns, looking rather incongruous, but at the same time, perhaps, making the ruin appear even greater in its grandeur from the force of contrast. Then we drove to the royal garden immediately surrounding the palace, where anyone is permitted to walk from 4 to 5.30 p.m. It is laid out with winding paths and shrubberies, leading to open spaces planted with rare exotics under the shade of high trees. The system of irrigation employed keeps all fresh and green even in this hot thirsty climate. We went to one or two shops, bought some photographs, and then had the very dustiest drive through the Street of Tombs back to the Piræus, where we all arrived looking like millers. It was a fine night, and much cooler.

Tuesday, October 13*th.*—We were so smothered with dust yesterday that we determined to try the train, and, starting at 9 a.m., reached Athens in ten minutes. It was then but a short drive to the Acropolis, where we spent a couple of hours, perfecting our pleasant impressions of yesterday. At 11 a.m. we went to the hotel to breakfast with some friends, and a capital breakfast they gave us. The table was beautifully decorated, and the cook must have been a real artist. We had the wines of the country to taste; some were very good, and some peculiar rather than palatable. The ordinary wine drunk by the common

Woman of Athens

people is largely mixed with resin, to preserve it. They say, when once you acquire the taste for it, you do not like anything else; but to the uninitiated it is very medicinal. We had honey, too, from Mount Hymettus. Anything more delicious you can hardly imagine. The perfume reminds you of a well-sunned bank of heather on a lovely

August day on the moors. We found that the trains, like everything else, had a siesta, and that there were none in the middle of the day ; so we had another dusty drive back to the Piræus. Before starting, we went to some greenhouses belonging to the Scotch gardener of the English consul, and bought some beautiful plants. He said that anything at all rare or curious came from London or Paris, as everything deteriorates so in this climate.

The yacht had steam up when we went on board, and Athens was soon many miles astern. The view, looking back, was exquisite, but outside the north-east wind was blowing hard, and as all the ships going before it had every sail reefed, and those wishing to go against it had mostly put in for shelter, Tom thought it prudent to do likewise, especially as night was coming on and it looked thick. So we ran under the shelter of Cape Sunium, a fine headland, rising from the sea, and crowned with the Temple of Minerva. We had hardly dropped anchor before a Norwegian barque that we had seen near Tromsöe recognised us, and began dipping her ensign most enthusiastically. An Austrian barque thought proper to follow her example, so for some time there was great exchange of salutations. Soon after, a large mail steamer came in for shelter from the fury of the gale.

Wednesday, October 14*th.*—Under way by 6 a.m. The lovely Temple of Minerva looked even more beautiful than it did last night, as the sun slowly rose and shone on its white columns, the cliffs rising red and brown from the deep blue sea. A few little sails, scudding gaily along before the breeze, under shelter of the land, made up a perfect picture. It was here that Lord Byron and his friends were nearly captured by robbers, and this was also the scene of Falconer's shipwreck. Outside it was still blowing a gale, right in our teeth; and, as it was impossible to proceed on our course, Tom decided to try a narrow passage between the island of Negropont and the mainland. We steered direct for it, and were soon in smoother water again, and under shelter of the high mountains, though the wind was still so strong that we could not make more than five knots under a full head of steam. We passed the plain of Marathon. It is separated from Athens by Mount Pentelicus, whose peaks form a background to the long plain and marshes. Then we passed near the white ruins of Rhadmis, gleaming among groves of myrtle and lentisk; by Delis and Apostoli, so called from the many voyages of the apostles; then close to Sycamino, where Mr. Vyner and his unfortunate companions were shot by the brigands in 1870—victims of the mismanagement of their friends, and of the want of faith of the Greek government. Shortly after, we came to a very narrow passage, with shallow water on each side. Some fishermen came alongside, but as we could not understand them or they us, we had to send the gig on before to sound, and then creep our way slowly after her, till we dropped anchor at Drokho, close to the site of the ancient Chalcis. We thought we were rather near the mountains, still said (and with truth) to be infested by brigands; the deck watch was therefore doubled and armed with rifles and cutlasses, with orders to call up the remainder of the watch if any boat approached. We were not disturbed, however.

Thursday, October 15*th.*—Tom and I were up early and off to Euripo, the town built on the site of the ancient

Chalcis, to try and get a pilot. We rowed up about two miles. As we approached, the town looked most picturesque, surrounded by old Venetian walls and battlements, now tumbling to decay. At the foot of the wall in many places were lying the stone cannon-balls, of enormous size, which had commenced the work of destruction centuries ago. The town is built on the right or south side of the strait,

The Promenade at Euripo (Ancient Chalcis).

and an old Venetian fort stands on the north. These are connected by a bridge about fifty feet long, which opens to admit the passage of ships. The moles connected by this bridge were first thrown out 411 B.C. Thus commanding the strait, the Bœotians were enabled to intercept the direct commerce of the Athenians with Thrace, Thessaly, and Macedonia, compelling their ships to navigate a stormy sea, where the same wind prevailed ten months in the year, and where, even in these days, it is no unusual thing for a sailing ship to wait six weeks for a passage.

We landed, and no one asked for our papers, though we were surrounded by soldiers and a motley crowd, even at that early hour of the morning. We were soon fortunate enough to find a man who could speak a few words of Italian, and he sent for a pilot, while we wandered about, first across the bridge to the inside of the fort, with curious white marble reliefs built into the brickwork, among which the winged lion of St. Mark was frequently repeated.

We then recrossed the bridge, and walked up the main street, in which were curious carved wooden overhanging roofs, and projecting rooms and lattices, to the mosque, a picturesque building, with a minaret, surrounded with stone cannon-balls. It is now used as a barrack. Close by there is a beautiful little Turkish fountain, shaded by a palm-tree and some beautiful Bella Sombras. The little *place* is very pleasant and shady, with stone seats, and tables in front of them, and stands for the band in the centre. The pilot arrived before we had quite finished our inspection of the town, and he fortunately could speak a few words of Italian.

Captain Mansell, the well-known hydrographer to the Navy, introduced himself to us, and asked for our papers, which the Greek authorities, having forgotten to demand them, were in great tribulation about. He has resided here seven years, and has a nice house in the town and a beautiful garden outside. He gave us rather an interesting description of life in this curious, out-of-the-world, old town. They enjoy a delicious climate, and have a very pleasant little society among themselves. Once a week a steamer passes through each way, which is a great and pleasing excitement. Once or twice a week earthquakes occur, which is not quite so pleasing an excitement, as they often do considerable damage. The houses are generally built only one story high, to avoid serious accidents. Another drawback to Euripo is the impossibility of going on the mainland, on account of the brigands who still infest the country. I really forget how many years Captain Mansell said it was since he had ventured to leave the island.

Castle of Euripo.

The current came running down under the bridge like a millstream, but we were told the tide would turn at about ten o'clock, when we could get through. We took a good many interesting photographs, and after breakfast steamed slowly up to the bridge, when the yacht shot through without any trouble. The coast north of Chalcis is certainly very fine, high mountains rising from the sea, covered with forests and myrtle-groves down to the water's edge.

It was a cloudless afternoon. A shoal of porpoises accompanied us for some time, and there were many land and sea birds flying around. At 4 p.m. we came out of the channel of Talanta into that of Orios, leaving the pass of Thermopylæ on our left. Unfortunately the sun set all too soon, the light failed us, and, the channel being very narrow, we were obliged to anchor in the bay of Gadakira. The young moon shone brightly, and the smell of myrtles from the shore, not fifty yards off, was perfectly delicious.

Friday, October 16*th.*—We got under way at 6 a.m., just as the sun was rising, tipping the snowy peaks of the Pindus chain of mountains with a lovely rose colour. For the first three hours the scenery was exquisite. We passed through the channel of Trikhiri, by the large town of Argalasti, standing on a hill. Thence we steamed across the entrance to the gulf of Volo, and among the islands of Skiatho, Scopelo, Ioos, &c. When once really out at sea, we lowered the funnel, and set the sails. The wind was blowing strong, and exactly in our teeth, so that the 'Sunbeam's' head was pointed for Scyros instead of the Dardanelles. Mount Athos was visible, rising grandly from the sea, 6,000 feet above Cape Santo. On the summit there is the strictest monastery in the world. Not a female animal of any kind is allowed within miles, so that the monks have to do without milk, or fresh eggs even, and travellers are not allowed to carry even *dead hens* on their saddles for provision. A few years ago two English ladies landed here from a yacht. As most of the men here wear petticoats, and the women trousers, and the monks have not a chance of much experience in such matters, they did not discover the sacrilege that had been committed for some time; and then you may imagine their horror and disgust, and the penances they had to perform—poor things!

About 3 p.m. we passed the island of Scyros, with its steep cliffs, from which Theseus is said to have cast himself into the sea. Almost every little island and rock is full of interest, not only from its mythological legends, but from the part it has played in Grecian history. After passing this island it became very rough, and we took more water on board than we had hitherto seen on the deck of the 'Sunbeam.'

Saturday, October 17th.—About 1 a.m. we passed the island of Ipsara, sighted Chios, and at 2 a.m. made the light on Cape Sigri, at the north end of the island of Mitylene. From then till 8 a.m. the wind was shifty, and we only lost ground. Fires were lighted, and by 11 a.m. we were under steam and running up the coast of the island, which is very large, and fertile in parts, with two splendid natural harbours. But it is little frequented, although it contains many interesting antiquities. We ran up the coast of Asia Minor, between the island of Tenedos and the mainland, passing the site of the ancient city of Alexandria Troas, and the plains of Troy. Close by was Besika Bay, where our fleet so often lies at anchor, and opposite to us rose Tenedos, on the island of the same name. It seemed a large town, and there were many ships lying there, waiting for a fair wind to carry them through the Dardanelles. About 8 p.m. we made the lights at the entrance, and steamed up the strait to Chanak-Kalesi, where two towers guard the narrowest part. Here we expected to be boarded for our bill of health. We went slowly, therefore, till a gun was fired across our bows. Then we stopped; but finding that nobody came, and that the current was carrying us backwards, we proceeded on our course, and heard no more about it. The passage is very narrow, in many places narrower than Southampton Water, and oftentimes crowded with ships, many of them not carrying lights. Though beautifully lighted, it is rather a difficult piece of navigation for a stranger in the dark, and people here are much astonished at Tom's having attempted it and done it successfully. But he was so confident, and the Admiralty charts are so good, that we went full speed all the way, and never hesitated for a moment. It was a great disappointment, coming through in the dark, but we hope to see it better on our return voyage.

On arriving at Constantinople we found we were very lucky not to have had a shot fired into our hull, instead of across our bows. By the strict letter of the law, I believe we ought to have paid a fine of 24*l*. for our mistake, but through the good offices of our consul the matter was arranged.

General View of Constantinople

CHAPTER IV.

CONSTANTINOPLE.

The city now doth like a garment wear
The beauty of the morning. . . .
Never did sun more beautifully steep
In his first splendour, valley, rock, or hill.

Sunday, October 18*th*.—We were on deck at daybreak, and saw the sun rise over the low lands on each side of the Sea of Marmora; but it was 9 a.m. before we got our first glimpse of Constantinople rising from the sea, and it was 11 a.m. before we were at all near enough to realise its beauties. Mosques in every direction, with their round domes surrounded by slender minarets towering one above the other, looking like sentries keeping guard over the shrine; cypress-trees, old fortifications, houses, and palaces in every style of architecture; towers, high, low, thin, thick, round, and square, with battlements and without;

gardens, ships, boats, steamers, barracks, and public buildings, all mixed together in the wildest and most picturesque confusion, make up one of the largest ports in the world. It has a great trade of its own, besides being the great highway to the Black Sea. The three towns of Stamboul, Pera, and Skutari are separated by such narrow arms of the Golden Horn and Bosphorus, that land and water appear completely blended. From a distance it is almost impossible to see where one ends and the other begins.

We steamed slowly along, past endless houses and gardens, with occasional patches of barren waste, where there had been a great fire, till we reached Seraglio Point, just at the entrance to the Bosphorus and the Golden Horn. Here a pilot and the captain of the port came alongside, and after some difficulty in threading our way among the crowds of shipping, and one very near shave of a collision, we dropped our anchor at 1.30 p.m. just off the arsenal at Tophaneh, where the men-of-war lay. Now we were able to look round at our leisure.

As usual, on coming into port, we were immediately surrounded by a crowd of picturesque boats, full of things for sale. The caïques shot swiftly by, sometimes with a load of merchandise, but more frequently with a muffled-up Turkish family on board. About 4.30 p.m. we landed, and, passing through streets which offered a picture at every corner, went to the public garden, where the band was playing, and all the European rank and fashion of Constantinople were assembled. We dined at Misseri's hotel, where we found many friends. As we walked down to the boat a Turkish regimental band was playing most discordant music in front of the officers' quarters. The streets were crowded, the mosques and minarets illuminated, and squibs were going off in every direction. It was the Fast of Ramazan, which some Mohammedans keep very strictly, neither eating, drinking, nor smoking (the last, perhaps, the greatest deprivation of all to an Oriental) from sunrise to sunset. Then the gun fires, and from having been half asleep all day, they rouse themselves to eat, drink, and rejoice all night long. The view from the yacht of the hundreds of airy-looking pointed minarets lighted up with myriads of tiny lamps was very beautiful. The dogs which abound here made night hideous by their cries, rushing about in large packs from quarter to quarter; and unfortunately we lay near enough to the shore to be kept awake by them.

Monday, October 19*th.*—On deck at daybreak. Even then (in spite of the Sultan's order that all steamers should consume their own smoke) the atmosphere was very murky, and though it was a beautiful, bright, clear morning, the city had a much more Manchesterian aspect than I liked to see, and put one rather in mind of Liverpool, seen from the opposite side of the Mersey. Before we had done breakfast the English vice-consul came on board, bringing us each a good supply of letters. He told us a good deal of gossip and news about the place, and then we went across the water to the celebrated bazaars of Stamboul. The crowd was very amusing—such numbers of Turkish ladies, attended by negroes, eunuchs, or old women, making purchases of all sorts, but mostly buying articles of European manufacture. It was amusing to see them admiring and bargaining for second-hand European dresses, all very smart in trimming and of the most gorgeous colours, though somewhat soiled. I have often wondered what became of old ball and dinner dresses, but now that I have seen the enormous quarter of the bazaar devoted to the sale of these articles of apparel, I cease to do so. The old saying that two of a trade never agree does not, it is to be hoped, hold good here, for there are streets in which reside sellers of saddles, slippers, silk, cotton, and woollen goods, embroideries, beds, chairs, handkerchiefs, and every sort of thing—rows of little shops on each side of a very narrow path, the proprietors of which all sell the same article. In this way you have the convenience of great choice and much competition among the dealers, but if you have many purchases to make you have to traverse an enormous area of ground, for the bazaars are miles in extent, and it is said that no one resident in Constantinople has ever seen the whole of them.

We were disappointed in the look of the things exposed for sale, but I fancy all the best are kept inside. The Bezistan, in the centre, is perhaps the most interesting. Here you find beautiful old weapons of every description, jewellery, furniture, and all sorts of things, especially clocks of the most elaborate construction, telling the hours of the day, the days of the week and month, and playing one or two tunes. They are of the best workmanship, made perhaps a hundred years ago in England for the Turks, who have a veritable mania for timepieces. I have seen twenty-six large clocks and candelabras in one room in the harem at Bardo belonging to the Bey of Tunis. But they are now to be sold very cheap, on account of some change of fashion. It is the most trying work going through the bazaars, standing, pushing, and being pushed; and very hot, for they are all covered, while large round holes in the roof admit the light in the most beautiful rays and streams on to the motley crowd and gay stuffs beneath.

From the bazaar we went to the Ottoman Bank, to take a letter of introduction to Mr. Foster, the chairman. He was out, but another director, whom we had known in Beyrout, and an old friend of Tom's father, came in. It is very pleasing and almost astonishing, even to us who

Tower in the Bosphorus

knew his worth so well, to find in what affection, respect, and esteem Mr. Brassey's memory is still held in every town, country, and continent we visit, and what kind consideration and attention the name always commands for us.

After lunch, we drove all round about and through Stamboul, past the various mosques, the curious columns of Theodosius and of the Three Serpents. The obelisk of Egyptian granite, about fifty feet high, in one piece, brought from Egypt by Constantine the Great, is close by, and from this point we went to the door of the Cistern of Constantine, now called the 'Thousand and One Columns' (from its numerous supports), but we did not descend into its subterranean depths. We went to see the Tombs of the Sultans, a large room under a dome, in the middle of a garden. It is beautifully carpeted, and in the centre is the large tomb of the late Sultan, with mother-of-pearl railings. All his family lie around him. The tombs are all covered with beautiful brocades and shawls, and are surrounded by richly inlaid praying-desks, or with illuminated copies of the Koran lying open on them. Close by are buried the three sons of the late Sultan's sister, barbarously murdered in infancy, according to the then existing law, to prevent their ever aspiring to the throne. When the late Sultan came to the throne, he had his five brothers bowstrung before his eyes, for the same reason. It is indeed a wonderful country, with its mixture of barbarism, luxury, and civilisation.

Our drive ended at Misseri's. After dinner we walked back to the boat, down the stony staircase-like streets, tumbling at every step over dogs which seem to be asleep, for they never take the trouble to move till you tread on them in the dark, and get an unpleasant snap at your legs. Most ladies have sedan chairs, which are very comfortable at night. In the day there are good horses for hire at the corner of every street. The carriage-roads are so few and far between that they take you miles out of your way, and so atrocious that they shake you to pieces. The moon shone brilliantly, and all the minarets were lighted up with small lanterns arranged in a different pattern from those of last night, but quite as beautiful.

Tuesday, October 20th.—Before we had done breakfast, some friends came on board, and at 10 a.m. we started with one of them, who had kindly promised to show us all that was best worth seeing in the bazaars. But it was a long time before the merchants would show us anything *really* good. They carefully barred and locked the door, and we had to sit for an enormous time looking at rubbish before they would bring out the real treasures. The embroideries, some eight, some five, and some four hundred years old, are the most beautiful ; prayer-carpets, with silk and gold embroidery and seed pearls ; Persian enamels and narghilis of the richest description ; pierced copper lamps, with the most delicate tracery, set with turquoises, surrounding quaint figures of men and beasts ; gold and silver gilt coffee sets, and clasps inlaid with coral and precious stones ; magnificent pistols, guns, knives, and daggers ; rare Oriental china ; in fact, every curious thing you can conceive. Then we went to what is commonly called the Pigeon Mosque on account of the thousands of sacred birds that crowd the court-yards and cover the roofs. During the present month, in which this year the Fast of Ramazan falls, the courts are full of little booths, in which all sorts of common toys, china, lamps, fruit, spice, pickles, medicine, are sold, and which are crowded with Turkish ladies and gentlemen. All this was a long morning's work. It was 2.30 p.m. before we reached the yacht, quite tired. In the afternoon we went for a drive outside the town, past one of the Sultan's kiosks, built only that he may go and smoke a pipe there once or perhaps twice a year. The view from the top of the hill was splendid, across the Golden Horn and the Bosphorus, and over the three towns of Pera,

Stamboul, and Skutari, with their suburbs of Galata and Tophaneh. We dined again at Misseri's, and found the table crowded with English people and foreigners, just arrived by the steamer. Among others were two most amusing people, one a travelling professor from Oxford, come out to see the transit of Venus, with very strong opinions of his own (among others, that Sir Isaac Newton was a fool), and a Brazilian, who had been in the army and navy, and had learnt twenty, and talked seven, languages indifferently well. Their discussions kept the whole table in a roar.

When we landed the first day in the arsenal, poor little Félise was immediately set upon by about twenty fierce dogs, looking like wolves. Strange to say, in a few days they learnt to know her, and came to the conclusion that she did not wish to settle among them or take away their food, but simply to go quietly by; so they allowed her to pass through them without molestation. These fierce dogs abound in every part of the three cities, and as they are the natural scavengers of the place, they are never interfered with, but are regularly fed by the inhabitants. They all have their own quarters, perhaps a dozen to half a street, and woe betide the unlucky dog who comes from another quarter in search of food. He is immediately set upon and devoured, unless he lies down on his back and puts up his paws in token of surrender. Then, in the thickest of the fight, his assailants stop and content themselves with walking round him and growling, and seeing him safely back to his own quarter. The puppies are innumerable, and when there are too many to be supported in one quarter, the parents desert their offspring, and fight their own way somewhere else, in order to leave them enough to eat. If you once throw one a bit of bread in passing, he never forgets you, but looks out every day to fawn upon you as you go by. These facts I have heard from many long residents here; so that, in spite of their ill-favoured mangy appearance, there is a good deal to be said for the intelligence of these animals, and their scavenging services are most necessary, for refuse of every kind is thrown outside the door.

Fountain St. Sophia.

Wednesday, October 21st.—The start this morning was an early one, for during the Fast of Ramazan Wednesday is the only day on which the mosques can be seen, and there is great difficulty even on that day in procuring the necessary firmans from the Sublime Porte, because the officials sleep all day and play all night, besides being in a horribly bad temper from fasting. However, the consul's cavass managed to bring ours just at the last moment, and we went first to St. Sophia, a building more beautiful within than without. An enormous dome, the largest in the world, is supported by arches of the most beautiful proportions. The space in the centre is perfectly clear, with the exception of large hanging circles of oil lamps, so that its vast proportions can be clearly seen. It is all lined with mosaics and tiles of exquisite colouring. Some of the pillars which support the arches are of green jasper from the Temple of Diana at Ephesus. Others are of porphyry, brought from the Temple of the Sun at Baalbec.

From St. Sophia we went to the mosque of Ahmedyeh, which is the state mosque, as St. Sophia is the court mosque. The Sultan always goes there at the Feast of Bairam. It is a beautiful building outside, surrounded by six minarets. St. Sophia has four, and the mosque at Mecca seven. Inside is another large dome, similar to that of St. Sophia, but not so richly decorated, and the pulpit is an exact copy of the one at Mecca. In the square of the ancient hippodrome, where the mosque stands, is the Museum of the Janissaries, containing a curious collection of very stiff wax figures, interesting only on account of their clothes, which are exact copies of those worn by the high dignitaries, officials, and court servants, for the last hundred years. A long drive along the streets parallel to the Golden Horn took us to the mosque of Suliemanyieh, one of the purest examples of Moslem architecture. By this time it was twelve o'clock, and the hungry and fanatical worshippers were beginning to arrive; so we prudently retired, having been warned that during this season of fasting it would be rash to remain in the mosques after that hour, the pious Moslem thinking he is doing Mahomet good service by seeking an excuse to insult a Giaour.

While at the mosque, another cavass came rushing after us with an order for the Treasury, procured only at the last moment; so we drove thither and inspected its varied treasures. It is in the court of the old Seraglio Palace, which was burned some years ago, when these treasures were rescued with great difficulty from the devouring flames. The first thing that meets the eye on entering is a magnificent enamel throne, inlaid with rubies, pearls, and diamonds. The cases round the room are full of velvet prayer-carpets, embroidered in gold and precious stones. They also contain guns, daggers, and swords, ornamented with priceless gems, emeralds as big as hens' eggs, and rubies as big as pigeons' eggs, but full of flaws, besides basins of loose turquoises, coral, agates, cornelians, aquamarines, topazes, and rows of amber beads of the purest quality. One case was full of agate, crystal, and jade vases, mounted in enamel and precious stones. Upstairs are saddles, housings, and horse-furniture of gold inlaid with coral and precious stones. But the greatest marvel was a dressing-table encrusted with diamonds and rubies, the pillars supporting the glass set with diamonds of large size, the frame of the glass a mass of rubies and diamonds, and even the fringe round the edge of the table, three or four inches long, composed of hanging strings of diamonds. It is said that the Empress of the French was presented with over a hundred thousand pounds' worth of things when she was there, and that the Sultan gave her everything she admired or liked, without her even expressing any wish to possess it.

From the Treasury we went to see all that is left of the Seraglio Palace since the disastrous fire. We all now began to think we had had more than enough sight-seeing for one morning; so we drove back beneath the large plane-trees by the station to the ferry, where we had left our boat. It was necessary to wait for it a few minutes, till it could approach the landing-place. While doing so it was very amusing to watch the busy scene. Owing to the one city of Constantinople being really three cities, situated on three points of land, the two bridges connecting Pera, Stamboul, and Skutari, are always crowded. The caïque is the cab of Constantinople, and is used by everyone, from the highest to the lowest. There are many beautiful carriages, with fine horses, and generally one or two men as an escort, which seem to wait at the various ferries at all times of the day for their respective owners.

Turkish Waist-clasp.

CHAPTER V.

THE BOSPHORUS AND ITS PALACES.

> *The European with the Asian shore*
> *Sprinkled with palaces ; the Ocean stream*
>   *Here and there studded with a seventy-four ;*
> *Sophia's cupola with golden gleam ;*
>   *The cypress groves ; Olympus high and hoar.*

Thursday, October 22nd.—We started at 10 a.m. from Stamboul, and crossed in the ferry-boat to Skutari. Once on shore, we drove up the hill behind Skutari, towards the pretty village of Chumleyjah, to the hill called Boolgoorloo, from which there is a magnificent view all over the Sea of Marmora and Prince's Islands to the Gulf of Ismed, Kadi Keui, and Skutari. At our feet lay Seraglio Point, Stamboul, the Golden Horn, Pera, Tophaneh, Galata, and the Bosphorus. Another steep climb showed us a lovely view up the Bosphorus, over Beylerbey, towards Therapia, Buyukdere, and the Black Sea. On the way down again we passed the dwelling of the Sultan's nurse—quite a palace—and then went to the pleasant little house of a friend, whence we drove by the high-walled gardens of one of the Sultan's palaces to the quay at Beylerbey. This is one of the best furnished and arranged of all the palaces, and in it the Empress of the French stayed during her visit. Stepping into various caïques (they hold, as a rule, only two persons, and are the most delightful conveyances in the world), the whole party proceeded down the Bosphorus and soon met the yacht, when all went on board, and we steamed slowly up the Bosphorus. It was a lovely afternoon, and the views were even more beautiful than I had expected, looking down from above. The shores are charmingly wooded and undulating, with little valleys running up into the high mountains beyond, and literally lined with kiosks and palaces. One of the most beautiful of these belongs to the Viceroy of Egypt, but is at present occupied by his mother. He was so ruined by backshishing everybody here last year, that he is afraid to come again, and has sent his mother and his yacht instead. One of the stories afloat is that he entertained the Sultan one day at dinner off a magnificent service of gold plate which he had ordered expressly from Paris. After dinner, the Sultan intimated that no one could eat off it after him, and requested it might be sent to the palace at once! This is only a small specimen of what the Viceroy had to go through, and shows how he was fleeced right and left by everyone from the Sultan downwards.

We passed Kandili, from whence a continual look-out is kept for fires, a certain number of guns being fired to indicate the particular quarter of the city in which one is occurring. There used to be one and sometimes two a day, but latterly they have not been so frequent, and only one has occurred since our arrival. The fire-engines are most primitive, carried and worked by hand, and the men, after rushing violently to the scene of action, sit down quietly till they are hired, before commencing operations. Soon after we came to Roomili Hissar, the narrowest part of the Bosphorus, where the towers were built by the Venetians and Genoese to take the tolls. This was the entrance to the Bosphorus, as Chanak is to the Dardanelles. Here the submarine cable passes from Europe to Asia. We rowed slowly by the Palace of the Sweet Waters of Asia, behind which is the green meadow, shaded by splendid plane-trees, where the Turkish ladies love to walk on Fridays and Sundays in late summer and autumn, just as they resort to the Sweet Waters of Europe, at the end of the Golden Horn, in spring and early summer, and to Mashleck in winter.

Passing palaces and kiosks innumerable, ever surrounded by lovely gardens, we at last reached Therapia. It is about eight miles from Constantinople by water. It seems almost a misnomer to call such narrow straits (barely a mile wide in parts) *sea*, even though the water is salt.

We dropped anchor about five. Our friends then left us, and at 7.30 p.m. we went to dine at the English Embassy. It is built of wood outside, but within you enter a marble hall, and go up a marble staircase, along a corridor with marble columns, filled with plants. The rooms are handsome, and the effect is very good. But the discomfort is terrible in autumn and winter, for no amount of fires will raise the temperature above 46°. The party was entirely diplomatic, and dinner was eaten off the service of plate saved with so much difficulty from the great fire in 1870. Fifteen hundred persons were killed in that fire, though it broke out at one o'clock in the day. Lady Elliot and her children and servants ran down to take refuge on board the 'Antelope,' without hats or bonnets, not saving a single article of clothing except what they had on, the fire having begun at the top of the house. The scenes of robbery and pillage were awful, and for days after, dead bodies were lying about the streets, their pockets full of watches, jewellery, and ill-gotten plunder. Yet this awful fire, which destroyed thousands of houses and hundreds of people, and desolated acres of ground, did all this damage in six hours, being entirely quenched by seven in the evening.

Friday, October 23*rd.*—We were off by the 9.30 a.m. steamer down the Bosphorus, to see the Sultan go to the

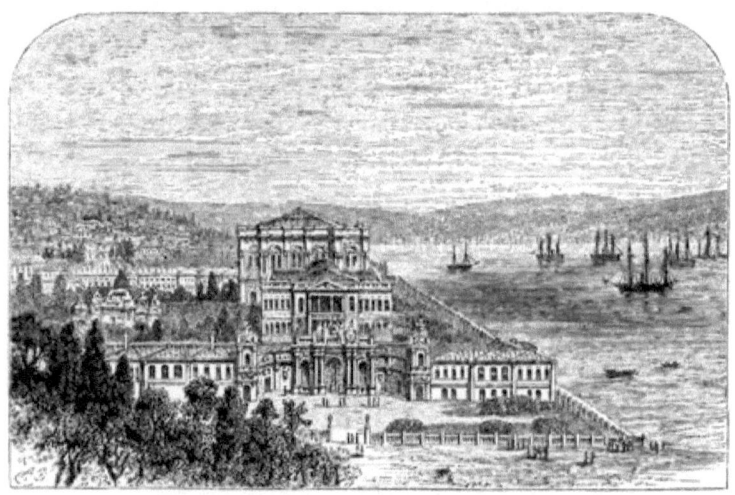

Palace of Dolmabagtcheh.

mosque, which he does every Friday at twelve o'clock. From fear of assassination he never makes up his mind before the moment of starting to which mosque he will go, or whether by land or sea, in a carriage or on horseback. Everything is therefore prepared and waiting for him both ashore and afloat, and the only chance of seeing the land or water procession is to station oneself in an open carriage outside the palace gates, having a caïque in readiness, and wait and see what turns up. This we did. There was no crowd, we had not long to wait, and it was delicious sitting in the shade of the avenue of *bella-sombras*, planted all round the Palace of Dolmabagtcheh, where the Sultan is now living. There were a great many smartly dressed troops about, magnificently caparisoned horses being led up and down, and officers on horseback and carriages waiting in all directions. Precisely at twelve the bugle sounded, and all the troops mounted; the fat pashas (dressed in light blue and gold, their horses having scarlet, white, and gold trappings) scrambled or were pushed up into their saddles, and everybody stood at attention. Immediately after, the Sultan's eldest son, a very ugly young man of about seventeen, gorgeous in purple and gold, his housings stiff with gold and precious stones, rode out, surrounded by a retinue of about forty gaily dressed officers on foot, and waited to salute his father. Then came the grand vizier, in almost equal state, followed by all the ministers, quite as gorgeous, but without so many attendants. At last the Sultan himself appeared, in a sort of undress uniform, with a flowing cloak over it, and with two or three large diamond stars on his breast. He was mounted on a superb white Arab charger, thirty-three years old, whose saddle-cloths and trappings blazed with gold and diamonds. He looked neither to right nor to left, and seemed to take no notice of the saluting and cheering. He is a fine intelligent-looking man of about forty-four, but looks nearer seventy, and has become terribly grey since we saw him in Paris in 1867. The following of officers on foot was enormous; and then came two hundred of the fat blue and gold pashas, with their white horses and brilliant trappings, the rear being brought up by some troops and a few carriages. The streets were all lined with soldiers, and different bands, about a hundred yards apart, took up the Turkish National Hymn as he passed.

We did not stay to see him come back, for he is as capricious in his prayers as in most other things, and might stay, we were told, half an hour or two hours and a half. They say he is quite mad, but he is sufficiently sane to be able to conceal it from strangers, and to talk with considerable intelligence. When he first came to the throne he was a very fine young man, and used to hunt and shoot. Now his chief amusements are cock-fighting, backgammon, and slicing off, with a sword, the heads of some unfortunate turkeys specially kept in a yard for his entertainment. His isolated life and his over-eating have reduced him to his present melancholy state. Nobody dares address him, even if he speaks to them, except in monosyllables, with their foreheads almost touching the floor, the only exception being the grand vizier, who dares not look up, but stands almost bent double. The Sultan is entirely governed by his mother, who, having been a slave of the very lowest description, to whom his father Mahmoud II. took a fancy as she was carrying wood to the bath, is naturally bigoted and ignorant, and tries to suppress all progress and improvement of every kind. and to immure the unfortunate women more tightly than ever. But the time is past for that, and before many years are over there will be a great revolution in manners and customs here. The thin end of the wedge is in already, and in spite of the Sultan Valideh's edicts the yashmaks get thinner and thinner every day, till in many cases they are little more than a tulle veil. The broughams containing the ladies from the harems draw up by the mosques of Bymzel at Mashleck, or the gardens at Chumleyjah, the negroes and eunuchs discreetly turn their backs, and a good deal of flirting and sign-making goes on.

There were some public gardens opened the other day, to which the Turkish ladies went with their husbands. This was speedily stopped by imperial edict. Then the gentlemen went inside the gardens, the ladies being left in their broughams in crowds outside. The coachmen, being well bribed no doubt, conspired together and got all their carriages into such confusion that, in spite of all the efforts of the police and soldiers sent on purpose to keep them moving, it was impossible to extricate them for more than an hour. This was repeated several times, till at last troops were sent in sufficient numbers to occupy the ground, to prevent the carriages going at all. The grand vizier or the ministers tell their favourite wives what they want done, and they go to the Sultan Valideh and try to persuade her, and she, if she approves, goes to the Sultan; and that is how things are managed in Turkey.

One of the Sultan's manias is a dread of fire. He has had acres of houses pulled down, and an enormous new palace built further out of the town, nor will he allow a single article of wood inside the palace. Even the wooden fez-pegs have been turned out. All the flat candlesticks must be surrounded by a saucer of water. He had two of the sultanas bowstrung the other day for transgressing this rule, and half murdered the wife of one of his colonels for the same offence. He knocked her down, and beat and trampled on her, so that the poor woman was ill for days after. One night, not long ago, he escaped from the palace in his night-shirt, and got into a common cab. He was immediately pursued by some faithful attendants carrying his clothes, but it was with great difficulty that he could be persuaded to put them on and return. It is not wonderful that he should occasionally suffer from nightmare, for though he neither drinks, nor smokes, nor takes coffee, he eats *eleven* times a day an enormous meal. There are always ninety-four dishes prepared from which he may make his choice.

Yacht's Deckhouse.

Whatever he selects is carefully sealed up in the kitchen by the Sultan's mother herself, the seals are broken only in his presence, some one tastes every dish before him, and he drinks water out of a prepared goblet, which poison would discolour or break. He is very anxious to change the order of succession, and make his own son the next heir, instead of being succeeded by the eldest male of the family of Osman; but as this is opposed to Mohammedan custom[1] generally, I do not think he is likely to succeed.

The unfortunate nephews, of whom there are four, the eldest thirty-four years old, are kept all together in a large palace, and have all their meals sent from the Sultan's kitchen. So afraid are they, however, of being poisoned, that they never eat them, but have an old woman to cook for them privately. They are allowed to go out in the daytime on the Bosphorus, with a strong guard. They have surreptitiously learned to play the piano and read French newspapers and novels, two things of which the Sultan would highly disapprove; and I fancy that if ever they should come to the throne they will be found to be very advanced young Turks indeed. Everything is kept from the knowledge of the Sultan which would be likely to displease him, for he would either publicly disgrace his informant, or, if the intelligence were very disagreeable indeed, have him bowstrung. The consequence is that no one has yet dared to tell him of the famine in Asia Minor, and he is in perfect ignorance of that fact.

The Sultan is not allowed to marry, but the slaves who become mothers of his children are called sultanas, and not allowed to do any more work. They have also a separate suite of apartments, a retinue of servants, besides carriages and horses; and each hopes some day to be the mother of the future sultan, and therefore the most prominent woman in Turkey. The sultanas may not sit at table with their own children, on account of their having been slaves, whilst the children are princes and princesses in right of

[1] That the eldest male of the house of Osman should always occupy the throne.

their father; and they do not receive the wives of the ministers for the same reason. The princesses may see men, and choose whom they like for their husbands. If they fix their affections on a married man, he is obliged to get rid of his wife or wives, and is not allowed any wife but the princess, who keeps him in the strictest order, and either disgraces him or has him bowstrung should he offend her seriously. Still, in spite of all these drawbacks, it is considered a great honour and advantage to marry a princess. I suppose that the marriage brings much patronage in its train.

Turkish time is extremely puzzling, for it changes every day. What is with us twelve o'clock of the night—that is, the close of one day and the beginning of the next—is with the Turks the moment of sunset. Consequently there is a daily alteration of a few minutes, and this makes it extremely difficult to keep your watch right, and not to be too late or too early for everything. No two clocks or watches in the whole town are, I believe, exactly alike. The consequence was that on this particular day we were three-quarters of an hour too soon for our boat, and had to amuse ourselves by watching the motley crowd. These boats are excellent, and are capitally steered and handled. Part of the stern is shut off for the Turkish ladies, and there they are penned up like sheep. They amuse themselves with eating sweets and drinking coffee and *eau sucrée* (when it is not Ramazan); and the waiter on board seemed much astonished that we did not take advantage of our liberty as Christians, and eat large lumps of rahatlakoum and sweet cakes, and drink *eau sucrée* all the time.

Soon after we reached the yacht, the British ambassador

and Lady Elliot, Count Pisani, and many other people came on board to see us and the yacht.

Saturday, October 24*th.*—Tom and I went ashore, paid some visits, saw the beautiful gardens and vines, and brought off handfuls of lovely flowers. About noon we started in the gig, and rowed across to Beikos, taking our lunch with us. We landed in the village, and, passing through, picnicked on a green sward, by the side of a stream, under the shade of some plane-trees, close to the Sultan's palace. After lunch, Evie and I mounted our horses, while the gentlemen walked to the top of the Giant's Mountain. It was a lovely ride, through green parklike pastures, and, as we climbed higher and higher, there were lovely peeps through the trees over the Bosphorus. When the shoulder of the mountain had been rounded, we could see right over to the Black Sea. At the summit of the hill is the tomb of a dervish, called here Joshua's Tomb. It is held very sacred, and the railings round it are covered with tiny bits of rag, hung there by the superstitious as a sure preventive against fever and ills of every kind. The view from the top is splendid, but after a short rest and a cup of coffee we were obliged to leave, so as to reach the boat before sunset. The mountain does not enjoy a good reputation, and we had been warned to take our revolvers and an extra man or two with us from the yacht. In spite of these precautions, however, we thought it better to be on the safe side and return by daylight, for only a few months ago one of the *attachés* at the Austrian Embassy, and his wife and daughter, having stayed on the mountain after dark, were attacked and cruelly maltreated by some Turkish soldiers.

On our return to the yacht, we found a letter from the Princess of Roumania, expressing much surprise that we had not already arrived, and begging us to be at Bucharest to-morrow for some special festivities. This was, of course, impossible; and as it appears our telegram could not have been received, we sent another, saying we would start on Monday in the yacht for Kustendje, instead of waiting for the steamer to Varna on Tuesday. The Danube is so low this year, that it is impossible for us to take the yacht up to Galatz, as we had first intended, there being only eleven feet in the mouth of the river at Sulina, while we draw thirteen.

A pleasant evening on deck, though the weather looked as if it might change.

At midnight we were awakened by a tremendous gale blowing, and by morning the whole of the narrow channel, generally so calm, blue, and peaceful, was covered with curling waves, foam, and spray, and torrents of rain were falling.

Turkish Lady

CHAPTER VI.

THE BLACK SEA, SKUTARI, BROUSSA, HAREMS.

By foreign hands thy dying eyes were closed,
By foreign hands thy decent limbs composed,
By foreign hands thy humble grave adorn'd,
By strangers honour'd, and by strangers mourn'd.

Sunday, October 25th.—The weather was so bad that we could not go to church on the 'Antelope,' as we had intended. After lunch we saw the ambassador and all his family go on board; we exchanged salutes, and the 'Antelope' steamed past us on her way to Salonica, with her party, for a few days' shooting. At 3 p.m. we started for a drive past Buyukdere to the forest of Belgrade, a lovely drive. We passed under the aqueduct which supplies all Pera and Galata with water, and then stopped at Bagtcheh Keui, where are the bends or reservoirs which collect all the water. They are merely walled-up valleys, into which all the water from the surrounding country drains, and is then let out through pipes into the aqueduct. At the top of one wall there is a beautiful marble terrace with iron railings, and indeed the whole scene would have been lovely had not the water been so low.

From Bagtcheh Keui we drove past a very large encampment of Hungarian gipsies to the village of Belgrade, and then on to the heart of the forest,[1] a most lovely place—a river running for miles through a green parklike

---

[1] The Russians, who were encamped here in 1878, used many of the finest trees for firewood.

sward, under magnificent plane and oak trees, surrounded by hills covered with beech, chestnut, and fir woods. On a fine day this spot is generally crowded with people, and even under the most unfavourable circumstances it must be always lovely. The rain, which had held up a little bit, now came down in torrents, and our drive back was very wet. The wind increased, and it was soon blowing a hurricane. Some guests came to dinner, but it was such a frightful night that we hardly liked sending them ashore, even in our big cutter; however, they insisted, and ultimately reached the shore safely.

Monday, October 26th.—It was blowing as hard as ever, but we hoped it might moderate by evening, and determined to start at night for Kustendje. So we sent the steward into Constantinople to get provisions, that we might be all prepared. About 1 p.m., however, we received a telegram from the Princess of Roumania, saying that they had been expecting us with impatience for days, that the Prince was so ill after the military manœuvres that he was obliged to go away for a change of air at once, and that with much regret they must ask us to postpone our visit. The first part was puzzling, the latter disappointing, as we should have liked to see them again; but nothing could be done beyond sending a telegram to say how very sorry we were to lose the pleasure of our visit. As the fires were already lighted, we proceeded to get up steam and go up the Bosphorus into the Black Sea, just to see what it was like; but we had quite enough of it in a very few minutes. The swell was rolling in horribly, and when we turned our head to go towards Constantinople instead of Kustendje, and were broadside to it, more things were

DINING SALOON

carried away than had been lost all the way from England. We steamed down the Bosphorus in a thick mist and heavy gale, and dropped our anchor with considerable difficulty, so crowded were the straits, among the men-of-war at Fundukli.[1] The steward was on shore, and as we had no provisions on board, we were obliged to land, late as it was, in the pouring rain and strong wind, to dine at Misseri's.

Tuesday, October 27th.—A high wind again, but we went

Dancing Dervishes.

on shore to a curious mosque in Pera, to see the dancing dervishes. Our seats were in a gallery next to those reserved for the harem. In course of time the dervishes appeared, and after an interval devoted to monotonous prayers and gesticulations to the high priest, seated in the centre, they divested themselves of their shoes and outer

---

[1] Fondook means a large nut; Dolmabagtcheh, which is close by, a hazel-grove. Probably, therefore, a large number of nut-trees were cut down when these suburbs of the palace were built.

garments, and walked solemnly round three times, headed by the high priest, bowing gracefully to each other as they passed the sort of altar where the sacred copy of the Koran is kept. Then they all started off twirling round and round, each keeping in his own orbit and never touching the other. It certainly was a most curious, not to say ridiculous, sight to see all these tall men in long white full petticoats, with high light-brown conical felt hats on their heads, spinning round and round with their arms over their heads, exactly like so many huge extinguishers.

After lunch at Misseri's we spent the afternoon at the bazaars and in the court-yard of the Pigeon Mosque, which was more crowded than ever. We were rather alarmed to-day at hearing that the Sultan had taken a great fancy to the yacht, and was anxious to possess her. As his every whim must be gratified, if the report were true, there were only three courses open to us: the first, to refuse to sell her, which would occasion the instant dismissal of the grand vizier and a general change of the ministry; the second, to sell her at considerable personal inconvenience, but of course at a profit; the third, to steam away in the dead of night and leave the Sultan to lament our departure and bemoan the loss of his new toy, while he would have nobody in particular to blame.

Wednesday, October 28*th.*—To-day we paid visits to some harems. The two nieces of the Viceroy of Egypt, Princess Nazli and Princess Azizieh, on whom we first called, were at their farm in the country. Madame Ikbal Kiasim, daughter-in-law of Fuad Pasha (the greatest statesman Turkey ever had), after keeping us waiting some time, sent first a slave and then a French *dame de compagnie* to tell us she was in her bath, and was therefore very sorry she could not receive us.

At Madame Hilmeh Bey's (granddaughter of Fuad Pasha) we were more fortunate. She was at home, and received us in a French *robe de matinée*, a blue cashmere beautifully embroidered with wreaths of roses, *crêpe lisse* ruffs and frills, a pile of dyed golden hair (naturally black) rolled and twisted and curled in the latest fashion. She laid down a French novel to rise and greet us—rather a contrast to the last harem I had been in at Tunis. All the women of the higher classes of the present generation are tolerably educated, have European governesses, and read European books—principally novels, I fancy—and all bemoan their present hard fate very much. It is a great mistake of the Turks to think that they can educate their wives and daughters, and still keep them in confinement and subjection. To hear this poor little woman talk of her own and her lady-friends' feelings, you would think the revolution must soon come. The children of the present day in Turkey are brought up to think the system of yashmaks and confinement a most tyrannical custom, and not to be endured. Still I am afraid education does not prevent their using the cowhide frequently and very cruelly on their slaves. During our visit to-day two slaves, attired in semi-English semi-Turkish dress, brought us in first some sweetmeats and a glass of water each, and afterwards a cup of coffee. Our hostess apologised for not sharing it with us, owing to its being Ramazan. After dinner at Misseri's, we went to the Turkish theatre, where we saw what appeared to be a very amusing piece, though of course we could not understand a word. The dresses were all Turkish, the actresses all Armenians. Ten years ago the Armenian women were veiled as carefully as the Turkish women, and it was difficult to tell them apart. Now it is equally difficult to tell the former from Europeans, either in dress or manners.

Thursday, October 29th.—Tom started early with Mr. Foster to call on the grand vizier and several of the ministers by appointment. He had rather an interesting morning. They all received him very kindly, and talked a good deal, either in French or through a dragoman. As it was Ramazan, the usual pipes and coffee were not served. However, a friend assures us that more than once during Ramazan he has been with one of the ministers who, getting tired during a long interview, carefully locked all the doors, opened the windows, and lighted a cigarette, having enjoyed which he produced a tiny brush, removed every scrap of ash, and unlocked the door.

The salary of the grand vizier is thirty thousand a year, that of the minister of finance fifteen thousand ; and as these officials are changed on the slightest caprice of the Sultan, their great temptation is to fill their own pockets during the short time they may be in office.

Their elevation is equally curious. The last grand vizier was a common chaouch, or sergeant in a line regiment. Another chaouch was presented with five hundred pounds and made colonel of a regiment, simply because the servant of a friend of ours happened to give him a pair of Aylesbury goslings, which in time grew up and had a family of their own. The Sultan, who is passionately fond of all animals, saw and admired them at the guard-house, and wished to buy them. The sergeant refused to name a price, but begged the Sultan to accept them, and accordingly was rewarded by promotion. The command of one of the largest ironclads was given to a common sailor because he had a very pretty cat, to which he had taught all sorts of tricks. He presented it to the Sultan, and was told to name his own reward. These stories sound like wild romances, but they are, I believe, really undoubted facts. Tom was much relieved to get away without having any proposal or offer made to him for the yacht.

In the meantime we went in the gig to Skutari, where the carriage met us. We drove through the dirty rough streets of the town to a mosque, to hear the howling dervishes; but

> Just at this season Ramazani's fast
> Through the long day its penance did maintain.

They were, therefore, not howling on this particular Thursday as usual. I believe we did not miss much, as, however curious it may be, the performance is not pleasant either to see or hear. We then drove on to the Turkish cemetery, consisting of acres and acres of cypress groves, thickly interspersed with graves, some painted with the gaudiest colours, but still picturesque enough. The Orientals believe that the aromatic odour of the cypress prevents all ill effects from the burial of the dead, and I think there must be something in it, as small graveyards are constantly met with in the midst of the most crowded cities, and, the Europeans say, no disagreeable consequences arise from them; but they are never without the protecting cypresses. One of the present Sultan's favourite horses is buried in the midst of the cemetery, in perhaps one of the grandest tombs.

The Sultan has eight hundred horses and seven hundred women belonging to him, and it is hard to say which are worse cared for, except a few special favourites.

From the Turkish cemetery we went past the Skutari barracks and hospital, the name of which was so familiar

Turkish Cemetery.

to English ears during the Crimean War, and left the carriage at the gate of the English cemetery, where the remains of so many near and dear to those in England rest. It was interesting to see, and I am sure it would be pleasing to those whose relatives are laid here to know, what a sunny, peaceful, well-cared-for spot it is, in marked contrast with the desolate, uncared-for Turkish graveyards. The cemetery occupies a large space in front of the hospital, and is shaded with trees and planted with flowers. It lies on the top of a precipice, the foot of which is washed by the Sea of Marmora, and commands splendid views over that sea, the Prince's Islands, the Golden Horn, and Con-

Soldiers' Cemetery (Skutari).

stantinople. After wandering about a long time, reading the inscriptions, and bringing away as a memento a tortoise which we found crawling about, we drove back to the town and walked through the streets, for the shaking was too bad to be endured a second time. Some of the little shops were rather interesting, and there was a good deal of game exposed for sale—hares, quails, woodcock, snipe, and pheasants. The latter are wild here, but rare and dear. We just caught the ferry-boat, landed at Stamboul, and Evie and I drove to the bazaar. We made sundry purchases for presents, and I bought a Turkish lady's summer cloak, lined with fur, for myself. The ladies here almost always carry a fur-lined cloak, thin in summer and thick in winter.

Friday, October 30*th.*—It was a lovely morning, and we were just thinking of going ashore, to see the Sultan drive to mosque, when the Grand Duke of Oldenburg came on board with his suite, saying he had received a message from the Sultan to tell him he was going by water to the mosque at Fundukli, exactly opposite, and about fifty yards from where we are lying, and that the Sultan had suggested he should ask our permission to see the procession from the yacht, as the best point of observation. The Grand Duke is a pleasant young man, about twenty-two, heir-apparent to the small duchy of Oldenburg. He is on his travels for two years, with Colonel Philipshorn, Professor Lutwig, and Captain Otto Hervig, commanding the Prussian gunboat in which he is going to Smyrna and the East. As he is thinking of building a yacht on his return, he was much interested in inspecting ours, and his two hours' visit passed pleasantly enough.

About twelve o'clock, five caïques glided alongside the steps of Dolmabagtcheh: the Sultan entered the first, which was white, lined with red velvet and gold, and having a gold canopy. The cushions were embroidered in gold and precious stones, and facing those on which the Sultan sat knelt two of the chief ministers, their heads bowed down and their hands folded across their breasts, in the most abject attitude. Behind stood the steersman, gorgeous in green and gold. The front caïque was manned by twenty-four oarsmen, dressed in very full white shirts and trousers, purple and gold jackets, and scarlet fezzes, who, prior to every stroke, knelt down and touched the bottom of the boat with their foreheads, then rose to a standing posture, and sent the oars in with a tremendous sweep. The pace is terrific (they beat easily the fastest steam launch afloat), and the exertion is equally

The Sultan's Caïque.

so; for though picked strong men, the rowers generally break down at the end of two years. The whole effect is one of the prettiest imaginable, and the boat looks almost too good for the use of mortal man.

The second caïque, with the Sultan's son on board, was very like the first, only with a rounded prow and a small bird, instead of a sharp prow and a large bird, and with a less elaborate canopy. It held only twenty rowers, instead of twenty-four. The three boats that followed were white and gold, without any canopies, and had only ten rowers each. They contained the ministers. Every available quay and spot near the water was filled with soldiers and bands; the ships were all dressed with flags, and manned yards and fired salutes as the caïques passed. Our men were busy painting when the Grand Duke came on board, but we took them off that work, and got the yacht dressed just in time, before the Sultan passed. When the Sultan landed, and walked on a red carpet kept down with little brass weights, he passed between two rows of pashas, who bent double as he walked between them.

The Sultan was so pleased at the yacht being dressed in his honour, that before going into the mosque he sent for the minister of marine and told him to come on board at once and thank us for the compliment we had paid him. As this minister spoke only Turkish, Aarif Pasha, the admiral commanding the ironclads, who spoke a little English, came instead. He was very pleasant, and spent a long time examining the yacht.

In the afternoon the men resumed their painting, and we went in caïques down the Golden Horn to the Sweet Waters of Europe. It was a pleasant row of about two hours, the latter part up a narrow river bordered with velvety turf and shaded by magnificent plane-trees. In the spring and summer, when the whole place is crowded with caïques and carriages, and the Turkish ladies are seated in groups under the trees on their carpets, eating sweetmeats and drinking coffee, it must indeed be a gay scene. At the Sultan's kiosk we got out and walked to the palace, a little higher up. The whole place swarmed with peacocks. There were hundreds of them in every direction, walking about the greensward, perched on the trees, on the walls, on the house-top, or running in and out of the mansion specially provided for them, adjoining the palace. They are great favourites of the Sultan, and, as such, are well cared for. The carriage met us here, and we drove back to Constantinople. Just as we were starting up the hill, our dragoman asked us if we had our revolvers. As it so happened, we had not thought it necessary to bring them; but though it had become quite dark before we reached the town, we did not meet with any molestation.

Saturday, October 31*st.*—After breakfast we set off in the gig to visit the new Palace of Tcheragan, as Aarif Pasha had arranged for us to do. We saw all over the harems, consisting of hundreds of rooms, with floors covered with matting, distempered walls, and very elaborate curtains, each furnished with a large four-post bed and numerous divans, covered with splendid satin brocades, all differing in pattern from each other, as well as from the curtains. Only one wardrobe, and not a single chair, was to be found in the whole palace. However handsome their clothes may be, the women just lay them in a heap on the floor. We wanted to look at the Sultan's apartments, which are the best worth seeing; but unfortunately he was coming to make a personal inspection, so we were obliged to retire with our curiosity ungratified.

As it seemed rather late to go on to Beylerbey, we went on board the flagship 'Osmanlieh,' to return the admiral's visit. The admiral was not on board, but the captain, who spoke very little English, and the doctor, who spoke still less French, received us most kindly, and entertained us in the admiral's cabin, with cigarettes, coffee, and syrups. At last the brilliant idea struck them of sending for the English engineer to act as interpreter, and then they showed us all round the ship, which was in the most perfect order, and would have done credit to the English navy. Her guns, carriages, shot, and shell, were miracles of polish, and the decks were exquisitely clean. On our departure the officers and crew were mustered: they saluted and presented arms, the ensign was dipped, and we were put into our boat with great ceremony.

After lunch we went by appointment to the studio of Mr. Chlebowski, who is painting for the Sultan an enormous picture of Mahmoud the Second entering Constantinople in triumph. This gentleman possesses an interesting portfolio of sketches in red ink, done by the Sultan himself, just to indicate roughly what he wishes the picture to be. Though in many cases consisting of only a few strokes, they were wonderfully spirited and showed great talent, particularly the battle-pieces. Mr. Chlebowski has also collected in Paris, St. Petersburg, and Constantinople, a vast quantity of pictures, china, arms, jewellery, stuffs, curtains, furniture, knick-knacks, all of which are arranged with exquisite taste. We were a long time looking over them, and could easily have spent hours more.

Sunday, November 1st.—We attended service at the chapel raised to the memory of the British officers who fell in the Crimea. After church we claimed our letters, the Varna mail having just arrived, and went to lunch with some friends, afterwards driving with them to see the Valley of Sweet Waters, and returning by Mashleck, one of the Sultan's farms, where he spends a good deal of time in the summer. It was a pretty drive, but a long one, and we were barely in time for the *table d'hôte* at Misseri's. We walked down to the boat after dinner, and, Félise being with us, we were accompanied by a running fire of barks the whole way, each pack of dogs seeing us a certain distance through their own quarter, and passing the word on to the next pack.

Among our letters has been one from the Princess of Roumania, explaining the telegram which had puzzled us so much. Our telegram was sent on a Tuesday, and in it we said that we should start on the next Tuesday. They interpreted it as meaning that we should start on the Tuesday on which the message was sent, and accordingly made all preparations, arranging two special trains, and setting everything in order for our reception. As the mistake was not discovered for three or four days, the people expected us at the stations, and the post-horses waited on the road. It is provoking to think that they should have had so much trouble for nothing, whilst we have been waiting and wondering in Constantinople at not receiving any answer to our telegram, and have not liked to start until it arrived.

Monday, November 2nd.—To save the trouble of getting up steam, a tug, the 'Sarah Smart,' took us in tow about 9.30 a.m., and brought us through the shipping and up the stream towards Beylerbey. There we hoisted sail, and glided down past the ironclads, exchanging salutes. After Pera and Seraglio Point had been passed, the course was altered, and the vessel's head turned across the Sea of Marmora towards Cape Boz. It was a perfect day for a

sail, with a fair breeze, and about 4 p.m. we dropped
our anchor just off the town of Moudania, in twenty-two
fathoms of water, and not three hundred yards from
the shore. It is a very bad place to anchor in, and only
possible on this one little patch, for to right and left of
us there were sixty fathoms of water. We went on shore
at once, with considerable difficulty, for there was a very
heavy sea running, and the steps on the pier were high,

Broussa, from l'Hôtel de l'Europe (Preziosi.)

old, and rickety, the handrail coming off when we touched
it. However, we landed in safety, were received by an
officer and seven very ragged soldiers as a sort of guard
of honour, and then proceeded to get the bill of health
viséd and to make arrangements for our journey to-morrow.
The dirty and uninteresting streets of the town did not
tempt us to remain long ashore, and as it was now dark
we returned to the yacht. Re-embarking was a great
business, the sea having risen and the waves coming more

than halfway up the very rotten steps, and dashing the boat about in a most unpleasant manner.

Tuesday, November 3rd.—At half-past eight we landed, and, some riding and some driving, climbed up the hill, through groves of olive and mulberry trees, for about an hour, past the pretty little Greek village of Missolonghi, nestled in a hollow among trees and gardens. From the guard-house at the top of the hill there is a splendid view over the fertile plain of Broussa, at our feet, stretching away towards the distant range of Mount Olympus. It was a quick run down to the half-way house, where we lunched under a magnificent grove of oak-trees. The owner of the little coffee-house had some beautiful poultry, and some curious little bantams with wings on their legs. I tried hard to buy some, but as they had only just been received as a draft from the Sultan's yard, it was not possible to come to a deal. One of the gamecocks had on a curious pair of laced silk stockings, with three steel spurs beside his own on each foot.

After an hour and a half's drive across the plain, we stopped at a well, under some plane-trees, to water the horses. All this time we were sometimes alongside and sometimes crossing a railway which is being made between Moudania and Broussa. Another steep climb through luxuriant vegetation, past the old mineral baths, brought us to the Hôtel d'Olympe, just on the outskirts of the town of Broussa, but perched on a hill sufficiently high to command a lovely and extensive view over the plain. We wandered through the town, visiting a silk manufactory owned by some French people, who have been settled here seventeen years, and who came from near Lyons. It was interesting to see the Greek and Armenian girls all hard at work, winding the silk off the cocoons, which are placed in boiling water, the very fine thread being led over a machine and wound off, generally without a single break if the water is hot enough. There are three different kinds and colours of silk—green, yellow, and white—according to the part of the country from which the silkworms' eggs come. We hardly reached the main part of the town, but the streets were crowded with all sorts of picturesque costumes and groups. On our return to the hotel we found there a large party of foreigners who had arrived during our absence, and soon after dinner we were all glad to go to bed.

Wednesday, November 4th.—After an early breakfast, we started to see the town. First we drove to the ancient baths, which are splendid, built of marble, over some very hot sulphurous springs. Thence we went to the bazaars. They are large, and full of beautiful embroideries and other curious things, and are much more Oriental in character than the greater part of the Constantinople bazaars. No Europeans come here, nor are there so many Jews, and the vendors sit with true Oriental indifference while customers are looking at their things, and take any amount of time to settle a bargain. We bought some lovely embroideries, and some ornaments made for mules, but which I mean to use to fasten back curtains with, besides a quantity of bags, pipes, &c., as presents for the crew and servants.

Leaving the bazaar, we peeped in at a splendid mosque, visited the Sultans' tombs, which are very handsome, saw a magnificent view from the terrace above the town, and returned to the hotel to a late lunch, for which we were quite ready. We had meant to stay another day, and to ascend Mount Olympus; but though the weather was lovely, there was a good deal of wind, and Tom got rather fidgety about the yacht, as the anchorage at Moudania is very bad. He feared Powell might be obliged to get up anchor and go off, leaving us on shore, uncertain where to meet again, and without sleeping accommodation of any kind. Directly after lunch, therefore, we started to drive down. Moudania was reached about 7.30 p.m., and as the night was dark as pitch and the wind blowing hard, it was rather a difficult job to get ourselves and our luggage off from the rickety old pier. We put two anchors down, with sixty fathoms of chain on one side and forty-five fathoms on the other, and so rode out the night in security.

Thursday, November 5th.— At 6 a.m. we began to get up our chain, an operation of immense labour, which lasted more than two hours. We ceased to wonder, when, attached to one of our anchors, a ship's chain, more than a hundred fathoms long, was raised to the surface. The vessel to which it had belonged had evidently been compelled by bad weather to slip her cable suddenly and leave anchor and all behind. As soon as we got outside the Bay of Moudania we found the Sea of Marmora very rough, with quite a heavy gale blowing. One of the hoops of the stays supporting the bowsprit gave way. The spar, after bending as much as its size would allow, snapped with a mighty crash, and fell with the sail right across the foot of the vessel, so that there was great difficulty in getting it on board. We spent a wretched day, without making much progress, and were glad to anchor in company with many other ships in the sheltered Bay of Silevri for the night.

Friday, November 6th.—We were off by daybreak, and had a delightfully smooth sail under the lee of the land to Seraglio Point, where we got up steam, and, passing the usual crowd of vessels, took up our old anchorage opposite Fundukli about 2 p.m. In the afternoon we landed, and went straight to the bazaars to complete our purchases, but found almost every shop shut up. Still, we managed to get what we wanted.

Just before we were going on shore to dine with some friends, a man who had been in the 'Eothen,' and was a friend of Rowbotham's, came on board with a most melancholy story of the unseaworthy state of his ship, the 'Violet,' a steamer laden with grain in bulk. He was chief engineer on board, reported her as very leaky and greatly overladen, and said he had just written to his wife to wish her good-bye, as he felt sure the vessel would go to the bottom before long. Finally, he implored Tom, almost on his knees, to interfere and stop her going to sea, saying that he and his mates would be for ever grateful, and would pray for him night and morning, if he would only come on board and speak to the captain. This he said with tears in his eyes, and with such earnestness, that Tom promised to do all that could be done in the matter.

We had an excellent dinner, and a pleasant party. Many people dropped in afterwards, and we enjoyed some first-rate music. Our friends have charming rooms, and, in the winter, give dances every fortnight. I give the bill of fare, to show that dinners in Constantinople do not differ much from those in London and Paris.

DINER DE VENDREDI,
Novembre 6.

Potage à la Reine.

Petites Bouchées à la Nesle.
Bar, sauce Bisque.

Croquettes à la financière.
Noix de bœuf sauce Malaga.
Côtelettes de bécasse à la suprême.
Aspic de foie-gras en Bellevue.

Punch à la Romaine.

Cardons à la Moelle.
Selle de Mouton.

Gâteau à la Richelieu.
Mont blanc à la Vanille.

Tom had a long chat with our consul-general about the unfortunate 'Violet,' and received full authority to act in the matter.

Saturday, November 7th.—This morning Mr. Crake arrived from Hastings to join us for a few weeks. He had had a very good passage in a comfortable boat, one of the Austrian Lloyd's. Tom went on board the 'Violet' at six, saw the captain, and asked leave to muster and address the crew. This was at once given to him, although the captain said it would ruin him with the owner. When they came on deck Tom told them that one of their number had made a complaint to him that the ship was overladen and utterly unseaworthy; that he had spoken to the British consul, who was perfectly prepared to stop the ship going to sea, if that was the general opinion of the crew. Several of the crew said it was, and that the pumps were always going. On this, the very same engineer who had come on board and complained to Tom, stepped forward and said she was one of the most seaworthy ships he had ever been in, that she was not at all overladen, that he had been to sea in bad weather in her when she was twenty-one inches lower in the water than at present, and that he never wished to go to sea in a better ship. He also tried to give an elaborate explanation to his shipmates that the working of the pumps had to do entirely with the engines, not with the leakage of the ship. After this there was nothing more to be done, though it was excessively annoying for Tom to have taken all this trouble for nothing. About ten the 'Violet' got under way, and, having first run foul of an Austrian steamer, steamed slowly out of the harbour, looking very low in the water, all on one side, and with the pumps going hard. In the Sea of Marmora she ran into an Egyptian steamer, and was towed back to have some trifling damages repaired, and to pay for injury done to the other vessel. We were told afterwards, on enquiry of Lloyd's agents here, that a hundred tons of cargo were taken out of her in the course of the night, and in the morning she started again. This time last year a sister ship belonging to the same line, and laden with the same cargo (rye from Nicolaieff in the Black Sea), sailed for Bergen, in Norway, and was never heard of again after passing Chanak-Kalesi.

We were to have ridden round the walls again; but as it was a pouring wet day, we wasted some time in debating and hoping it would clear. The expedition round the walls had to be abandoned, and in the afternoon Evie and I went to pay some visits in the harems, having previously sent notice of our intention, as the Turkish ladies like to be fully prepared to receive visitors. We first went to the

Princess Azizieh's, and, having passed through several doors and climbed up innumerable stairs, found ourselves in her reception-room, commanding a beautiful view over the Bosphorus. The Princess received us in an elaborate blue velvet *toilette de matin*, trimmed with undyed ostrich feathers, her hair being very much frizzed. She is a decidedly stout but pretty woman, with lovely eyes, teeth, hair, and expression. Soon after our arrival a long jasmine stick pipe, with a beautiful amber mouthpiece, studded with diamonds, was brought in by the slaves and handed round. Sweetmeats followed on a gold tray, in gold dishes, thick with large diamonds and rubies, and finally coffee in eggshell china cups, encased in exquisite gold filagree stands, pierced with holes, each hole filled with a large diamond, set clear and swinging, so that the effect was most brilliant. The Princess had a pleasant little French companion, Madame Boyer, and she herself, for a Turkish lady, talked very well; so the visit was pleasant, though a long one. It is considered an insult to your hostess to remain less than an hour, and we stayed longer. The Princess had some of her slaves dressed up, that we might see their costumes. One little black page, about nine years old, in a gorgeous Albanian dress, stiff with gold lace and embroidery, and a remarkably full white petticoat, was very droll. The Princess herself smoked cigarettes the whole time, and was interested about the yacht, which she is extremely anxious to see. She asked many questions concerning our manners and customs in England, our travels, and London and Paris, both of which cities she is dying to visit, though she has very little chance at present of doing so, I fear—poor thing! The conversation turned, as usual, on the wrongs of the Turkish women, and the most ardent longings for freedom and liberty were expressed by all.

Madame Kiasim unfortunately being again engaged, our next visit was to the Princess Nazli, sister of the Princess Azizieh, quite as pretty, perhaps even better educated, certainly more advanced in her ideas, and speaking English as perfectly as her sister does French. Her rooms are as beautifully fitted up in light blue satin and brocade as her sister's are in the same materials of a red colour. The furniture was all French; and very handsome, but here many books and flowers might be seen, and the place had altogether a more European and home-like look. The Princess, who wore a plaid dressing-gown, received us kindly. The numerous slaves were not particularly well dressed, but the pipes, the sweetmeat and coffee services were resplendent with rubies, diamonds, and precious stones. She, like her sister, smoked all the time, and conversed pleasantly and frankly, telling us many details of the interior of Turkish life, and of her own history. Her father, Mustapha Fazil, is only twenty days younger than his brother the Viceroy of Egypt, and was his heir-apparent till the Sultan changed the order of succession and made it pass to the Viceroy's eldest son—a step which he is anxious to take in his own case, but which, I should think, would never be allowed by the Mussulmans. Princess Nazli, who is a grand-daughter of Mehemet Ali, was engaged to her cousin, the heir-apparent, and all her trousseau was prepared, when the Viceroy was seized with a sudden fear of being poisoned if surrounded by too many near relations; so the match was broken off, and she was engaged to Halil Pasha, who, when his father died, is said to have had two millions and a half sterling left him in gold, packed in boxes. He went to Paris, spent a million and a half in that most fascinating of cities, then returned, married the Princess, and settled down to spend the remaining million.

Izzet Bey, who married the sister, seems much nicer, though he is not so rich. He is the son of a most charming mother, a Circassian slave, who was brought up and educated by Fuad Pasha, and was ultimately chosen by him to become his son's wife. Fuad Pasha accompanied the Sultan to England and Paris in 1867. Among many other reforms, he wished to bring about the freedom of women. He even said, in a memorable speech on a public occasion, that Turkey would never take its proper place till the walls between the Selemlek (or men's apartments) and the harem were broken down, and the softening and purifying influence of women was allowed to be felt. Consequently his relations, the ladies of the harems I have visited to-day, are allowed more liberty than any others in Turkey.

One of my hostesses, talking about things in general, said, 'How odd it must be to you Europeans to hear us talk about our brothers and sisters and their mothers, for there are just as many of one as of the other;' and then, speaking of religion, she said, 'I have read the Koran straight through thirty times in the original Arabic, and many expositions. The priests try and teach us to believe that there is one God, neither man nor woman, but a spirit, and that Mahomet is His prophet. But how are we to believe *that*, when everything is for man, and nothing for woman? A good God could not be so unjust. He must be all man, and a bad Turk too. We are told that we must kneel to our husbands and kiss their hands. If they kiss ours (as mine always does, he having lived in western Europe), their lips will be burnt, and our hands also, with the most horrible torture. We are to walk, even when weak and suffering, while they ride; and we must carry their parcels too. It can't be right. As I don't believe that, how am I to believe anything?' It was a difficult argument to answer, and I think she was only expressing the opinion of many of her sex in Turkey who have had any education. This discontent will assuredly bring about a revolution, in spite of the special services for women in the mosques and the special preachers to address them on the duty of subjection. Another lady amused me greatly by saying, 'Though my husband is not so very particular himself, I don't believe he will ever do anything to emancipate us, or get us places at the theatre. They are all alike—such *Turks!*—and are too glad of an excuse to go out alone and enjoy themselves.'

CHAPTER VII.

VISITS FROM TURKISH LADIES.   FEAST OF BAIRAM.
WALLS AND PALACES OF CONSTANTINOPLE.

*Here woman's voice is never heard: apart,
And scarce permitted, guarded, veil'd, to move.*

Sunday, November 8th.—Our experiences of last Sunday had not inclined us to make another attempt at church. We therefore had service on board, and afterwards went to look at Mr. Preziosi's sketches. He is an artist who has lived here for many years, and some of his costume pieces and landscapes are beautiful. We had a large and unexpected party to lunch. Having asked a few friends, several others dropped in, amongst them Mr. Chlebowski, the Polish artist.

Monday, November 9th.—A wet morning, but we had an early breakfast and were off to the bazaars, which are all under cover, though very dark and muddy. We spent a long time there and made a good many purchases. This being the last day of Ramazan, the traders were all so anxious to get money to spend at the Feast of Bairam that there were wonderful bargains to be obtained, and the things were much cheaper than when we were here last. The Pigeon Mosque was more crowded than ever with stalls, and our wanderings took up so much time, that I was obliged to go straight on board to receive some Turkish ladies. Izzet Bey, grandson of Fuad Pasha, and husband of the Princess Azizieh, came first, and stayed to receive his mother, Madame Kiasim, a wonderfully handsome young-looking woman, about forty-five, but not appearing thirty. In the cabin, when, with doors closed, she took off her feridjee and yashmak, she looked exactly like a Frenchwoman, being beautifully dressed in two shades of brown, with a black lace bonnet, and having all the manners and conversation of a European. Her remarks about books, pictures, and things in general were extremely clever and sensible, and it was difficult to imagine how she had gained her knowledge, or to believe that she was only an educated slave, bought when young by Fuad Pasha to play with his son, and afterwards married to him on account of her superior talent, tact, and manner, as well as of her extreme beauty. She was accompanied by a white slave and a black eunuch.

The Princess Azizich sent her little black slave in Albanian costume, on purpose to please Muriel, she herself being too unwell to come on board. This was a great disappointment to her, for she had experienced considerable difficulty in procuring leave to come, these being the first visits ever paid by Turkish ladies to a European. The Princess Nazli arrived next, dressed in delicate blue satin and Brussels lace, with pale pink feathers in a blue satin pork-pie hat to match. She had also her white slave and black eunuch in attendance, and was immensely interested in everything she saw, admiring most things greatly. She smoked nearly all the time, but did not seem to approve either of our coffee or our tea. After visits of more than two hours' duration, our guests departed, I think highly gratified; at all events, they had had quite a novel experience, and, fortunately, the day was so fine that they had no nervous fears in going backwards and forwards in the boat. All the afternoon and evening guns were firing and bands playing, to announce the end of Ramazan and the commencement of Bairam. As we are anchored in the midst of the men-of-war, the prospect of deafening salutes five times a day and night for the next three days is not a pleasant one. Just before dinner we had a lottery for the crew and the servants, which I think they enjoyed immensely, especially the uncertainty as to whether they would draw a caïque, pocket-handkerchief, bag, pair of slippers, or what not. After a glass of wine all round, Mr. Rowbotham made a speech, and then they all retired to the forecastle for a merry evening together among themselves.

Tuesday, November 10*th.*—It has been the custom of the Sultan from time immemorial, on the first morning of Bairam, to start from the Seraglio Palace at break of day, and to ride in state, with all his ministers and a great many troops, past the mosque of St. Sophia to the mosque of Achmed and back. We had made all our arrangements accordingly, ordered horses, procured a cavass from the Sublime Porte, and were called at 5.30 a.m. Just as we were going to start, at 7 a.m., our dragoman came on board in a great hurry to say that the Sultan was going by water, and only as far as Tophaneh. Again we dressed ship in all haste, and the Sultan with his five lovely caïques passed close by the yacht. His own caïque in particular diverged from her course and came very close, to have a good look at us. He kept his head turned in our direction, and saluted us all repeatedly, so that we had the opportunity of indulging in a good look at him.

As soon as he had passed we landed, mounted our horses, and went to see the crowd on shore, which was very amusing. Such a mass of carriages!—I could not have believed there were so many in all Constantinople—all full of Turkish ladies, in their smartest dresses and jewels, and attended by black eunuchs on black horses, and white eunuchs on white horses. Some of them appeared to be dressed to suit the colour of their carriages, and the effect of a bright red, yellow, green, or blue carriage, lined with red, yellow, green, or blue, and the liveries of the servants outside, and the ladies' feridjees inside, all to match, was very striking. It was impossible to get about, except on the footpath, and even then only slowly, among the dense crowd, all in their holiday best.

The Sultan returned from the mosque at Tophaneh to Dolmabagtcheh by water, passing close by the yacht again, and then the crowd on land moved gradually towards the palace, to see the ladies of the harem return, and all the ministers and officials pay their congratulatory visits. First came the Sultan Valideh, 'the mother of the Sultan and of her country,' and for that reason the one Turkish lady allowed to go without a yashmak. For as every son is allowed to look on the face of his mother, so the people are allowed to look on the face of their general mother. Her carriage was very handsome, drawn by four black horses, with handsome harness, and attended by a large retinue of slaves and soldiers; but all the blinds were down. The other sultanas were in almost equally gorgeous carriages, mostly drawn by white horses, and surrounded by crowds of attendants. Then came the Sultan's eldest son, commander-in-chief of the army, followed by the next son, a boy about seven years old, who is lord high admiral of the fleet; and the procession was filled in and closed by carriages full of ministers of every degree, in their most gorgeous uniforms.

After riding about for two or three hours, we went on board, dressed, and rowed in the gig up to Kandili to lunch. It was a pleasant row up in the eddy till we reached a particular point, Roomili Hissar, where the 'devil's current,' as it is not inappropriately called, ran like a mill-stream, and obliged us to have a rope and be towed by two men. Then we shot across and down, and landed on the quay at Kandili. A short steep climb brought us to our friend's house, which commands lovely views on every side, up and down and across the Bosphorus, and to the mountains behind.

Wednesday, November 11*th.*—Before breakfast, Ali Bey came on board with a message from the Sultan, to know on what day and at what hour we should like to see his palace at Beylerbey, that it might be in order for us. The Sultan had sent his aide-de-camp to Aarif Pasha between twelve and one last night, waking them all up, to tell him to make special arrangements for us to see it; and therefore Ali Bey came on board the first thing to know our wishes. It was a very wet morning, but the weather cleared up at about 11.30 a.m., when we started for our frequently postponed ride round the walls. As the horse I rode yesterday had been down in the interim, and was dead lame, I had to wait while they found another. We drove the first part of the way, across the bridge into Stamboul, and along the narrowest and dirtiest streets for miles, till we got to the Seven

Towers. There we stopped, climbed up the walls, saw the towers, admired the view, back over Constantinople, and forward over the Sea of Marmora, took some photographs, and ate our lunch. Then we mounted our horses and rode along the most execrable road, outside the walls. Of course we stopped at the Greek church of Balukli, to see the miraculous fishes swimming about in a dark pool inside a chapel. They are *said* to be eight hundred years old, and to be red on one side and brown on the other, in consequence of having leaped from the frying-pan, not into the fire, but into the water, when Constantinople was taken!

We then rode on round the walls, which are triple, and which form an interesting monument of the work of the Middle Ages. They are of enormous size, with square towers at intervals, and were of considerable strength in former days. But they have been actually sold by this present Sultan to his mother for the paltry price of the building materials, and she was rapidly having them destroyed, when this act of vandalism was stopped by the British minister in 1869. Past the Gate of Adrianople and various other gates, up and down steep hills, through graveyards, full of dogs and magpies, but always on a frightful road, we rode, till we reached Eyoob, the mosque, where the new Sultan is not exactly crowned, but girt with the sword of Osman, which ceremony answers to the coronation of our kings and queens.

The way home lay along a real road, but knee-deep in mud, and full of holes, some very deep. We crossed the new French bridge, and rode up into Pera, arriving just in time for dinner, at Misseri's. Rustem Pasha, governor of Lebanon, was there, holding forth on the mismanagement connected with the rebuilding of the Embassy here, of which he said even the Turks would be ashamed. The mistakes and the delays are really so ludicrous, that they furnish the main subject of talk everywhere here. After tea I was carried in a sedan-chair down to the yacht, and found it a very pleasant mode of conveyance. The men went at a smart pace, but very smoothly, over the rough ground ; so I do not wonder that people prefer these chairs to the jolting of a carriage in this badly-paved town.

Thursday, November 12*th.*—Aarif Pasha, high admiral of the fleet, was on board by eight, saying he had received another message from the Sultan, to fetch us himself and take us round the palace and gardens of Beylerbey at eleven. At that hour he returned, and took us in a twelve-oared boat up the Bosphorus to Beylerbey. We were received on the steps by half a dozen servants, who first showed us a seal in a large salt-water tank, and then took us inside the gardens, which are in excellent order and full of flowers, though it is late in the season. We then went into the kiosk, which is built on the terrace overhanging the Bosphorus, with enormous plate-glass windows, each forming as it were the frame to an exquisite real landscape. It is luxuriously furnished and has a highly decorated ceiling. The palace itself is magnificent, especially the staircase, the steps and balustrades of which are inlaid with the finest marqueterie. The hall, too, resting on large marble columns, is very fine : it is surrounded by numerous rooms, each handsomer than the last, with ornamental ceilings, and pictures of ships let into the walls in every direction. Having seen all the apartments in the Selemlek, we went into the apartments of the Harem, containing a still larger and more spacious hall, in which were a most splendid table, chandelier, candelabra, and clock, in frosted silver, a present from the Viceroy of Egypt; also two handsome cabinets, in which are kept many of the Sultan's jewels. The rooms surrounding the ladies' hall are just as handsome as those surrounding the men's hall, with the exception that all the walls are whitewashed, instead of being painted in designs or hung with silk. By another staircase we descended into a third magnificent hall, the centre entirely occupied by an enormous fountain, easily convertible into a bath. It must be deliciously cool in summer, and here sometimes the Sultan has theatrical performances. On the women's side are the apartments of his mother, on the other those of his son.

We sat down for a time in one of the rooms, while coffee, sweetmeats, and cigarettes were served to us. Then we went through the gardens, all laid out in terraces, with miniature lakes and splendid bronzes, and so on to the upper kiosk, which overlooks the public park, and where the Sultan delights to sit and observe the people. He goes there frequently, but never enters the palace since the visit of the French Empress, being afraid of the evil eye, her misfortunes having come soon after her visit. He has even had part of the outbuildings pulled down, to try and avert any ill consequences. The proportions of the palace are so good that it is really spacious inside, and contains many suites of rooms, surrounding two enormous halls, all on one floor. Outside it does not look larger than an ordinary country house.

Leaving the kiosk we passed a small lake, about three

feet deep. There are boats on it in the summer, and the Sultan sometimes amuses himself by sitting on the bank, while some of the ladies of the harem are rowed about and purposely upset for his amusement. They are all dressed very smartly for the occasion, and he always gives them new dresses afterwards. There was another kiosk, decked out with paintings of animals and birds, and bad copies of Landseer's pictures, while the grounds were full of pigeons and curious birds in aviaries, and wild beasts of all kinds. They were removed from Tcheragan a few weeks ago, because they roared and disturbed the Sultan at night. When the Empress was staying here, the Sultan visited her every day. One day she went to see his mother, and saluted her on the cheek. The Valideh was furious, and said she had never been so insulted in her life, especially by a Giaour. She retired to bed at once, was bled, and had several Turkish baths, to purify her from the pollution. Fancy the Empress's feelings, when, after having so far condescended as to kiss the old woman, born one of the lowest of slaves, she had her embrace received in such a manner. One of the Sultan's titles, of which he is very proud,—why, I know not—is 'Son of a Slave.'

At the steps of Beylerbey we parted from Aarif Pasha, who sent us back in the same boat we came in, whilst he returned on board the flag-ship, alongside of which a perfect fleet of captains' gigs was waiting, to receive their orders for the annual move of the fleet from the Bosphorus into the Golden Horn for the winter. This is one of the only two cruises they ever make in the year, so that it is an important event; and though it is only about three miles from above Tcheragan to the dockyard, the ships generally contrive to do a good deal of damage to themselves, to each other, and to the two bridges. When his business was over, Aarif Pasha returned to lunch, and we found several other friends on board. After they left, it being nearly dark, we went in a caïque to see the sunset from the Golden Horn. Nothing could be more lovely, with all the shipping about. The smoke of the steamers even was gilded, and looked picturesque at this hour.

We went down as far as the French bridge, over which the contractor lost an immense sum of money in the following manner. The bridge was to have been finished by a particular day, but the contractor found that this would be impossible with Turkish workmen unless he worked day and night. This he obtained leave to do, and the necessary lights and torches were supplied at the Sultan's expense. All went well for a time, till the unfortunate contractor was told that he must open the bridge to let a ship from the dockyard pass through, some time before the bridge was finished. He said it was impossible, as he would have to pull everything down, and it would take two or three months to replace the scaffolding and pile-driving machines. He went to the ministers of marine and finance. They only said, 'If the Sultan says it must be done, it MUST, or we shall lose our places if not our heads.' So the ship came out, at a cost of a little over a hundred thousand pounds and a delay of three months in the completion of the bridge, all because the Sultan found his small son crying in the harem one day, the child's grief being that, though he had just been promised to be made an admiral, he could not see his flag hoisted on his own particular ship from the nursery windows. So a large ironclad was brought out from the dockyard and moored in front of Dolmabagtcheh to gratify his infant mind, thus causing enormous inconvenience to the whole town for months, to say nothing of the waste of money, of which the Sultan paid very little, and for the loss of which, I imagine, he cared still less.

The Sultan's youngest son.

CHAPTER VIII.

THE SEA OF MARMORA, DARDANELLES, SMYRNA, EPHESUS, CHIOS, AND MILO.

There is a temple in ruin stands,
Fashioned by long forgotten hands;
Two or three columns and many a stone,
Marble and granite, with grass o'ergrown.

Sunday, November 15th.—We had service on board, as usual. Soon after, Madame Cassanova and a French maid arrived from Madame Ikbal Kiasim and Madame Hilmeh, with a feridjee and yashmak, all arranged ready for me to put on, and the most lovely embroidered dress as a present. They are really all exceedingly kind. Madame Kiasim had already sent me a towel beautifully embroidered in gold, and the Princess Azizeh another embroidered with a picture of Noah's Ark as a paddle-wheel steamer with smoke coming out of the funnel, and the dove returning with the olive-branch.

We landed about 11.30 a.m., and drove to the Sweet Waters, where we all met (some on horseback and some in carriages, a pleasant little party) for a pic-nic. It was another lovely day, though cloudy, very warm, with occasional gleams of sun. The peacocks were more abundant than ever, and we tried hard to take some photographs of them, but failed from lack of light. Several friends drove by while we were at lunch on the bank of the river, and stopped to have a chat. We were obliged to drive back early, to go on board, dress, and attend a small pleasant dinner-party, followed by a large assembly after dinner, with some very good music. We were very sorry to say good-bye to all our kind friends at night, for though we have talked of going for some time we are still here. We really mean, however, to make a start to-morrow.

Monday, November 16*th.*—We drove up into the town after breakfast, to pay bills, make farewell visits, &c., and, after lunch at Misseri's, went to wish Mr. Chlebowski good-

Original Sketch by the Sultan Abdul Aziz.

bye, and thank him for the kind present he had made me of an original marine sketch by the Sultan Abdul Aziz, a great compliment, as he has always hitherto refused to part with one of these sketches. He was delighted to see us. The inspection of the grand picture he has in hand, and then of his most choice and varied collection, took some time. He told us about his life in the Sultan's palace, which seemed almost like that of a state prisoner. He was always hard at work, and was scarcely allowed time for his meals, and never permitted to be ill or tired. The Sultan immediately dismisses any official, *employé*, or servant, who is so unlucky as to be ill even for a day. At the end of five years he saw the Sultan for the first time. After that he used often to drop in, and make rough sketches of the pictures he wished painted. On Friday the Sultan used to say : 'You are a Christian, so you can work, though it is our Sabbath ; '—on Saturday : ' You are not a Jew, so of course you work to-day ; '—and on Sunday : ' I know this is your day of rest, but it is not mine, as I am a Mussulman ; so you must work for me.' Consequently, at the end of nine years, he was obliged to give up his appointment, quite broken in health.

It was nearly 5 p.m. before we reached the yacht. Everybody was on board, but, instead of everything being ready, the two anchors were so foul of one another (for want of a proper swivel) that neither of them was half up, and it was more than 6.30 p.m. before we were really on our way, and steaming slowly away from Constantinople, past the Seraglio Point and down the Sea of Marmora. We were very sorry to leave on some accounts, and wondered when, if ever, we should return and see the beautiful city and our numerous kind friends again. It was almost a calm when we started, with a slight breath of contrary wind ; but in the night it shifted a little, and freshened so much that, though close-hauled, and with but little canvas, we sailed forty knots (forty-five miles) in three hours by the log, independently of the current—not bad going at sea—a mile in less than four minutes. Tom kept an extra watch all night, besides being on the bridge himself ; for this sea, which is very narrow and a great thoroughfare, being the highway to the Black Sea, is crowded with ships, and very few of the Greek or Turkish vessels carry lights. A few years ago one of the Viceroy's small yachts, the 'Muffa,' going fifteen knots, cut down an English ship so effectually that she sank almost instantaneously, although not completely cut through, and the crew, thirteen in number, who were happily all on deck, were saved by clinging to the yacht's anchor chains as she went through. None of the officers, except those on deck, were in the least aware of any collision, and in the morning there was only a slight scratch on the bow of the yacht, hardly removing the paint, to show what had happened in the night.

Tuesday, November 17th.—The wind dropped, and we were obliged to steam again. Then, before we passed Gallipoli, a burnt-up white-looking town on the top of brown cliffs, it came dead ahead and pretty strong, with pouring rain and a thick fog. Tom therefore thought it better, when we reached Chanak-Kalesi (the narrowest part of the Dardanelles, where we were obliged to stop to give up our firman and bill of health), to remain there for the night. We landed about 3.30 p.m., in the pouring rain, called on the vice-consul, Mr. Cortazzi, who was most kind, posted our letters, gave us the latest papers, and went with us to buy some of the coarse pottery for which the place is famous, Chanak-Kalesi in fact meaning 'Earthenware Castle.' The place has been much improved of late years. The cemetery is removed from the middle of the town, and a high road has been carried through it. The inhabitants objected strongly to this change, and when the late governor proposed to remove the tomb of a very sainted dervish, there was a regular revolution. He was therefore obliged to let it remain exactly in the middle of the high road, with a railing round, and a lamp at each end, to keep passers-by from tumbling over it at night. The rain came down harder than ever as we went on board, but ceased after dinner, and we had a fine night.

Wednesday, November 18*th.*—By 9 a.m. we were off again, under steam. The wind was contrary (N.E.), so that, with a falling glass, we expected a gale all day, and indeed came in for a small one in the afternoon, which changed the wind, when we were able to feather our screw and set sail. We held on all through the night under canvas, sailing sometimes fast, sometimes slow.

Thursday, November 19*th.*—At 7.45 a.m. we got up steam, and at 10.30 a.m. we dropped our anchor in the lovely Bay of Smyrna. The tops of the hills were covered with snow, and it was bitterly cold, with heavy showers of rain. We landed about 11 a.m., and paddled through the mud, over planks across torrents running down the streets, to the British consul's, where, to our great disappointment, we found no letters, only a telegram about the Birkenhead election. From the consul's we went to the bazaars, which, though under cover, were dirtier and wetter even than the streets, torrents of water running down, and occupying almost the whole width between the dullest and most uninteresting of small shops. Of course there were pretty things, but they were few and far between. Even the jewellers' shops were not interesting, though we found a few of the celebrated Smyrna bracelets and chains. More than once we had to squeeze ourselves almost into nothing against the shop-fronts, to allow long droves of camels to pass by—splendid big fat creatures, covered with curly hair. They were sleek and well cared for, carrying their heads with an air of dignity, very different from their small African brethren.

We waded back to the hotel, thoroughly dirty and wet, and as it cleared up a little after lunch we went for a drive round the town, over the roughest of streets, and then outside through the marshes, full of oranges and myrtles, along the side of a canal, till we reached a large orange

Smyrna Camel.

and myrtle grove, in the centre of which are the remains of Diana's bath, a beautiful 'silent pool' of transparently clear water, full of fish swimming about. In spite of the cold wet day and the snow on the hills, the gardener gathered a large bunch of beautiful roses, and boughs of oranges, nearly ripe, besides quantities of myrtle. We returned on board, and found Mr. Bigliotti had kindly been to arrange for a special train to Sardis (the ancient capital of Lydia, where there are a few interesting remains) for to-morrow at 7 a.m.; but the weather was so bad that we thought it better to decline the kind offer with grateful thanks.

Friday, November 20*th*, was rather finer, though bitterly cold and showery. All the morning was occupied with making arrangements about one of our men who has been sick for some time with Asiatic fever, and we thought it might be better to send him home by the Cunard boat lying alongside, or else to place him in the hospital on shore. But the man is very anxious to stay on board with his shipmates, and as the doctor does not think it will do him any harm, we have decided to let him stay. When we came on board yesterday the first thing we were told was that a snake about two feet long had been caught coming out of the port in Allnutt's berth. How it ever got there is a mystery. We can only imagine that it must have come on board in one of the pots from Chanak-Kalesi, where it had probably settled itself for the winter, but had been disturbed by being brought on board. Anyhow it is not a pleasant idea, as there is a popular theory that where there is one there are sure to be two; it makes us very careful as we step about, get into bed, or look into any dark corner. As a precaution, we have ordered the pots on deck each to be filled with water and then repacked.

We landed about noon, and went first to the Persian khan, and then to the great *dépôt* for Turkey carpets, a small shop, in which sat an old Turk cross-legged, who allowed us to purchase his wares with the most sublime indifference. The carpets certainly were far better than I had ever seen imported into England, and much cheaper. After lunch the consul sent his cavass, and Muñie and I on donkeys, the rest of the party on foot, went through the town and up the hill to the Genoese castle, which once commanded the town and bay, but is now in ruins. It is alleged to be the restoration of a fortress of the Cyclopean period, but no traces of the fortifications are to be seen now, though numerous remains of Greek and Etruscan pottery and statuettes have been discovered, and we bought a beautiful little head of a terra-cotta statue from a

Aqueduct near Ephesus.

shepherd boy on our way down. The view from the summit is very fine, not only over the town and bay of Smyrna, but over the surrounding country.

Saturday, November 21*st*.—About 2 a.m. it came on to blow a hurricane, and at 5 a.m., when we were called, it was blowing still harder, and pouring with rain ; so we reluctantly gave up our intended expedition to Ephesus, sent notes to the manager of the railway, and then turned over and went to sleep again. After breakfast we had an answer from him, saying that the barometer had not been so low in Smyrna for years, and that he expected worse weather to follow. All day it blew, rained, thundered, lightened, as if all the fury of the elements had been let loose on our devoted heads. At least three thunder-storms seemed to break over our little ship, the thunder crashing and the lightning flashing almost simultaneously. It was next to impossible to land, and we were busy all day writing letters, copying out journal, arranging old, and developing new photographs, &c. Towards evening the wind moderated, and though we had thunder-storms and rain during the night, with a considerable amount of wind, the fury of the gale had moderated, and the morning broke bright and clear. About 1 p.m. to-day (Saturday) we dragged our anchor, and as it was some time before anyone perceived what was happening, we had full way on, and were drifting with great force against an Austrian steamer before we knew where we were. She let out more chain, we let go another anchor, and at last, after much excitement, the terrible collision which it seemed impossible to avert was avoided, with barely three inches to spare, as the end of our mizen-boom glided by her bowsprit. All hands on the decks of both craft of course did their best to help.

Sunday, November 22*nd.*—The sea was still breaking over the quay with so much force this morning that it was difficult to land before noon, and we had to row up quite behind the breakwater in order to effect a landing dryshod. The walk to the English church was long and very dirty. After service we went to the Point Station of the Smyrna and Aidin railway, where we found our special train waiting for us, and the manager ready to receive us, with luncheon provided at his private residence. We started about 2 p.m. through a pleasant low country between ranges of mountains. We met a long string of fine camels, packed with tents and bright-coloured rugs and carpets, and led by their owners, accompanied by all their women and children, dogs, domestic animals, cocks and hens—evidently changing their camp. A splendid eagle rose from the plain and slowly flew towards the mountains. Our line passed the railroad to Magnesia and Sardis, always winding along the valley where once the river flowed. Other Arab encampments were dotted about, but neither villages nor houses except those connected with the railway were to be seen, till Ayasolook, the station for Ephesus, had been reached. Just before arriving a tremendous jolt caused a stoppage, and we found we had run over a cow. The poor creature's body, completely cut in half, was soon further divided and taken possession of by the guards and bystanders.

Horses were in readiness for us, and we rode first to the top of the hill near the station, to get a general view of the ruins—the remains of many Mohammedan mosques and tombs, some in very tolerable preservation, and those of modern date of very good architecture. At the bottom of the hill stands the temple of Diana of the Ephesians, excavated by Mr. Wood, 23 feet below the surface of the surrounding plain. It was once one of the seven wonders of the world, and though burnt eight times, it still contained many treasures of art and sculpture to reward the excavator. As these have been mostly removed to the British Museum, there is not much left to see on the spot. On one of the small hills above, the guides point out the ruins of the church of St. John, and, close by, his grave and that of the Virgin Mary. We bought some of the marble remains (not thought worth taking to the British Museum) from Mr. Wood's agent, took some photographs, and saw the Turkish aqueducts, all tumbling to pieces, but with beautiful bits of Greek sculpture built in here and there. Even in the small cottages and fountains you find lovely specimens of Greek inscriptions and sculpture let in anyhow into doorsteps or lintels, or built into the wall.

A Camp on the Road.

We left Ayasolook at 5 p.m. and reached Smyrna about 6.45 p.m., found the boat waiting for us at the Point Pier, a nice smooth place of embarkation, and reached the yacht after a long row by 7.45 p.m.

Monday, November 23rd.—We had intended to start at 8.30 a.m., but, as usual, there were many delays. The steward did not come on board till 9 a.m., and the water-boat was not alongside till nearly the same hour; so it was just 10.30 a.m. before we were really off, under steam, with pouring rain, but not a breath of wind. It cleared up about the middle of the day; the breeze freshened, and we were going twelve knots when off the island of Chios, about 7.30 p.m. After some debate we decided to throw away (so to speak) our fair wind, and lie-to off the island till morning, to land and see its beauties. It was a most lovely moonlight night, and as we glided slowly about, with the full moon shining on the sails, and a delicious aromatic fragrance wafted from the shore on either side, it was exactly one's *beau idéal* of what cruising in the Archipelago ought to be, if only the thermometer were 15° higher—80° instead of 65°.

Tuesday, November 24*th.*—Breakfast was over by 8 a.m., and we landed at 9 a.m., sending off a doctor to see another of our men, who had unfortunately caught the country fever, and was very ill. Evie, Muñie, and I rode, and the gentlemen walked, for about an hour and a half, along dirty lanes, between high walls overhung with orange, lemon, pomegranate, fig, and mastic trees, affording tantalising peeps through latticed gates of lovely gardens, still full of scarlet cloves, geraniums, and other bright flowers. The mastic is the chief product of the island, and is a speciality. It has been tried in many other places, but has almost always failed.

At length we reached our destination, and were admitted through one of the large and jealously guarded gates into a lovely orange grove, where we wandered about and gathered oranges to eat and boughs to take home at our own sweet will. Then, after taking some photographs, we mounted our donkeys again, and turned our faces homewards. At the quay we bought some eggs, chickens, and bread, and were prepared to go on board, when the

French vice-consul came with a piteous appeal, to beg us to give him a passage to Syra or Tenos. He had been waiting to take his little girl to school for three weeks, during which period the bad weather had prevented the steamers touching. It was rather inconvenient, and we represented to him in the strongest terms that we had neither bed nor room on board, and should probably go straight to Corfu, without touching at Syra; but he continued to plead so hard that at last Tom gave way, and we consented to wait ten minutes for his daughter, her *malle*, and her *matelas*, all of which speedily arrived, with the accompaniment of the vice-consul's own very small valise, and a basket full of the odds and ends without which foreigners hardly ever seem able to travel. I think the poor man had taken us for a trader, and he was rather astonished when we went below to lunch. Afterwards, when shown round the yacht, he said, 'But you are all cabins; where does your cargo go?' It was quite calm, but the daughter was very ill, and retired shortly to bed in Mabelle's berth.

Wednesday, November 25th.—At 3.30 a.m. we were off Tenos. Tom called our passengers, and took them himself ashore in the cutter. They were terribly frightened, and very ill. When they reached the landing-place, everybody on shore was asleep, and when they were roused they told us that the senior health officer had been superseded yesterday, and that the new one only commenced his official duties at 8 a.m. to-day. Hence there were great delays, one not knowing the proper form, and the one who did know not being qualified to sign it. In the end the matter was satisfactorily settled. The gratitude of our temporary guests was immense. To this day I have occasional letters from them, with a photograph or a little gum mastic.

Tom returned on board, and we were under weigh again about 6 a.m., passing between the central island of Syra — from whence almost all the commerce of the Archipelago

Muffie, Mr. Crake, Evie, and Fcliso.

is conducted — and the anciently sacred island of Delos. All the islands of the Archipelago send their produce in small boats to Syra, there to be reshipped in steamers for ports in England and elsewhere, bringing back various kinds of cotton goods and iron tools, as well as money, in exchange.

We had been going fourteen knots ever since 6 a.m., the

gale gradually increasing, till at 9 a.m. we hove-to, to take in reefs and hold a council of war, whether to run back to Syra or struggle on to Milo, 25 miles further on. As the wind was fair, we decided to keep on, and a terrible tossing we had. A nasty short sea, a great deal of water on board, and a gale of wind, made us all very thankful to get into the shelter of the splendid harbour of Milo. The entrance to it is very beautiful, and takes you between abrupt volcanic rocks, of the most varied tints of red, green, purple, and yellow. So brilliant and intense was all the colouring, but especially the red, that, till we looked through the glasses, we almost thought the rocks were overgrown with Virginian creeper of the brightest scarlet. A little town perched on the very apex of the highest and sharpest-peaked mountain seemed to domineer over the whole island, making one wonder how the inhabitants ever climbed up to their craggy houses; and the effect was altogether very beautiful in the setting sun. A few miles up the bay we dropped anchor near the old capital, a ruined town depopulated by the plague in former times, and now a nest of malaria and fever. There are a few new houses built among the ruins since the Greek occupation, though the majority of the inhabitants have removed to the town far above and away, to secure themselves alike from pirates and malaria. The weather cleared at sunset, the wind lulled, and we had a lovely moon for a time. But soon the rain came down again in torrents, and continued to do so throughout the night.

Thursday, November 26th.—We landed at 9 a.m., and Evie, Muñie, and I on donkeys, the gentlemen on foot, soon left the dirty little town behind, and proceeded up the

THE 'SUNBEAM' IN A GALE (OFF MILO).

'A vessel in mid ocean, her heaved prow
Clamb'ring, the mast bent, the rattl'n wind
In her sail roaring.'

hill, along narrow paths, with walls on each side, all built of the brightest-coloured marble and stones. In a little while it became necessary to dismount and scramble down a still narrower and more rocky path, where the donkeys could not go. This track led to a curious subterranean grotto, which seemed to penetrate many hundreds of yards into the earth. There was unfortunately no time to explore it. Another short walk brought us to massive tufa walls, apparently of the Cyclopean period. Soon after, on turning a corner, the theatre itself was disclosed to our view. Here the beautiful Venus of Milo (now in the Louvre at Paris) was discovered. At the present time there are nine rows of semicircular seats, tolerably perfect, remaining. All are of pure white marble, and there are numberless slabs and blocks, beautifully carved, lying about all over the ground. Though there are but few, if any, travellers, many of the peasants had beautiful little figures, jars, lamps, coins, and seals to dispose of.

The situation of the amphitheatre is very beautiful, on the side of a hill commanding a lovely view of land, sea, and islands to the south. We wandered about a long time, took several photographs, and then scrambled up the hill again and remounted our donkeys, to climb a steep rocky path to the little town above. The ground was covered with wild cyclamen and white crocuses, and the walls festooned with the *Clematis montana*, while myrtles and lentisk grew in abundance. Half an hour's climb took us to the town, and a very funny town it was, up and down the very steepest crags. It was inhabited by a race of good-looking men and women and pretty children, who all came out to look at us. They had the regular Grecian type of countenance, straight noses, pretty mouths, and lovely large dark eyes, and all were scrupulously clean. Most of the women's garments were white, and there was not a speck of dirt on any of them. The people not only followed us down the streets, but placed themselves in all conceivable nooks and corners. On every house-top, in every balcony, out of every window, peeped heads, not annoying us in any way, but simply indulging their curiosity.

Ruins of Amphitheatre (Milo)

We took some photographs—a process which greatly interested the natives—then mounted our donkeys and hurried back to the yacht. We should all have liked to remain another day, but Tom thought it better to take advantage of the fine weather (which at this season of the year is very precarious) to pursue our voyage; so by 3.30 p.m. we were under weigh, and steaming slowly out of the lovely harbour of Milo. As there was a light air outside, the screw was feathered and sails hoisted, and we sailed slowly on through the remainder of the afternoon, and all through the calm, lovely night.

Friday, November 27th.—The sun rose, a few minutes before 7 a.m., out of the sea, and in a perfectly unclouded sky, near Cape Malea. The wind was dead ahead, and as we could only beat slowly against it, it was 9 p.m. before we rounded Cape Matapan. The wind afterwards fell light, and we got up steam again. It had been very pleasant all day, for though we had a contrary wind we were close under a very lovely shore, and in perfectly smooth water.

Saturday, November 28th.—Soon after midnight it began to pour in torrents, with thunder and lightning, which continued till about 10 a.m., when the rain stopped, and as the wind rose fresh and fair, all sail was again set. About 3.30 p.m. we dropped anchor in the harbour, or rather bay, off the town of Zante. The boat lay alongside, ready for us to land, when first arrived the officer about the bill of health, then an officer from the American man-of-war 'Alaska,' with many kind offers from the captain. We begged him to send their doctor on board, to see our poor sick man, who is still suffering from fever. By the time all these visits were over, a terrific storm of thunder and lightning burst over us, accompanied by a deluge of hail and rain. We therefore determined, in fact were obliged, to remain on board the yacht for this evening. The 'Alaska,' Captain Carter, has been out from America a year, and is on her way from Alexandria to Malta and Villa Franca, to join the squadron there, under Admiral Worden.

The doctor gave a very good report of his patient, who

has had the Smyrna fever badly. It is now on the turn, and it was satisfactory to know that Tom and I had given him exactly the right remedies. The other man is quite convalescent. Happily this fever, though lowering and disagreeable, is neither dangerous nor contagious.

The 'Sunbeam' when first launched.

A Church at Zante.

CHAPTER IX.

ZANTE, ITHACA, CEPHALONIA, CORFU, AND ALBANIA.

All green was it and beautiful, with flowers far and wide,
A pleasant spot, I ween, wherein the traveller might abide.
Flowers with the sweetest odour filled all the sunny air,
And not alone refreshed the sense, but stole the mind from care.

Sunday, November 29th.—A lovely morning after a wet night. We went on shore to the English church at 11 a.m. The service was held in a low damp room near the seashore, and there were but few people present. After church we strolled up the town, through dirty ill-paved streets, with a great many churches, and one or two apparently good hotels. There is a nice market-place, with quantities of fish, poultry, game, fruit, vegetables, and lovely flowers, for sale. The inhabitants are not nearly so good-looking as those of the other Greek islands we have visited, and there were marvellously few women about.

After lunch on the yacht, we returned the Americans' visit, on board the 'Alaska,' and then went ashore. It was rather late, and the carriage we had ordered had gone away, tired of waiting for us. While we waited on a doorstep for another, a violent shower came on, and a lady sent her servant to ask us to come and take refuge in her house. We did so, and found she was the wife of the principal merchant of the place. She spoke Italian only, but was most kind, and told our new coachman where he should take us. The drive was lovely up to the citadel, through vineyards and olive groves. All the terraces were covered with purple cyclamen and white crocus in full bloom, the stones were carpeted with lycopodium, and wherever there was a tiny stream of water, the wall formed a perfect curtain of maidenhair fern, the long fronds waving in the wind. The citadel (a Venetian fortress) is now old and dismantled, but there is a beautiful view from the top over the island in every direction. It was nearly dark before we left, and we went straight on board the yacht. We found that while we had been away our kind acquaintance of this morning had sent us a huge basket full of the most lovely flowers, principally exquisite rosebuds, violets, heliotropes, and some green roses, which are not so uncommon here as in England, besides a quantity of delicious pears and apples.

Monday, November 30*th.*—Another most lovely day. We were very anxious to go and see the 'pitch wells,' a curious natural phenomenon, described by Herodotus more than two thousand years ago, and remaining exactly in the same state at the present day. The pitch may be seen bubbling up through several fathoms of clear water, like a great india-rubber bottle, till it bursts on reaching the surface, when the inhabitants collect it and carry it away in jars. Unfortunately, the Greek government does not keep in repair the excellent roads made by the English, so that the recent heavy rains have completely washed them away in many places, and it was impossible to get to the wells. We took, however, a lovely drive through vineyards, orange and olive groves, all along the plain. The further we went the more we were struck with the immense fertility and beauty of this lovely island, which richly merits its name of 'Flower of the Levant.'

Every respectable person to whom we have spoken bitterly laments the departure of the English from their occupation of the islands, and gives the most dreadful account of the Greek government, which, in these islands, is hardly a government at all, but simply a system of bribery and corruption. Robbers and marauders who can pay a few piastres to the so-called police are never taken up, while poor but innocent men are put in prison and punished in their stead. At the time of the elections, the bribery and corruption are worse than ever, and the soldiers go into the houses with fixed bayonets, to drive the unfortunate voters to the poll. Under this system, of course, everything is going to ruin, roads, ports, public institutions, &c. They are, however, building a fine new opera-house here, and for the present a very good Italian company are playing at a minor theatre.

Soon after midday the anchor was again weighed, and the yacht on her way to Cephalonia. It was a perfect day, and Zante looked lovely as we sailed along close under the coast till nearly past Cape Skinari (the northern extremity of the island), and then made for Cape Seakeas (the southern extremity of Cephalonia). Here we felt the force of the wind more, and came in for a considerable roll, till we turned into the sheltered bay leading up to the harbour of Argostoli, the modern capital of the island. It was quite dark before we dropped our anchor in this almost land-locked harbour.

Olive Gathering, Cephalonia.

Tuesday, December 1st.—Another very wet night, followed by a lovely hot day. After an early breakfast we landed and drove into the town. There is not much to see, only a few dirty shops and some insignificant-looking buildings facing the sea, the road in front forming a quay, about a mile long. The bay is crossed at the end by a causeway, about seven hundred yards long. Over this we drove, and slowly climbed the steep mountain on the opposite side. The island of Cephalonia is very rough and rugged, and though every scrap of ground is cultivated and made the most of for the currant vines, the general effect is bleak and bare—very different from Zante. There are no orange-trees, only old gnarled grey olives, like forest-trees. From these the natives are now gathering the fruit, and a curious picturesque sight it is—boys in the trees, men below beating the branches with long sticks, and women and girls picking up the olives as they fall into cloths spread underneath. They are then taken to the mill and crushed. The first good oil is sold for exportation, the second pressing is kept for home consumption by the peasants, or else the olives themselves are eaten without being pressed again. Olives, either pressed or unpressed, form, with bread and a little sour wine, the staple diet of the peasants here; and when really ripe they contain so much oil as to be almost as nourishing as a meat diet, besides being much more wholesome in a hot climate.

A three hours' crawl up what had been once a good road, but is now a very bad one, took us to the top of the mountain ridge, which runs across, or rather along, the island. Here is a fine view of the harbour and town beneath, with sea and islands beyond. We had lunched, and taken some photographs, when a smart shower of rain came on. As this seemed likely to last, we drove rapidly down the hill again; but in less than half an hour were quite out of the clouds, with blue sky above us and the sun shining, and we spent some time collecting ferns and common objects by the sea-shore before going on board the yacht.

There is a very good Italian opera company playing

here as well as at Zante, and we were anxious to go and hear them; but this being the first night of 'Rigoletto,' it was quite impossible. Every seat was taken. Some of the servants went, and said that the theatre was small, and the scenery bad, but that the acting, singing, and dresses were all good, and that the ladies in the boxes were very well dressed. Cephalonia appears to be the least interesting of the islands, and has the fewest classical associations. Still, there are one or two pleasant excursions to be made. Perhaps the best are to the old Venetian fortress of St. George, and to the house Lord Byron occupied at Melaxata, from which there is a beautiful view.

Wednesday, December 2nd.—Still calm and beautiful weather. The anchor was up by 6 a.m., and we steamed out of our sheltered harbour, down the coast of Cephalonia, round Cape Seakeas, along to Cape Monda, and then up the other or eastern side of the island, towards the Bay of Damos. Here are the remains of a Grecian town of the same name, the ancient capital of the island. We stretched across to Ithaca, and, running up the eastern shore, soon came to the narrow entrance of the gulf and port of Bathy, or Vathi, scarcely visible among the surrounding rocks. We steamed up about a mile and a half, till we were close to the town, and had entered the most perfectly land-locked harbour I ever saw. It reminded us rather of Norway, but the mountains were all burnt and brown instead of green, and there was not any snow. In fact, these islands generally are in many of their features very like Norway, though, at all events at this time of year, not so beautiful.

Directly after lunch we landed, intending to make a

long excursion to the Grotto of the Nymphs and Ulysses' Castle; but, alas! we found on landing that, as in Homer's time,

> Rough is the land; nor can we drive a car
> Through the rude ways, for steeds impassable;

and that all the horses, mules, and donkeys were employed all over the island in gathering in the olive harvest. After considerable delay they found a very small but rather nice black donkey, which carried Muñie, and a miserable specimen of a horse, which carried me, very safely, however, up and down the steepest places, while Evie and the gentlemen walked to the Grotto of the Nymphs. At first the road led to some windmills, and then up extraordinarily craggy paths, till we turned the shoulder of a steep mountain, and soon after reached the grotto. The views all the way up were lovely, looking back over land and sea. We crept into the grotto through a tiny little hole, and though there are several apertures that admit daylight, we were obliged to have candles to see the stalactites. It was not so beautiful as we expected from Homer's description, though it answers to it in all material points, with the light of heaven seen through the blue veil supposed to have been worn by the nymphs.

We scrambled down to the town again, and walked about among the dirty streets, which rise gradually from the water's edge to the top of the hills behind, with terraced gardens of oranges, lemons, and flowers between, and with lovely views over the quiet little bay, where the water is deep enough to moor a big ship alongside the quay. We passed the cathedral, saw the 'Café of Telemachus'—(what an idea! fancy Telemachus and his Mentor taking their after-dinner coffee and 'fine champagne' on a straw chair in the principal street of Vathi!) We took some photographs, bought some coarse pottery, and went on board again. Many other interesting excursions may be made in the island, but of course all on horseback. No antiquities are to be found here, no lace or silver ornaments or cups. Everything has been collected by a Jew and taken to Corfu.

To look at this harbour, doubly surrounded by high mountains, you would think it impossible that the effects of any tempest would be felt. For a hundred years or more this has been the case; but last week, during the terrible gales, this place, like many others, came in for a perfect hurricane, which did a great deal of damage.

Thursday, December 3rd.—The night has been lovely, and to-day is still more beautiful. We were under weigh at 6.45 a.m., and the little harbour looked exquisite as we left it, just as the day was breaking, and still more fair half an hour later, when the sun rose, gilding the mountain-tops or tinging them with rose colour, leaving light clouds and mists hovering among the valleys. We steamed out of the harbour, but as we found a strong fair breeze outside, the screw was soon feathered, and we were bowling along ten knots an hour under the rocky coast of Santa Maura. About 11 a.m. the breeze fell light, and we lay for a long time off Fort St. Maura, looking at Prévésa and the ruins of Nicopolis on each side of the Gulf of Arta, and almost on the classic naval battle-field of Actium, where 'the world was lost for a woman.' The lofty peaks of the mountains of Thessaly stood up in the background, thickly covered with snow to a very low level. In consequence, I suppose, of a westerly gale, there was a very heavy roll, and it was a great relief when, about 1.30 p.m., the breeze freshened and we were bowling along again ten knots, the additional wind on the sails keeping the yacht steady. Early in the afternoon the islands of Paros and Madonia were passed, and soon after we entered the channel of Corfu at its southern extremity, where it is only five miles across. The island here ends in abrupt white cliffs. The mountain of San Salvador rises boldly up three thousand feet from the sea, and, indeed, the whole of the surrounding scenery is most striking and beautiful. It seemed very sad when the short day came to a close, for during the remainder of that night's voyage it was too dark to see anything of the scenery. In fact, Tom had great difficulty in picking up the anchorage between the island of Vido and the principal town of Corfu, which is called by the same name. We dropped anchor at 11.30 p.m.

Friday, December 4th.—I was on deck before daybreak, and saw the sun rise over this beautiful harbour. The town is pretty in itself, crowned by the picturesque old citadel. The island is all fertility and luxuriance, and on the opposite coast, barely six miles off, the snowy mountains of Albania form a lovely panorama. It was a lovely morning, and after an early breakfast we read our welcome letters from home, landed, and strolled about the town, before driving out to Pelleki, where we lunched and spent a most enjoyable day. The drive itself was lovely, principally through groves of hoary old olive-trees, over three hundred years old. At the village we left the carriage and climbed up, in about ten minutes, to the top of the mountain, from which we had a magnificent view of land and sea on every side. On our way down we had a better opportunity of noting the wonderful luxuriance of the country, the valleys being in the highest state of cultivation. We looked in at one or two shops, but found them all kept by Jews, and the prices too absurdly high to lead one into much temptation. We dined at the *table d'hôte* at 1.30 p.m., in a front room, with a lovely view over the promenade to the sea and the mountains of the opposite coast beyond. The old palace of the Lord High Commissioner of the Islands is a beautiful building, and looks over a luxuriant garden at one end of the promenade, full of palms, cacti, orange and lemon trees, and semi-exotics of all kinds.

Saturday, December 5th.—Yesterday Tom had engaged the services of an experienced sportsman, who, with two nice dogs, came on board by 5 a.m. By 6 a.m. we were under weigh, and soon after 8 a.m. we dropped anchor near the river Butrinto, in Albania. During our short steam across, one of the side-lights was unfortunately left open. I was in my room, when I suddenly heard and saw a wave dashing along the passage, and on going outside my maid and I found ourselves ankle-deep in water, which was pouring in in torrents through the open port-hole in Mr. Crake's berth, and was rapidly overflowing everything. Assistance was speedily called and the side-light screwed up, but not before Mr. Bingham, who performed that operation, had received a most uncomfortable bath, and the cabin and everything in it had been flooded. At 8.30 a.m. we got into the large cutter, for it was blowing hard, and by 9 a.m. we had landed the gentlemen, with some sailors to beat for them, while Evie, Muñie, and I rowed on in the boat to the mouth of the Butrinto, and then up the river itself.

It was rather fun, exploring by ourselves, though the banks of the river were marshy and uninteresting. The numerous birds, however, quite made up for the want of scenery, and they were all so tame that they let us approach quite near. Flights of wild ducks, cormorants, magpies, turkey-buzzards, hawks, curious black ducks, lovely white birds of the hawk tribe with long white tails, exquisite light-blue kingfishers, flitted to and fro, besides many other small birds. About a mile and a half brought us to the

An Extra Bath

large fisheries established at the exit of the river from the lake of the same name. There our further progress was barred by an elaborate system of fisheries. We got out, bought some fish, took some photographs, and asked if neither love nor money would persuade them to open us a passage. I could not speak Greek, and our interpreter's persuasions were not effectual. But we found that by landing on the opposite side, and engaging a soldier to show us the way and protect us, we could reach the top of an old ruined

Byzantine castle, from which a fine view of the lake might be obtained.

This we accordingly did, but on relanding we found a sort of morass, or rather shallow lake, between us and our path. This looked rather formidable, but as we were determined not to be defeated in our object, Evie and I took off our shoes and stockings and waded through, rather to the disgust of the soldier, I think, who thought he was going to earn his pay with very little trouble. A quarter of an hour's walk brought us to the top of the castle, where a fine view of the lake rewarded us. It is really a beautiful piece of water, surrounded by mountains, and bordered by forest trees of every description, now gay with their autumn tints. It was a very showery day, and as the rain soon began to descend in torrents, we paddled back to the boat as fast as we could, and set sail down the river again. A violent squall of wind, rain, and hail came (luckily from a favourable quarter), and we flew down the river with two reefs in our sail, the task of steering taking all my time. When we got outside in the open sea, it was fearfully rough, and we shipped a good deal of water trying to get off to the yacht. We therefore turned the boat's head round and crept along the shore, under lee of the land, till we saw the gentlemen waiting for us. The bad weather had compelled them to give up their sport sooner than they intended.

They had had a pleasant morning on the whole, and saw quantities of game—three and four woodcocks rising from one bush at a time. They brought home a good many woodcock, and a few snipe and quail, but failed to secure any wild duck. Pigs they did not attempt. Last year Sir David Baird and his brother killed five hundred head in four days, pig, wild duck, woodcock, snipe, and quail; and five guns of another party killed four hundred and twenty couple of woodcock in two days. This is just the season for woodcock, and I can fancy nothing more delightful to the sportsman than a month on this coast, shifting his anchorage to a different bay, each lovely, every few days, and, if he wants more change and excitement, going up into the mountains after deer, ibex, and chamois. Ladies, too, might amuse themselves very well. There are many charming excursions, good paths, and no fear of brigands. If they were artists, botanists, anglers, or photographers, they would find more than enough to occupy them.

It was very pleasant to get on board, change our wet clothes, and lunch in front of a warm fire. Our short voyage back to Corfu in the yacht was not pleasant, there being a strong gale ahead and torrents of rain, so that, though there was not much sea in this narrow channel, we pitched and rolled considerably. We dropped anchor about 5 p.m., and went ashore, to dine at the *table d'hôte*, intending to go to the opera afterwards. Unfortunately, however, the tenor and baritone were both ill (perhaps because it was such a bad night), and there was no opera. There seems a fate against our opera-going in the Ionian Islands. When we went off to the yacht, the gale had ceased, it was a flat calm, and the stars were shining brightly.

Sunday, December 6th.—A lovely day. One friend sent me a very large and lovely bouquet, and another the most enormous lemon I ever saw, weighing four pounds. I took the opportunity of photographing the men in their Sunday clothes before going to church. The English church is a pretty little building, well fitted up inside, the choir very good. We met several acquaintances coming out of church, and went with some of them to the citadel, to see the beautiful view and the old English church, now used by the Greeks, and the barracks. The first thing that strikes the eye on entering is the place whence the English arms were cut down, their outline being still clearly visible. Scarcely anyone in England, perhaps, knows how bitterly these poor islanders lament the loss of British rule, under

Some of our Crew.

which at one time they used to complain that they were only slaves. They find the difference now, when the Greek government neglects them utterly, except to impose enormous taxes; and the patriotic idea of being governed by a Greek king does not seem to console them much.

Our drive took us from the citadel to Garousta, a village eight miles off, near which we lunched on a sort of natural terrace, beneath the shade of some olive-trees, overlooking a most luxuriant plain. After luncheon we went on through the village and found the women most picturesquely dressed. Their hair was done into thick plaits, interwoven with red ribbon, arranged on each side of their faces; over their heads they had a long white handkerchief, with open-work embroidered ends. A dark blue petticoat, a black striped apron tied with broad light

Citadel, Corfu

blue ribbons, a black velvet jacket with little tails, something like a habit, and embroidered with gold at all the seams, worn over a full white shirt, and sometimes a coloured waistcoat in between, completed their costume. The women themselves are very good-looking while they are young, though they age somewhat prematurely. In the towns there is little noticeable in the way of costume, but at all the wells in the country the traveller meets beautiful groups of picturesquely dressed girls bearing pitchers on their heads, and having the 'immemorial gossip at the fountain side.'

We drove to the house of the present Greek minister in London. He owns a large amount of property in the island. His house stands in lovely gardens, the walks about which command a series of fine views over the sea, the adjacent islands, and the mainland. The drive home was very pleasant, looking through the trees on to the sea. In one of the bays is an island which bears a fancied resemblance to a vessel, and claims to be the ship of Ulysses, or rather the Phæacian galley which was sent to convoy him and became suddenly petrified. We stopped at the King's palace, which looked like a pleasantly furnished country house, with a beautiful terrace commanding the most exquisite views, and with winding paths leading, through orange and myrtle groves, to the beach. From the palace to the One Gun Battery is a charming drive of about a mile and a half.

But it was now quite dark, and there was no time to go to the river on the way to Govino, where Nausicaa is said to have met Ulysses. We were therefore obliged to go straight on board the yacht, to receive some friends to dinner. At 10 p.m. we had to say good-bye; they went ashore, and soon after we were steaming away down the narrow strait on our way to Cape Bianco. It seems a pity to be obliged to leave Corfu so soon. I should have liked to stay some time longer. I hope it may not be many years before we are able to see more of the beauties and sport of this highly favoured island.

Both here and at Zante green roses are grown. I had several sent me in bouquets, exactly like pink or red roses, only the petals were a bright green. They are more curious than beautiful; but their rarity would make them valuable in England.

An unpleasant Demand for Ammunition.

CHAPTER X.

PAXOS, SPARTIVENTO, MESSINA, AND NAPLES.

Tossing about on the roaring sea,
From billow to bounding billow cast,
Like fleecy snow on the stormy blast;
The sails are scattered abroad, like weeds;
The strong masts shake, like quivering reeds.

Monday, December 7th.—I am sorry to say we must consider our pleasant voyage nearly at an end, for we are really 'homeward-bound' now, and our only consideration is how to get home as fast as possible, with a due attention to comfort, and not being at sea too long at one time. Since we left England, on September 13, we have been exceptionally fortunate in the weather at sea; and though we have of course had some rough gales, and they have this year been even more severe than usual in the Mediterranean, they have always occurred when we were in port or under shelter of islands. The number of narrow straits we have navigated, and ports we have entered, both by day and night, would have been creditable to a professional, much more to an amateur. By occasionally heaving-to for meals, Tom has enabled all his passengers to appear at dinner every night since our departure from England, however ill they may have been at other times of the day. All our expeditions have proved successful and a great enjoyment to us all. Our only disappointment has been missing the visit to Roumania, especially as everything had been arranged so pleasantly for us, and the unfortunate misreading of the telegram caused the Prince and Princess so much unnecessary trouble.

Of course, with forty people on board, we have had numerous cases of illness incidental to hot climates, but the patients have all recovered wonderfully well. One or two of the men have caused us some anxiety for two or three days, when out of reach of a doctor; but when we have arrived at a port, and the doctor has come on board, we have each time had the satisfaction of hearing that the case could not have been treated better. The Board of Trade and Dr. Lankester's medical books, with Dr. Wilson's medicine chest, are simply invaluable. Muñie has not had a day's illness the whole time, and is wonderfully grown and improved, as strong as a little horse, and a most independent plucky little thing. She goes out with us for long expeditions quite alone, and is as happy as possible at a picnic, or in charge of the ruffianly-looking Turk or Greek to whom her donkey may happen to belong. She will not condescend to ride the same animal with anybody else; and finding that the strange men cannot understand her chatter, she amuses herself by singing the whole way.

If only our voyage ends as prosperously as it has begun, and gone on so far, and we find ourselves safe back in Old England early in the new year, we cannot be sufficiently thankful. We are sorry not to have time to go up the Adriatic, or to Venice; but it leaves for another year a pleasant cruise, which would bring us near these lovely islands again. Some of them are very beautiful, especially Milo, Zante, and Corfu; but with others we have been rather disappointed. They are not to be compared with Sicily, which is a capital cruising ground for a yacht; and if only the brigandage could be put an end to, so that one might move about without fear in the interior, it would be, to my idea, the most perfect winter residence in the world.

At 3 a.m. we left Paxos behind. About 9.30 a.m. we were all called in a great hurry to see a waterspout. The sea was rushing up violently like an immense fountain jet, while from the cloud above, which was intensely black, an inverted cone came down to meet the sea. Another waterspout, farther off, looked like a long black trough, pouring down from the heavens above into the cone-shaped fountain in the sea beneath. While we were all gazing at these over the starboard side, another small waterspout rushed by under our stern, so close that the man steering, using the sailor's proverbial expression, said 'you could have pitched a biscuit into it,' and before he could even call us to look, it was miles away, so swiftly was it flying. It was a fortunate chance it missed us, for these waterspouts are very dangerous, the force with which the water falls often driving ships' decks in, and sometimes causing them to founder. Men-of-war frequently fire into and break them to prevent such an accident.

At noon we were 128 miles from Corfu. Latitude 38° 42′ N., longitude 18° 33′ E. The sea was fairly smooth, with a long roll from the westward, telling of recent gales. About 3 p.m. a breeze sprang up. We then ceased steaming, and set all sails as quickly as possible.

Tuesday, December 8th.—This is one of the days so trying to everybody on board. A heavy swell from one quarter, and a short confused sea from another; the wind flying round to every quarter of the compass, sometimes violent squalls, sometimes no wind at all ; so that the men were setting sails and taking them in all day, and the funnel was up and down more than once. Altogether it was a most unpleasant, laborious, and unsatisfactory day. Everybody was more or less uncomfortable, and nothing was gained. At noon we had sailed 130 miles since noon yesterday. Latitude 37° 13' N., longitude 16° 11' E. Soon after sunset the wind really dropped for good, and by midnight we were steaming along full speed.

Wednesday, December 9th.—Shortly after midnight we made the light on Cape Spartivento, having sailed since noon a distance of 99 miles. We steamed up the straits, and at daybreak I came on deck. The weather was beautifully fine, and soon after the sun rose clear and bright, and shone on Mount Etna, now much more covered with snow than when we passed it two months ago. At 7.30 a.m. we dropped anchor in the harbour at Messina, and the steward went ashore for some fresh provisions. Soon after breakfast we landed, posted some letters, got some money at the bank, and then drove to some lovely gardens just outside the town beyond the Marina. They are all laid out in terraces down to the sea, and planted with orange, lemon, and myrtle trees, with rare and beautiful shrubs in between. Some of the hedges were of mandarine oranges, beautifully trained over wire fences, with the clusters of green and golden fruit hanging down in profusion. There was a shrub called Duranta, with leaves like a bay, and long clusters of pale yellow berries like grapes ; another smaller shrub, with black berries on coral-coloured stalks ; and curious lilies, whose flowers more resembled the head of some tropical bird with a gorgeous crest than any known blossom. The camellias were not quite out, but there was a profusion of heliotrope, carnations, roses, and geraniums. We gathered and ate as many oranges as we liked. We had large bouquets given us, besides the flowers we plucked for ourselves, and when we left the people were more than delighted with five francs —a very pleasant and not an expensive morning's entertainment.

The steward arrived soon after our return on board, and by 1 p.m. we were steaming away out of the straits. On getting outside we set sail and ceased steaming, and soon began to feel a most disagreeable roll. The glass fell, and there was a bad sunset; but as the wind was fair, and the yacht was running along before it, Tom did not like to turn back. By 7 p.m. we were close to Stromboli, which was sending out flames and smoke. By 10 p.m. we had all retired to bed. The wind freshened and veered to the north, and the glass fell rapidly. Tom put the yacht's head round, and we flew back towards Messina, tossing and tumbling about in the heavy swell. At 1 a.m. the wind shifted again to the southward, and at 2 p.m. everything looked brighter and the glass rose. Isaac, the mate, woke Tom, and urged our turning round. This we unfortunately did, and pursued our course towards Naples again. We went a tremendous pace, in spite of the heavy head swell, but it was most uncomfortable.

Thursday, December 10*th.*—At 9 a.m. we had nearly regained the sixty miles we had run back in the night, but were consequently again nearer the centre of the storm. The glass fell, and the wind rose. Tom thought of turning back, but, the wind still being fair, determined to continue towards Naples. At noon a very heavy squall struck the yacht without any previous warning. Luckily we were able to put her down before the wind, and lower everything on to the deck, before much harm was done. The sea now became terrific, with thunder, lightning, and torrents of rain. The wind flew round to the north again, and then Tom put her head round and determined to run back for Messina. The yacht had behaved beautifully through it all; but it was very miserable on board, and the prospect of being hove-to for three or four days in the middle of this stormy sea, if the gale continued or increased (which seemed only too probable from the look of sky and sea and the behaviour of the mercury in the barometer), was not cheerful. The afternoon and night were wretched; the wind whistling, the sea roaring, the thunder and lightning increasing, and the rain flowing down in sheets. The sea was intensely phosphorescent, causing Tom to remark that when the water came over her deck, deckhouse, sails, and canvas, all looked as if they were on fire. We never shipped a real sea all the time, though we had plenty of water on board, and we went tearing along, sometimes up and sometimes down, sometimes through and sometimes over the waves, with only a little pocket-handkerchief of a trysail and a rag of a jib, all reefs down. Stromboli was fortunately in the full blaze of an eruption, and served as a beneficent lighthouse, to guide us through the inky darkness of the night.

Friday, December 11*th.*—We were off the Faro of Messina about 3 a.m., and hove-to till daylight. Steam was then got up, and by 10 a.m. we were once more safely anchored in the harbour of Messina. Very thankful we were to be there, though it is provoking to have endured so much discomfort for forty-five hours, only to find ourselves back at the place whence we started. Tom, however, was glad to have so thoroughly tried the yacht, and found what a fine sea-boat she is. We were all good-for-nothing for a while, but we landed, lunched on shore, and went for a stroll through some lovely gardens, stretching up to the summit of a hill commanding a fine view over the town and bay. On the way down we stopped at the church of

The Smoking Room

the Greci, the whole of the walls and ceilings of which are beautifully inlaid with mosaics of the choicest marbles, as well as lapis lazuli, malachite, and agate. There is a large convent attached, and some of the nuns came and spoke to us through the grating. We dined at the *table d'hôte*, went on board soon after, and retired to bed early, thankful for the prospect of a quiet night.

Saturday, December 12*th.*—To our mutual regret Mr. Crake decided to land and find his own way home, our return being so very uncertain in this bad weather, and he being tied to time. As the day looked favourable, it was determined to make a start. Fires were lighted, and we went ashore to post some letters. At noon, on returning on board, the day had completely changed and the glass gone down, so our start was postponed. We went ashore and walked to the Capuchin convent on a hill behind the town, from which there is a fine view. As a steamer from Naples, on her way to Malta, had arrived during our absence, we sent on board to enquire about the weather. All her boats were stowed inboard, and her skylights and hatches battened down. She had had a terrible passage, and, after waiting three days at Naples for the gale to break, had been three days coming from that port, her average run being eighteen or twenty hours. No cooking of any sort could be done on board, and the passengers seemed in a most abject state of misery. She brought news of the mails being stopped and the telegraph wires broken by the gales.

In the evening we went to the Italian Opera, at a nice, clean, well-ventilated little theatre. The large house is shut up for want of funds. This theatre was crammed with nice-looking people. The opera, by a man named Domenio, was a rather amusing travesty of Rossini's 'Barbiere di Siviglia,' and was not badly performed on the whole. It was a lovely moonlight night, as we walked back to the boat and rowed on board, and we hoped to make a fresh start in the morning. Not long after we were in bed, however, there came a tremendous downpour of rain, accompanied by thunder and lightning. About 2 a.m., a violent squall struck us, making the yacht heel right over, even though everything had been housed, and topmasts struck, so as to offer as little resistance to the wind as possible. The deck was flooded with water from hail and rain, which came down in sheets. It was certainly a terrific night, and we were all most thankful that Tom had taken so much trouble to pick out the very snuggest corner in this well-sheltered harbour.

Sunday, December 13*th.*—Day broke and the sun rose on an apparently fine morning; but as the glass was again down, Tom thought we had better go and see Taormina, one of the finest ruins in Sicily. We took our lunch with us, and went by train to Giardini, along the pretty coast line close to the shore. From the station a good carriage road leads to the town of Taormina and the ruins of the ancient Greek and Roman amphitheatres above. Evie and I drove along the carriage road, while the gentlemen took the short cut. Our road commanded exquisite views at every turn. From the village a steep walk of a few hundred yards took us to the theatre, which is certainly built in one of the most beautiful situations in the world. It is the only Greek theatre of which the *scena* still remains, as well as the seats, with all the Roman additions and alterations. The dressing-rooms and entrances for the actors may still be seen, with the water-clock by which their performances were timed, the seats of the vestal virgins, the entrances for the ladies, gentlemen, plebeians, patricians, and senators, and stalls for the sellers of playbills or refreshments. No words can describe the exquisite loveliness of the view on all sides. Fancy stepping out of your private box at a theatre on to a narrow ledge of rock at the top of a sheer precipice of 900 feet, facing the sea, and commanding most lovely views up and down the straits to the Faro on one side and to Cape Augusta on the other, while the eye ranges to Etna, and other mountains and valleys stretch away, with villages dotted about in every direction. We had a long chat with the intelligent old *custode*, who has been there thirty-eight years, and who superintended all the excavations and restorations himself. He has plans of the whole as it was under the Greeks, Romans, Saracens, and Normans, and as it is now; and

Amphitheatre, Taormina.

under his guidance it was most interesting to trace all the transitions which it has undergone. It was a glorious day in spite of the wind, and we were all very sorry to be obliged to tear ourselves away to catch the 3.30 p.m. train. Our drive down the hill to the station was very rapid, and we were back at Messina in time for six o'clock dinner.

Monday, December 14*th*.—Though the glass was low, the fair wind and the beauty of the day determined us to make another start. As soon as we got outside the harbour we gave a most tremendous roll, which was so unexpected that it sent many things adrift. We got on pretty well through the day, and by sunset found ourselves off the Lipari Islands. They are very picturesque in form, and but little known, there being, I believe, only one good harbour, that at Lipari itself. Stromboli was more than usually active, and looked really very grand. The weather was still gloomy, and continued squalls of wind and rain passed over our heads, accompanied by thunder and lightning in the distance. About 11 p.m., just as everybody except the watch had gone to bed, a most terrific squall struck us and threw us on our beam-ends, lee-rail and boats' davits being under water in an instant. Happily the boats were on board and well secured, or they would have been lost and the davits carried away, as in the case of the ill-fated 'La Plata.' Everything had been made safe on board, canvas having been lashed over all the skylights and doors; and as we were running under a three-reefed trysail on the mizen and a rag of a staysail only, the yacht was down again before the wind in a minute, and no harm done. We had several more squalls during the night, but none quite so bad as this.

Tuesday, December 15*th*.—In the morning the glass was still falling, and Tom thought it better to run for shelter to Naples, instead of trying to get on to Leghorn. After a very rough, disagreeable morning, we were off the island of Ischia about 2 p.m., and dropped anchor inside the Mole at Naples just after dark. The weather had cleared a little at sunset, and the far-famed bay looked very lovely as we came in past the islands of Ischia and Procida, the bays of

Baiæ and Posilippo, &c. We had some difficulty in getting *pratique* after sunset, but succeeded at last, and were able to send the steward ashore and get our letters and newspapers—a large and welcome bundle, filling a very big bag.

Wednesday, December 16th.—Soon after breakfast we landed and went to the Museum, to look at the beautiful bronzes and statues, which appear more lovely every time we see them. The Museum is beautifully done up and re-arranged, and when the alterations are finished it will be greatly improved. In the evening we went to the opera, and saw 'Marta' at a very pretty small theatre, well sung, and well put on the stage. The present government cannot afford to open San Carlo this year, but is doing much to improve the city. All the dirty houses between Santa Lucia and the Chiaja have been pulled down, a fine promenade has been made, and the gardens of the Villa Reale, instead of being right on the sea, have now a large esplanade and sea-wall in front. Altogether the place is much altered since we were here five years ago. The shops for antiquities, tortoiseshell, and coral, however, are just as numerous and as tempting as ever; but the price of coral has at least trebled in the same number of years, and it is difficult to get it of good colour. There are a few splendid things in the best shops, but then the prices are fabulous—five thousand francs for a single string of not very pale beads.

Thursday, December 17th.—The yacht 'Zantha' arrived from Nice during the night, and just as we had done breakfast the 'Ione' came racing in under close-reefed canvas. We called alongside on our way ashore, and heard a very bad account of the weather outside. They had experienced strong north-westerly gales all the way, so it was lucky we had come in here. We landed and drove up to San Martino, situated on the top of the hill overlooking Naples, and close to the castle of St. Elmo. It was formerly one of the richest Carthusian convents; now all its revenues are confiscated for the good of the Crown. Most of the monks are dispersed, a few of the oldest being allowed to drag on a miserable existence with the munificent allowance of a franc a day from the government, which they supplement as best they can by begging. The wood carving in the church is very beautiful, principally the work of the monks themselves. The sacristy was full of curious relics. The view from the windows of the galleries over Naples and its lovely bay and environs was very fine, and the drive down was delightful.

It rained so heavily in the afternoon that we could only wander about among the shops. In the evening we went to see 'La Fille de Madame Angot' at a small theatre. Tom treated half the crew and half the servants last night, and the other half to-night. They made quite a sensation each night, so many sailors trooping in one after another. It was still very stormy when we returned on board, though the rain had ceased.

Friday, December 18th.—We landed directly after breakfast, and went straight to the museum, to look at some beautiful pictures which are still left there; but a good many of our old favourites, like the statues, have been removed to other towns. After looking at the pictures, we went to see all the rooms, which are newly arranged, and full of the most interesting objects recently discovered at Pompeii. Whether it is that they understand the art of excavating better now, and that the things are consequently in a more perfect condition, I do not know; but I have never felt so much interest in the collection before. One sees figs, olives, plums, currants, and nuts of all kinds, blackened and dried up of course, but with the form of the oil drops still visible on some of the olives. The loaves of bread, the cheeses, and the eggs are in a perfect state of preservation. In another part are all the cooking utensils, mostly in bronze, the handle of each being a lifelike model of the fish, flesh, or fowl for cooking which it is supposed to have been used. The scales and weights, too, are made to represent the articles they were intended to weigh, such as bread, cheese, pork, goat's flesh, mutton, beef. One finds here cooking stoves, which would be not at all a bad model for an economical kitchener now; braziers, all exquisitely modelled, and a most ingenious arrangement for warming water, with a tap to draw it off, exactly like those in use at the present day. There are gridirons and frying-pans, flat irons, goffering-irons, curling-tongs, and every sort of domestic utensil, besides beautiful vases, bronzes, jewellery, cameos, and intaglios. Anyone might spend days and weeks among them, and all the time be learning the minutest details of the life lived by a people nearly two thousand years ago. One of the rooms contains over three thousand papyrus rolls, found in Herculaneum. Experts are busily engaged in unrolling and deciphering these, and the contents may perhaps throw much light on the times in which they were written.

At the hotel we saw the 'Daily News' of December 15, and the first thing that caught my eye, at the head of the shipping disasters, was the 'Total Loss of the Steamer

"Violet:" crew all saved in boats.'[1] This is the steamer in which we had taken so much interest at Constantinople. As Tom and I were watching her leave that port, I said, 'I only wish that she may go to the bottom, that all the crew may be saved, and that the wretched story-telling engineer may have an extra fright for his life.' We have not heard, and perhaps never shall hear, his special adventures, but otherwise my wish has been fulfilled to the letter. It only shows what boats can live through, for we all agreed that the 'Violet's' boats looked as unfit for an emergency as most boats on board traders do; and all feared that if anything happened to the ship, as seemed only too probable, the poor men would be sacrificed as well as the steamer. Happily, however, the result proved otherwise.

As the day had improved, we drove after lunch towards Resina. The weather was too bad for Vesuvius, and as we wished to see as much as possible of the last eruption, we drove along the bay, which might be pretty if it were

---

[1] The following is a detailed account of the wreck given by the 'Daily News':—'The steamer "Violet," of Glasgow, Edwards master, bound from Nicolaieff for Bergen, laden with rye, foundered about 30 miles south of the Lizard on Sunday morning. The crew landed at Penzance harbour yesterday afternoon in an exhausted state, having taken to the boats, and been exposed to the gale for thirty hours. The vessel had experienced strong gales since December 8, and became leaky, and the cargo shifted. They passed Wolf-Rock Lighthouse on Friday last, only making slight progress. On Saturday morning they made for the Lizard, and a steamer then passing tried to take the "Violet" in tow, but this the violence of the gale prevented. A portion of the cargo and starboard anchor and chain were thrown overboard, with the hope of saving the vessel, but the water gained, and the fires in the engine-room were put out. The crew, seeing the steamer sinking fast, abandoned her on Sunday about 10 o'clock. The "Violet" was 974 tons register, and was built at Newcastle in 1871. Her crew consisted of captain and twenty-six hands all told.' After our return home, Tom had to go to Glasgow to give evidence for the Board of Trade. There was so much doubt about the matter, and so many people were involved in it, rendering it impossible to put the blame on the right shoulders, that no legal proceedings could be taken.

not for a perfect street of dirty little houses, preventing a view of the sea, except in occasional peeps. However, the crowd was amusing. Carioles full of people going out to the country, eighteen or nineteen in one vehicle, some hanging on behind and on to the shafts ; itinerant vendors of every sort of ware ; macaroni makers and sellers ; fishermen making and mending their nets ; everybody doing or pretending to do something, for the weather was too cold for even the Neapolitan lazzaroni to indulge in their favourite occupation of doing nothing.

At the end of five miles we turned off from the main line towards the villages of Massa and Somna. Soon piles of ashes appeared upon either side, the remains of the eruption of Mount Vesuvius three years ago. After driving two or three miles further, the great stream of lava could plainly be seen running down from the crater at the summit. It must have been serious work for those engaged in taking their observations in the observatory at the Hermitage that night. Many travellers, who had gone up from curiosity, were killed, together with twelve horses, as the lava changed its course rapidly and suddenly. The whole valley still presents a most wonderful sight—bits of walls and houses cropping up here and there, all crushed and overwhelmed by the lava in its relentless course. It seemed to have turned and twisted in the most capricious manner, without any apparent reason, sparing a house in its direct course, on purpose to knock down a larger one to the right or left.

We left the carriage, and walked over the still smoking lava beds. When the outer crust was stirred, we could still burn our fingers, take casts of coins, or, if we went deep enough, find quite a little fire, hot enough to cook by. It was very curious and interesting, and we wandered about a long time. The weather had quite cleared up, and the drive back to Naples was delightful.

At the *table d'hôte* Tom, who had been on board for a short time, said that before leaving the yacht he had made all arrangements for starting in the morning, but that, as the wind was momentarily shifting round and becoming fairer, he thought it would be almost better to start at once. He therefore went on board directly after dinner to make arrangements, and we followed him at 10.30 p.m., after staying to write and post some letters. At 12.30 a.m. we started under steam, the sea being calm, with a light wind from the S.E.

Harbour at Bastia.

CHAPTER XI.

BASTIA, NICE, PARIS, AND HOME.

*The man who, with undaunted toils,
Sails unknown seas to unknown soils,
With various wonders feasts his sight.*

Saturday, December 19th.—Steaming between Ischia and the mainland all night. At 8 a.m. we were off Mount Cecillo, and ceased steaming, proceeding under sail alone, with a very strong wind from the S.W., accompanied by occasional squalls and showers. At noon we were off Port d'Ango, and continued a northerly course all day, the sea being very rough and disagreeable, and nobody venturing into the saloon. Neither was the deck as pleasant as usual; for all the boats were inboard, and everything, as far as possible, stowed away and battened down and covered with canvas.

Sunday, December 20*th*.—At 4 a.m. we were off Pianosa. There was a tremendous gale from the S.W., and though we were under the lee of Corsica we made bad weather of it, the sea being rough, the wind howling through the rigging, and the barometer falling. Tom therefore determined to run back for the harbour of Bastia, which we entered at noon. Distance from Naples, 282 miles. The entrance is extremely narrow, and, once inside, there is hardly room to turn; so we were a long time settling ourselves, or rather being settled, by various officials and their underlings, with warps, ropes, chains, anchors, kedges, and all sorts of appliances.

The sudden start from Naples had made Tom forget that all-important document, the bill of health, and it was rather to be dreaded that we might not be allowed to land, or even that we might be sent back to the port from which we came. Fortunately for us, the senior health-officer proved most kind, and gave us permission to land at once, while he telegraphed to Naples to know that all was right. After lunch we took advantage of this permission, and walked up the steep streets, or rather staircases, leading from the harbour to the best part of the town, where the streets are wide, with handsome houses. We got a carriage after some difficulty, and drove along a lovely road by the sea-shore; but the cold was so intense that we were soon glad to turn back and remain quietly by the fire till dinner-time.

The consul dined with us, and told us a good many

interesting particulars about the island and the islanders. He had been at Ajaccio for a year, and came on here in August. At Ajaccio there are a good many English and foreigners in search of health. The climate is good in winter, but somewhat feverish in summer, on account of the large lagunes, which, however, afford excellent wild-fowl shooting. In winter the living is bad, but very cheap. English servants will not stay, as a rule. The natives make bad servants, but cost little either for pay or keep. The drive from Bastia to Ajaccio, about 94 miles, across the island and over some high mountains, is very beautiful, and we had some thoughts of making the expedition, which can easily be done in a carriage in two days. But on enquiry it was found that at one point the road was blocked with snow, and that we should have to walk for about four hours, and be transferred to another carriage on the other side of the mountains; so the idea has been given up. There is a great deal of pleasant society here and at Ajaccio. The law courts are held at Bastia, and a good many judges and officials of one kind and another residing there are employed under a *sous-préfet*. The inns are very small, as well as bad and dirty, and the cooking is atrocious.

It blew a perfect hurricane at night, and thundered, lightened, snowed, rained, hailed, and sleeted. In the morning the ice was half an inch thick in many places on the deck where the water had accumulated.

Monday, December 21*st.*—An intensely cold morning. The hills were all covered with snow, quite low down, close to the town, and all the people were in a state of astonishment, as many of them had never seen snow so near before. A servant, who came from Ajaccio, where the climate is much milder than it is here, could not make it out at all, especially when she got some snow in her hand and it all disappeared between her fingers. The consul had kindly arranged a great *chasse* for the gentlemen to-day, but unfortunately the weather rendered it impossible. It was, to compare it with our own climate, a bitter April day— hot sun, with a wind so strong that one could hardly stand against it, and constant thick snow showers. Yesterday, at a *chasse* on a lake of an estate not far from here, the sportsmen killed over one thousand head of wild fowl, including coots, moorhens, wild ducks of every kind, snipes, woodcocks, partridges.

In the afternoon it cleared up a little, and we went round the town with the consul, and made a few purchases of myrtle sticks, pipes beautifully carved from the heath roots,[1] which grow here to an enormous size, and stiletti. The making or selling of these poignards is specially prohibited, on account of the use which the inhabitants are inclined to make of them; and thus there was considerable delay before we could get any. The *vendetta* is still in its full force. There are few families which have not a feud existing, and all are ready with a dagger. Only this morning some men in a ship next to us were teasing a boy of ten or twelve, when he drew his stiletto and sprang at them, but fortunately was stopped in time by the gendarmes.

We started between the showers to drive to a grotto about six miles off, the gentlemen walking. The road was well macadamised, and ran along the sea-shore at the foot of the mountains. On a fine day it must be lovely, but to-

---

[1] These are what are called in England briar-root pipes, a corruption of the French *bruyère*, heath.

day there was no good opportunity for seeing its beauties. After driving a few miles we reached the grotto in the midst of a terrific storm of thunder, lightning, hail, and snow. The grotto, though small, is very pretty, and is beautifully kept and lighted. The stalactites are very fine and well preserved. As it was a steep climb up a very wet path, the water pouring down the steps in torrents, Muñie and I stayed in the carriage while the others went to look at it. The semi-tropical vegetation looked very much the worse for this most unusual weather. Aloes and prickly pears have a miserable effect in the snow, and the handfuls of maidenhair which we gathered must have felt very uncomfortable, coated and stiff with coagulated hail and snow.

We got on board the yacht just about dark, and were all glad to gather round the fires. I must mention that our open grates are a perfect success. They draw capitally, and we have had just as good fires as on shore, instead of the miserable little stoves so often seen on yachts.

Tuesday, December 22nd.—There was a slight improvement in the weather, so Tom thought it better to make a start. This was a great disappointment to our newly made kind friends, who had arranged an expedition for us. But we were pressed for time, and after a pleasant farewell luncheon the operations of pulling, hauling, and warping were repeated, and we emerged from the mouth of the very narrow harbour on to the still much-agitated ocean. We all very shortly disappeared into our berths, for it was bitterly cold and wet, and the short winter's day was soon over.

Wednesday, December 23rd.—Tom called me at daybreak of the most beautiful morning it is possible to imagine.

Sky and sea were alike of the loveliest blue, and the moon still rode high in the heavens, while Corsica and the Italian coast in the distance, and the nearer range of snowy mountains along the coast of the Riviera, were tinged with the light of the rising sun, as were also the sails of the numerous vessels gliding about in different directions. We were just off Bordighera, and as we steamed along close to the coast, each point we passed opened out a new scene of beauty.

It was quite difficult to tear oneself away from the deck and go below. There was an idea of going into the splendid harbour of Villa Franca, but Tom thought it would be better, in spite of its many inconveniences, to go into that of Nice for the sake of being close to the railway station on the main line. We arrived soon after 9 a.m., but it was nearly 11 a.m. before we were safely moored alongside two other yachts. Soon afterwards we landed, and made the best of our way to the consul's, and to the post-office for our ever welcome bundle of letters. We strolled along the Promenade des Anglais and looked into the shops, filled seemingly with the very same articles to be found in the various countries we had recently visited. There were Moorish shops, full of Moorish rugs, brass-work, arms, harness, and curiosities; shops for Spanish mantas, lace, and figures; shops for Sicilian lace and models; shops for bronzes and Grecian antiquities; shops full of amber, embroideries, lamps, carpets, rugs from Constantinople, Smyrna, and the Eastern Archipelago; shops full of coral from Naples; and, lastly, the most lovely flower-shops, full of violets, roses, orange-blossoms, heliotropes, carnations, mignonette, and every variety of summer blossom.

The sun was intensely hot, though the wind was cold, and white umbrellas were the order of the day. After another stroll we went to Monaco. Getting out of the train at Monaco station by mistake, we had a long walk through the pretty little town as far as Monte Carlo, where the hotel and casino are situated. It was a splendid clear night. The wind had gone down, and the moon was at its full, so that the gardens, full of palms and aloes and semitropical vegetation, quite transported one back to the East. After dining we went to the gambling-rooms, made a small, very small, venture, and lost, amusing ourselves afterwards by watching the other people gambling. It was delicious walking in the garden, which has seats in every pleasant nook, with lovely glimpses over the moonlit sea. We left by the 10.30 p.m. train, starting from the right station this time, and reached the yacht soon after midnight.

Thursday, December 24th.—We were called before daybreak, our luggage was on shore by 7 a.m., and we followed soon afterwards to see it through the custom house. It was a hard frost, yet the sun was hot enough to burn even at that early hour. At 9 a.m. we started by the train, which kept close to the sea-shore for some distance. The little pools seemed frozen hard, though the south side of the carriage was quite hot. The through carriages are most comfortable, and by taking a *coupé-fauteuil*, not a *coupé-lit*, you can enjoy the luxury of arm-chairs by day and beds by night.

Friday, December 25th.—When we arrived at Paris, the day was cold and snowy; but though the frost was the hardest that had been known for years, the rooms in Meurice's Hotel were as warm and comfortable-looking as usual, and there was not much temptation to stir out of them, especially as both Evie and I had very bad colds.

Saturday, December 26th.—The children arrived in the evening from Hastings in great spirits, and the next few days were devoted to showing them all the sights, indoors and out, breakfasting and dining at several of the *cafés*, going to see some of the best pieces at the theatres, and trying to see the new opera-house, about which everybody was quite mad just then. It is certainly very handsome, and for the opening night there is not a ticket to be had.

On the evening of *January 1st*, 1875, we left Paris for Calais. The cold was still intense; a nasty sleet was falling at Calais; and the ground was covered with a singular coating of *verglas*, which made it almost impossible to stand. Everything seemed turned to ice. All the porters had on list slippers, and it was only with their aid that we managed to embark safely, though it was nervous work going down the glassy wooden steps with the children. After a disagreeable crossing we reached Dover about 4.30 a.m., and later on in the day, January 2nd, we arrived at our house in St. Leonards all safe and well, after a voyage of 13,000 miles, north and south, occupying a period of exactly six months. The time has been full of pleasure and, I hope, profit to us all; but still it is delightful to be at home once more for a few months, before the wish to go further afloat and to see new countries comes on us again, doubtless as strong as ever.

PART II.

CYPRUS. CONSTANTINOPLE.
1878.

*Wherein of antres vast, and deserts idle,
Rough quarries, rocks and hills whose heads touch heaven,
It was my hint to speak.*

SHAKESPEARE, *Othello.*

VIGO BAY

Last of the 'Eurydice.'

CHAPTER I.

PORTSMOUTH, BREST, AND VIGO.

*Like ships that sailed for sunny isles,
But never came to shore.*

IN the summer of 1878 I was very ill, and we lay for many weeks in and about the Solent, unable to leave the vicinity of the shore and the doctor. There is good in everything, if one will only look for it, and during that weary time I learned to see how much of beauty there is in the well-known harbour of Portsmouth, and how much food, not so much for the imagination as for the memory, the mere sight of the ships bearing names so well known and celebrated in history and in the wars of old may afford. There they are, laid up in ordinary, ready to be fitted out when required, or to be used as hulks, or even doomed to be broken up. Many a pleasant little sail and row we had among them when I was well enough to make a move. It was just at the time when the disaster to the ill-fated 'Eurydice' was still fresh in all minds, and day after day the steam-launch passed us, towing the covered barge with its melancholy freight of bodies recovered from the wreck. A terrible task it must have been to make the sea give up her dead after so long an interval. At last one day the 'Eurydice' herself was towed past us, and a few days afterwards we went to see her being broken up. The decision that no attempt should be made to restore her was surely wise, for no sailor could ever have set foot in her again without a feeling of horror. It was sunset when we beheld the sad spectacle. Men were using crowbars, hatchets, pickaxes, and instruments of every sort, to pull to pieces those unfortunate but still strong and sound timbers. It was not a scene to linger over, nor was it altogether a cheering one to those about to face the perils of the sea.

One morning, about 8.30, while lying moored to a Government buoy, kindly lent us by the Dockyard Admiral in Portsmouth harbour, we had a very narrow escape of going to the bottom. I was lying helpless in my bed, where I had been for three weeks, and seemed likely to remain another three weeks, with the exception of being carried up on deck for a few hours daily. Some of the party were in bed, others preparing for Goodwood, the servants engaged at their usual avocations, the children at breakfast in the fore-saloon, when I heard some of the men shout, or rather scream: 'She is into us!' 'We shall be sunk!' 'Fetch the children!' 'Lower the boats!' 'Get the missus on deck!' Then I heard the rattle of the falls through the davits, and the splash of the boats in the water. Then two stewards rushed through the engine-room passage, each carrying a child, and followed by the affrighted maids, all saying: 'She will cut us through by the fore-companion.' Then two men came flying down to carry me up, and the nurse appeared with a quilt to wrap me in. There was a scare, a scurry, a terrible fright, a crash, but not so bad a one as we had anticipated, and then a cry of relief: 'She has not cut us below the water-line; we shall not sink after all.' The 'Assistance,' a troop-ship bringing soldiers from Ireland, in trying to avoid a sailing barge, had been caught by the tide and come stem on into us, but fortunately very far forward, where our over-hanging bow protected us. She had reversed her engines before she touched us; for had she not tried to alter her course and been going astern at the time she ran into us, we should have been crushed like a walnut-shell and sunk in a few seconds. It was a *mauvais quart d'heure* such as I hope never to experience again, specially when unable to move or to do anything to help myself or anybody else.

When an examination came to be made, it was found that the 'Assistance' had run into the 'Sunbeam' just forward of the foremast, carried away some of the rail and fore-rigging, and cut a gash in the bulwarks, while our white paint on her bow below her second line of portholes showed where she had struck us. You may imagine what a monster she looked towering above us. The dockyard authorities repaired our damages at their own expense ; so, beyond a most terrible fright, and the inconvenience resulting from the presence of workpeople on board for some days, there was no great harm done after all.

Nobody could have been more kind and sympathising than all the officers of the dockyard, or more annoyed and vexed than all the officers of the 'Assistance,' but it really was not their fault. She was in charge of the deputy harbour master, who was also terribly distressed about it.

The 'Assistance' running into us.

Portsmouth harbour is a difficult place to get in and out of when a strong tide is running, and it is crowded with shipping.

Towards the end of September I was pronounced to be better, and change was prescribed as the best thing for me. So on *Friday, September 20th*, we started.

Never, we thought, had the Isle of Wight looked more

lovely as we sailed past Sandown with its trim little houses, Luccombe Chine, Shanklin, and Bonchurch peeping out amid the trees, and sheltered by its tall cliffs. The weather had improved much during the last twenty-four hours, and a fair breeze gently filled our sails and wafted us quietly down the harbour, past the 'Victory,' 'Duke of Wellington,' and ' St. Vincent,' with whom we exchanged sea courtesies —past the Old Spit Buoy and Bembridge Ledge, where the poor ' Eurydice ' lay so long after she had been moved from her first sad resting-place.

After passing St. Catherine's Point the wind freshened, the sky became clouded, the rain came down, and we had rather a dirty night.

Saturday, September 21st.—To-day was fine and calm. Fires were lighted, and we steamed pleasantly along, though we had to encounter a long Atlantic roll and frequent showers. During the night the wind rose and freshened from the southward, with a nasty cross sea.

Sunday, September 22nd.—In the morning, as the wind was dead ahead, and the barometer low and falling, Tom decided to take the inside channel, between the island of Ushant and the mainland, and to go into Brest. This port has been our frequent refuge in a storm, and as such it seems ungrateful to speak ill of it ; but the town of Brest is by no means interesting, and the steps leading from the harbour to the town are very fatiguing. The only alternative to making use of them, however, is to go a long way round outside the walls. We passed through the roads, where there were several training-ships at anchor, besides ' La Gallicionère'—which we last saw at Kobe in 1877—and dropped anchor in the inner harbour at 1.45 p.m.

In the afternoon we went ashore to listen to the military band in the great avenue, from which there is a fine view of the bay and of the surrounding country. The *place* was crowded with people of all classes, dressed in their Sunday best. Muñie and Baby were quite delighted with the little French babies, which were wonderfully numerous, most of them 'voués à la Vierge,' and therefore dressed in white and blue. The afternoon was lovely. The wind had changed to N.W., and we began to regret our delayed voyage, but after dinner the sky clouded over again and the rain fell in torrents.

Dining under Difficulties.

Monday, September 23rd.—The glass was still low, but the wind fair; so, after hesitating for a few hours, we weighed anchor at 10.30 a.m., and cleared Point St. Matthieu soon after noon. Sometimes we tore along before a favouring gale, through squalls of rain so thick and black that one could scarcely see, and sometimes the wind nearly died away and even shifted to quite another quarter. The sails were perpetually up and down, and it was a trying day for both crew and passengers. Towards evening the violence of the gale increased, topmasts were housed, boats taken inboard, trysails set, and every preparation made for a dirty night. The wind blew heavily from the N.W., fortunately driving us before it in the desired direction, and the old 'Sunbeam' rode through the sea like a cork, now rising on the top of one enormous wave, then diving so deeply down into the trough beyond, that it seemed as if she would never rise again.

The two younger children, Muriel and Baby, have been ailing for some time, and are to-day pronounced by Dr. Hoffmeister to have chicken-pox. This at sea, and in the present state of the weather, causes us great anxiety, as it is impossible to give them any medicine, or to do anything but keep them warm, and try and coax them to eat something and keep it down—a very difficult matter, as they are sea-sick, which is quite unusual with them. We must look forward to getting into the nearest port, and finding a more genial climate, as quickly as possible.

Tuesday, September 24th.—By noon to-day we had the satisfaction of finding that we had run 220 miles, with scarcely any sail set. During the afternoon the weather moderated, but no observation could be taken. In the evening the lights at the entrance to the harbour of Coruña were seen. We had been driven further to the eastward than we expected, owing to our having had to put the yacht off her course, in order to run before the numerous violent squalls. We were still knocking about a good deal, and lay over to the wind so much that the balancing powers of the cabin tables were for the first time tested to the utmost, while the stewards in attendance had to sit or kneel, as best they could, much to the amusement of those who were well enough to appreciate the absurdity of this domestic yachting scene, without being worried by its discomfort. Steam was ordered, the course changed, and in a few hours we were steaming along the north coast of Spain, partly under shelter of the land.

Wednesday, September 25th.—A lovely morning, almost calm, a heavy roll being the only trace left of the recent gale. The children were very unwell. Poor little Muriel was quite exhausted, unable to take any nourishment whatever, or even to speak or move, and looking so white and miserable that it made one's heart ache to look at her.

About 10 a.m. we made the lighthouse on Cape Finisterre, and by noon we were abreast of it. To recruit the strength of the invalids and to give some rest to Tom, who has had hard work the last few days, we talked of going into Corcubion—the spot where the one boat containing the survivors of the ill-fated 'Captain' landed in 1870—but we finally decided to press on to Vigo, 60 miles further down the coast, a far better harbour, and a more likely place for fresh supplies. About 4 p.m., accordingly, we saw the Bayona Islands in the distance, 25 miles off, at the entrance to the magnificent bay of Vigo, and two hours later we were steaming between them and the mainland. The Bayona Islands are rocky and peaked, a lighthouse standing on the highest point of one of them. In size and form they reminded us all of Eimeo, one of the lovely islands of the South Pacific. The air was rather thick and misty, and after the sun had set it was with difficulty, and only very slowly, that we crept some ten miles up the bay to the town of Vigo itself. Great caution was necessary in order to avoid the hundreds of fishing-boats, which, with their nets, nearly covered the entire surface of the bay. The whole place seemed alive with them, and millions of silvery sardines and pilchards must have been hauled into the boats, even while we were passing through the busy little fleet. The fishermen burned great flaring torches in the prows of their boats, both to attract the fish and to indicate their whereabouts to their companions. It was a most picturesque scene, reminding us, in the dim uncertain light, of the graceful dusky fishermen on the coral reefs of the South Sea Islands. The smell of the land was almost as fragrant as the spicy isles of the far south. The miseries and discomforts of a two or three days' hard gale at sea are well recompensed by the intense pleasure of gliding quietly into a landlocked harbour like this, and hearing once more the sounds and smelling the odours of the land.

The cathedral clock chimed eight just as we dropped anchor, and throughout the night the old Spanish watchmen went their half-hourly rounds, proclaiming the time and the state of the weather, and doubtless giving good warning of their approach to ill-disposed persons and affording them ample time to escape.

Thursday, September 26th.—I was roused by the sun shining brightly into the cabin, and became conscious of a delightful feeling of rest and stillness, in strong contrast to the gloomy weather and rough knocking about that we had lately experienced. The views on every side as I looked out were lovely; and a large fleet might be anchored here in a spot as tranquil and as beautiful as any of the Italian lakes. The surrounding hills are all cultivated to the water's edge with vines and Indian corn. Not for a single day in the year is it impossible to go out sailing here, so sheltered is it by surrounding mountains, and every little bay and creek has a fresh beauty of its own. On seven of the most conspicuous mountains are little white chapels, said to have been built by seven sisters, in order that they might lead a holy life and yet occasionally gaze upon one another, though from a respectful distance. Each chapel is now occupied by a sainted hermit, whom crowds of pilgrims come to visit from all parts of Spain.

About noon we went ashore, paying a visit to the picturesque but odorous fish-market on our way. The boats are all drawn up on the sand in front of a row of low arcades, the intermediate space being filled by an ever-changing chattering crowd, dressed in the brightest colours, while nearer the shore a few graceful, barelegged, but brilliantly petticoated girls are raking in the floating sea-wrack, or leaning on their implements, gazing at the novel spectacle of our boat and flag. We proceeded to the modern part of the town, and landed on a fine new quay, close to the Hôtel de l'Europe, kept by an English-speaking Swede and his French-speaking wife.

Vigo is built on a steep hill, crowned by a fort, and has quite an imposing appearance from the water. The streets are generally narrow and dirty, but one street has fairly good shops.

After lunch we took a drive round the bay, and then up to the fort. The view from the spot where we stood was very fine, extending over the town and the bay, the latter of which, divided into two arms, stretches some eight or ten miles further up into the country, its shores being indented with numerous smaller bays and inlets. At its mouth the

Bayona Islands, purple in the afternoon light, stood out, sharp and beautiful, against a golden sunset sky, while the surface of the water, shining like molten gold, was dotted with hundreds of black fishing-boats.

A short drive brought us again to the town, where we found all the population enjoying the cool evening breezes on the pretty Alameda. Tom paid a visit to the English vice-consul, while we went to look at the cathedral—a fine building, the interior of which was seen to especial advantage in the dim religious glow of the early autumn twilight, the effect being heightened by the little lamps, shining like glowworms among the columns, and faintly showing the dark figures of the worshippers.

By the time we got on board again it was almost dark.

Friday, September 27th.—It was like looking at a panorama to watch the market boats this morning as they sailed past us, crowded with peasants from the different little villages around, and their great awkward-looking sails scarcely filled by the light air. The rig of the boats here is most peculiar. The one mast slants right back, and has a sort of square-sail with flaps attached to it, which appears to combine the powers of holding the smallest quantity of wind and giving the greatest amount of trouble. The arrangement, clumsy as it is, must possess some sort of advantage, which we cannot perceive, or surely it would not have been so universally adopted by the natives.

The children went ashore for a little while this morning, and certainly felt all the better for the change, though they were very tired afterwards. The doctor stayed on board to look after them and one of the men who is ill, while the rest of us started at noon in the cutter for

Redondela, a town picturesquely situated on a little river of the same name that runs into one of the many heads of the bay. The weather was hot but pleasant, with enough air sometimes to fill our sails. Each point that we passed revealed a fresh view. The quarantine island and lazaretto we saw only in the distance. They are most beautifully situated, up the other arm of the bay, close to the mouth of the river Paya. In all the streams hereabouts there is good trout-fishing. Having found a charming spot under the cool shade of some overhanging trees, we lunched in the boat, whilst the peasant girls, with their dark eyes and gay-coloured handkerchiefs, came to peep shyly at us during our meal. Lunch and cigarettes over, we gathered ferns and strolled about for a time before proceeding on our voyage.

At Redondela the railway crosses the valley on an enormous single-rail viaduct, a stupendous example of engineering skill. Close by is the station; and here an open carriage, drawn by a pair of dear little cream-coloured ponies, was waiting to take us back to Vigo, and so enable us to see the bay and the surrounding country from the heights above. It was certainly an expedition which we did not regret making. The pretty little town of Redondela, with its picturesquely dressed inhabitants, is always worth a day's journey to see, and the whole of the road thence to Vigo is beautiful, especially as we saw it, in the afternoon light, the long purple shadows of trees and hills varying the brilliancy of the landscape. The way itself was gay with groups of brightly clad peasants returning from market with their purchases, all looking cheerful and animated, and some of them dancing and singing to the music of a tambourine played by one of the party. The banks and cuttings through the rocks were covered with many varieties of ferns, amongst others the *Osmunda regalis*; and we gathered splendid fronds and roots of the haresfoot fern (*Davallia canariensis*).

As we were sailing along, one of our men noticed a small object floating on the water, which puzzled us all as to what it could possibly be. We steered down on it, and found a child's toy boat, evidently home-made. It was very carefully constructed of cork bark, rigged like boats of the country, and carried a blue sail and tiny red flag. There was no one anywhere near to claim it, and it was very evident that the constructor and owner would be most unlikely ever to find it again. So we laid hands on the small derelict, and took it back, to the great delight of the little ones on board.

A small Derelict.

The Vigo railway station is just at the entrance of the town, and though it has been built for more than two years, it is evidently still a source of great amusement and amazement to the inhabitants, whose favourite afternoon walk is under a fine avenue of trees, running parallel with the railway, whence they can see the train and the *machine*.

It was nearly dark by the time we got on board, and the

fishermen's lights were shining all over and around the bay.

Saturday, September 28*th.*—The children and I landed at 10.30 a.m., and, provided with the all-important permission of the governor, drove up the hill towards the fort. All the way, as we climbed up, we met men, women, and children, either leading or carrying a pig, sheep, lamb, chicken, duck, goose, or goat, from the fair, which was being held on a piece of flat ground near the top of the hill. Many were the amusing scenes we witnessed. Refractory pigs made frequent and frantic efforts to commit suicide beneath the wheels of our carriage, or a sheep or a goat would effect his escape, butting at anybody and everybody, and knocking down many whom he met. Fowls of all kinds cackled and quacked; while little wee pigs, carefully and fondly carried by their chattering owners, added to the noise and hubbub of the motley crowd.

I sat under the shade of the trees, while the children and servants visited the fort, and admired the lovely view of the Sierra on the opposite side, after which we drove rapidly down, and then proceeded through narrow and very dirty streets to the fish-market. Mabelle and Mr. Bingham had been spending the morning sketching from a boat close by; for though the feast of colour in the market itself may delight the eye, the disagreeable smell is hardly to be borne.

Our intention had been to make a start at midday, and all the sails were set in readiness, but not a breath of air disturbed the mirror-like surface of the bay. There were a few final settlements to be made, which turned out to be rather unsatisfactory, the one idea of everybody being to estimate the value of every article supplied and every service rendered, of however trifling a character, at one pound sterling—no doubt a highly convenient arrangement for the mere calculation of accounts. Thus a carriage for four hours, a carriage for one, a boat for a day, a dinner which we had not ordered, and the services of a guide whom we had found useless, were all charged for at the one fixed rate, the final result being that the bumboat man left us in an extremely discontented frame of mind.

A light contrary breeze sprang up about 4 p.m., and enabled us to make our way slowly down the bay among our old friends the fishermen. Gorgeous sunset tints succeeded the bright sunlight, and the purple shadows gradually deepened on the mountains and on the Bayona Islands, until the new moon rose, and the fishermen's torches once more shone brightly in the semi-darkness of the early autumn evening. At 10 p.m. we were obliged to get up steam in order to pass through the narrows. At midnight a thick fog came on, and the steam whistle and fog horns were going the whole night. A fog, with its inevitable risk of collision and disaster, is the one thing that makes me feel really nervous at sea. We have had one or two very narrow escapes in the course of our yachting experience, specially on the night when the 'Vanguard' was run down by the 'Iron Duke.' I always fear a real catastrophe.

Sunday, September 29th.—This was a grey morning, turning into a fine hot day as the sun rose. The breeze was fair, and it was quite perfect sailing.

Muriel is much better for her stay at Vigo, and

plays about merrily on deck, but Baby has a nasty sore throat and cough, and is again confined to her cabin, a mode of treatment of which she does not at all approve.

We had the litany and hymns at 11 a.m., evening service at 4 p.m., with a short sermon, translated from the French, by Tom. Mabelle presided at the piano, and, though she is rather nervous as yet, she is careful and painstaking, and will no doubt gain both skill and courage

Off the Bayona Islands.

as time goes on. There were some good voices among the crew, but there has not yet been time to train or organise them.

We saw some large grampuses and several shoals of porpoises in the course of the day, and in the afternoon passed quite a line of fishermen's buoys. These were saplings stuck into large blocks of cork, which seemed intended to mark some fishing-ground on a bank. This was at a distance of thirty miles from the shore, a long way for them to come, particularly as the marks must be difficult to find in thick weather.

Monday, September 30th.—The wind freshened, and we rolled about more than was pleasant, especially in the afternoon. The breeze kept fair, however, and by noon we had made 162 knots. It is very cold, and we are all glad to resume once more the English wraps so recently discarded.

Tuesday, October 1st.—It proved a flat calm early this morning, and fires were ordered to be lighted; but no sooner was steam up than, as usual, a fair breeze began to blow, enabling us to sail all day in weather which made mere existence a pleasure. At 11.30 a.m. we found ourselves off Cape Sagres, near Cape St. Vincent, where our return voyage from round the world was so nearly brought to an abrupt conclusion last year. The light-house keeper seemed to be asleep to-day, for he would not make the smallest response to our signals; unlike the man at Cape Peniche yesterday, who was quite frantic and peremptory in his repeated request by signal that we should spell our name out as well as make our number.

Baby is a little, and Muriel much, better to-day. Tom and Mabelle are in the best of health and spirits. I am gradually picking up in the sunshine, and the remainder of the party are very well. There are a few invalids among the crew, but that is almost always the case with vessels going suddenly into a warm climate.

Wednesday, October 2nd.—A fine morning, with a contrary wind; then a calm; steam up, and then a fair wind; much to Tom's annoyance, as he would have liked to make the whole voyage under sail. We were becalmed in the midst of a crowd of vessels, on board of which some surprise, and perhaps annoyance, must have been felt at seeing us, doubtless imagined to be companions in distress, raise our funnel and steam away, an operation which did not occupy much more than a quarter of an hour, as our fires had been banked since the day before.

In the afternoon, after another spell of calm, the wind freshened, and at 4 p.m. the tall lighthouse at the entrance to the Guadalquivir came in sight. There had been an idea of going up this river to Seville, but upon enquiry we found it would be better to go on to Cadiz and to make the journey thence by rail. It became dark when we were fully six miles from the port, and as there are no leading lights by which a vessel can be guided into the harbour at night, blue-lights had to be burned for a pilot, who came after some delay, and anchored us safely inside the harbour, though a long way from the landing-place. A smart breeze was blowing, but it was quite hot near the land, and we missed the freshness of the open sea at once.

CHAPTER II.

CADIZ, SEVILLE, AND GIBRALTAR.

*Who builds a church to God, and not to fame
Will never mark the marble with his name.*

Thursday, October 3rd.—At 6 a.m. the view of the snowy-white Moorish-looking town was very lovely; later on, as the sun rose and became hotter and brighter, it was almost too glaring and dazzling. The fishermen were at first trolling up and down the harbour, in small boats, with long bamboo rods; but as the breeze increased to a gale they were all driven to seek shelter on shore.

We had not brought a bill of health from Vigo, Tom, the doctor, and the mate each thinking one of the others had it. Some of the party, therefore, went towards the shore in a boat to try and see the chief health officer, but were met half-way by the quarantine boat. The officials made a great fuss about quarantine. First they said we could not land at all; then they offered to allow us to do so if we would state that we had come to Cadiz not for pleasure, but simply because we were wind-bound; and finally they promised to go and consult the governor and chief doctor, and to obtain permission for us to land in about an hour. Meanwhile we managed to persuade them to send us off some fresh provisions, as we were beginning to run short, having left Vigo on Saturday provisioned for two days only.

We find it a great saving, both of trouble to ourselves and of grumbling from everybody on board, to leave the men to provide their own food. They do not live nearly so well as when they were dependent upon us. Still, as they have chosen their own caterer, and buy their own things, they cannot now very well complain.

At about 10.30 a.m. we landed in the big cutter, with two reefs in the mainsail, men in oilskins, ourselves in mackintoshes, reaching the shore just by the old water-gate, near the fish-market. Here we found a carriage waiting for us, and also a guide.

The heat on shore was intense, very different from Vigo. We went first to see the fine modern cathedral, to which Queen Isabella has lately presented a splendid baldacchino of Carrara marble, with a centre altar of metal gilt. We next attempted to drive round the town, but the wind, heat, and dust were so great that we went instead to the Fonda de Paris, to see some English papers and hear the news. The place is not a bit changed from what it was years ago, and there even seemed to be exactly the same little yellow water-wagtails and fly-catchers darting about the floors, and catching the innumerable flies.

We returned to the yacht, and then took a fresh departure by the 3.45 p.m. train for Seville. The gale was blowing harder than ever, and the few trees bent before its fury. On the isthmus which connects Cadiz with the mainland nothing could be seen except a few muleteers hurrying home from market, struggling against the violence of the wind, with hats tied on and heads bent down. Later on we came to the Salinas, or salt-pans, where the water is allowed to evaporate and the salt is piled up in large pyramids, which in the moonlight looked like vast tombs scattered all over the country. Even at this hour a glance from the window was enough to show that we were in Spain, from the dry, thirsty, burnt-up appearance of the land. This year the evidence of drought is especially remarkable, as no rain has fallen for months.

In the salt marshes a peculiar kind of crab abounds, of which the hind claws are considered a great delicacy. These claws are pulled off while the poor creature is alive, and he is set free to develope another pair, thus economising the supply. At the stations these crab-claws are offered for sale in large quantities.

After Puerto Santa Maria, we passed through a vine-growing district, where the grapes are cultivated from which sherry is produced. The vines are small and stunted, but cover the hillsides for miles, each vineyard having its watch-house set in the midst. At Xeres the train stopped some time, and most of the passengers descended and drank sherry from the cask. We tried it, and found it very good, without any spirit in it.

After a journey of 90 miles, accomplished in five hours and a half, we reached Seville about 9 p.m., and drove to the Hôtel de Paris.

Friday, October 4th.—Tom and Mabelle started early to have a peep at the cathedral, and ascended the Giralda tower. Later, we all went together, and spent much time in this matchless building, first in wandering about and enjoying a leisurely look at its splendid design and proportions, and afterwards in going round in due form with the *custode* to see all the chapels and pictures, which are not very numerous or important. It is the grand whole which is so magnificent, so soul-satisfying. The painted Gothic arches, of stupendous height, and the exquisite combinations of form and grandeur, seen by the light from the coloured glass windows only,[1] compose a spectacle which is unequalled by anything else in the world. Every time one comes back to this beautiful building, whether the interval has been long or short, it affords increased pleasure and delight. A special interest and grandeur are attached to the place, I think, from the fact that the name of the designer is entirely unknown. He worked for the love of God and of his art, not for the sake of personal fame, and the creation of his brain is now admired by thousands and thousands as each year rolls on.

The exterior is certainly a curious conglomeration of all styles and periods of architecture, some hideous, some possessing a beauty of their own in spite of their incongruity. The view from the stately Gothic interior to the Moorish courtyard, with its marble fountain, its orange-trees, and its horseshoe doorway in the distance, is as beautiful as it is curious; while many equally interesting but incongruous peeps may be obtained from various nooks and corners of the edifice by anyone who cares to look out for them.

From the cathedral we went to the hospital of the Caridad, to see Murillo's two celebrated pictures in the chapel attached to the building—'Moses striking the Rock,' and 'The Miracle of the Loaves and Fishes.' They certainly deserve to be classed among his finest works. They were

---

[1] There is not a single plain glass window in the cathedral.

shown to us by a very pretty little nun, who, having drawn back the curtains and placed chairs for us, retired to the high altar, where she knelt undisturbed at her devotions until we had finished looking at the pictures. From the Caridad we went to the Museo, where there are twenty-four of Murillo's pictures. They are wonderfully beautiful; but somehow, hung as they are in a row, on a vast high white-washed wall, and placed in a bad light, they seem lost.

The Alcazar was the next place we visited. It has been splendidly restored in the old Moorish style, and though the colouring of the plaster is rather coarse, the delicate tracery, the marble columns, the flat carved wooden roofs, the brilliant *azulejos*, and the beautiful *patios*, with their central fountains and gardens, bear ample testimony to the original magnificence of the design. Some of the rooms have been partially furnished and used during the last two years by Queen Isabella; but the satin-covered chairs with gilt legs and marqueterie ornaments looked very much out of place on the red tile floors and against the tiled walls. Those that were covered with Turkish stuffs, or with coarse braided brown holland, looked far better. The bath of Maria de Padella, and the fountain of Pedro II., were alike dry and empty; and the quaintly cut figures of the time of Charles V., in box and myrtle, appeared also to have suffered considerably from the long drought.

We returned to the hotel fairly tired of sight-seeing, and exhausted by the heat. In the evening we went for a lovely drive in Las Delicias, by the old Torre d'Oro (where the gold from America used to be landed in the olden time), to the Triana suburb, or gipsy quarter, where all the inhabitants were enjoying the evening air, sitting on their doorsteps, chattering, singing, and laughing, their hair always elaborately dressed with flowers, however squalid their attire might be.

Saturday, October 5th.—In order to see something before the heat of the day began, we made an early start, and went first to the Casa de Pilato, so called from its being supposed to have been built exactly after the model of Pontius Pilate's house in Jerusalem, by one of the dukes of Medina Cœli, after his return from the crusades, in the thirteenth century. They point out to you the place whence the cock crew, and the balcony from which Pilate showed Jesus to the assembled multitude, or rather the facsimiles of those spots. Be this as it may, it is certainly a perfect specimen of a Moorish house, and, after the cathedral, quite the thing best worth seeing in Seville. The views into the gardens, through the arched Moorish windows, from the cool tile-covered seats in the recesses of the dark airy staircase, are most charming. The work has never been defaced or restored, and the gardens and *patios* are better arranged, and the *azulejos* far finer, than at the Alcazar. The tiles are wonderful—such depth of colour, such brilliancy, such transparency, I never saw before. One seemed to be able to look into their depths, as if they were mother-of-pearl. In the centre of the garden stood a shady ivy-covered arbour, beneath which a marble fountain was playing, full of lilies, amongst whose broad shining leaves the gold fish glided. Here you might sit at any hour of the day, and listen to the cool splashing of the water, without fear of a single ray of sunshine. At night, charming as it might be in some respects, you would inevitably be driven away by the mosquitoes, which swarm in this city. In spite of curtains and all sorts of precautions, I could hardly open my eyes this morning, and my fingers were quite stiff and swollen from the bites of these horrible insects.

From Pilate's house we paid another visit to the cathedral before returning to the hotel. Later on we went to see the tobacco manufactory, where some five thousand women and girls are employed. It is curious to see them all busily engaged in rolling cigars, at hundreds of little tables, each

Tobacco Manufactory, Seville.

occupied by five or six women, in a lofty spacious room, more than a quarter of a mile long, and supported by numerous arches. A merry light-hearted lot they seem, kept in order by a certain number of matrons or overseers, who patrol between the tables, and see that they do not make too much noise or get into mischief. The women take off their dresses as they enter the workshop, to save them from being spoilt by tobacco juice, and perform their task in a very light airy costume. Many bring their babies, and though the tiny occupants of the cradles and chairs were pretty numerous, I did not hear a single cry. Others bring cats and dogs, who curl themselves up in the tobacco baskets, and wait patiently for the departure of their mistresses. The work is all paid by the piece, not by the hour; and the earnings vary, according to the skill of the worker, from sixpence to six shillings a day. After being rolled, the cigars are dried on open frames in long rooms above and below where the women work.

Both here and at many other places we saw red-legged partridges shut up in small cages, hardly big enough for them to turn round in. Upon enquiry, we found that they had been caught in traps, and were now being trained for call-birds to decoy others. When perfect they fetch from ten to twenty pounds each, and, if extra good, even as much as thirty pounds.

From the tobacco manufactory we went to see the Duke of Montpensier's palace, to which, however, we could not gain admittance, as it was in all the bustle of preparation for the expected arrival of the Duke. The *custode* committed us to the charge of a small boy, who showed us all over the extensive gardens. They are laid out rather in the English fashion, with the addition of tropical plants and trees, and the general effect is good; but grass will not grow here, and they have had to resort to all sorts of expedients and experiments to find a substitute. There are pets of all kinds in every corner—peacocks, pigeons, poultry of various sorts, macaws, parrots, deer, Alderney cows, &c.

Everybody here seems to expect another revolution

shortly, and to think that either Don Carlos or the Duke of Montpensier would stand a good chance of success in any attempt to gain the throne.

Leaving Seville by the 6.30 p.m. train for Cadiz, we reached the yacht about 11 p.m. The wind had at last gone down, but we found that it had been blowing a gale from the east all the while we were away.

Sunday, October 6th.—The feast of San Rosalio, and a great holiday. Tom and the children went to early mass at the cathedral, which was crowded with worshippers, some of whom scandalised the younger children considerably by walking about and talking between their devotions at the various chapels, an experience quite new to their English ideas. There was no singing, but the organs were very fine. We had morning service on board at 11.30 a.m.

In the afternoon we drove across the Salinas to San Fernando, a large old-fashioned Spanish town, where many of the inhabitants were promenading the streets and the Alameda, dressed in their Sunday best, and chattering volubly, while their less energetic neighbours gazed upon them between the grated bars of their prisonlike windows.

After dinner at the Fonda de Paris, Cadiz, we strolled to the Plaza de Minas, to listen to the band. The garden is really beautiful, full of fragrant and gaily-flowered shrubs and plants. All Cadiz seemed to be there; pretty Spanish girls with mantillas and fans were numerous, as also were ugly Spanish dandies, with large cigars and high narrow turned-up-brim hats.

Monday, October 7th.—We were off at 7 a.m., but as it was a flat calm we went ashore about 10 a.m., to visit a sailors' hospital. It is a charitable enterprise, calculated to be of immense service to sailors of all nations visiting this port, and I hope it will be liberally supported by shipowners trading this way. The state of things in the single hospital existing hitherto is really too disgusting for description; but even to this institution, such as it was, Protestants were denied admission by the Spanish authorities.

People here seem even more apprehensive of an immediate revolution than they were at Seville. A lady told me to-day that she feared they might soon see repeated the sad scenes of a few years ago, when the pretty flowery Alameda was filled with the wounded, the dying, and the dead.

By noon we had slowly drifted out of the harbour, after a very narrow escape of going on to Las Puercas (the pigs), as the dangerous rocks at the entrance are called from their fancied resemblance to pigs' backs. A fresh fair breeze sprang up, before which we were soon bowling along through Trafalgar Bay.

Shortly after 10 p.m. we were agreeably surprised by a serenade, got up by some of the servants and crew in honour of its being my birthday. They sang some songs very nicely, and finished up with congratulations for me and cheers, I think, for nearly everybody on board.

By midnight we had passed Tarifa Point, and entered the straits of Gibraltar.

Tuesday, October 8th.—At 1.30 a.m. we dropped our anchor just outside the New Mole, and went ashore. The weather, which had been very bad, having by this time begun to improve, Tom and Mabelle walked up to the signal station, whilst the rest of us went for a drive to the North Front, where the children were delighted, first with the camp, then at seeing all the hounds out at exercise, soldiers running foot-races, horses being trained for the race meeting next week, &c. I paid a visit, in the meanwhile, to the cemetery, to look for the grave of a very dear friend. It was the first time I had ever been there, and I had no idea before what a quiet secluded resting-place it is. Jews, Mohammedans, Catholics, and Protestants repose there side by side, a light iron railing forming the only separation between the graves. Once inside the gates, the trees and shrubs form a complete screen from the outer world, of which nothing is visible but the grand old rock itself, keeping watch as it were over her children sleeping at her feet, and the mountains of Spain stretching away into the far distance. Here and there one catches an occasional glimpse of the sea, and of the masts of the vessels lying at anchor in the bay or sailing away to the far east.

We have had many invalids on board lately, and have only to-day learned that the water at Vigo (where we got our last supply) is so bad—except from two sources—that an Admiralty order exists prohibiting the vessels of the Mediterranean and Channel fleets from refilling their tanks at that port. Captain Edie not long ago had seventeen men down at once with typhoid fever, on board a comparatively small ship, the sickness in that case being clearly traced to the use of the Vigo water.

Wednesday, October 9th.—The anniversary of our wedding-day, duly celebrated on the part of the crew and servants by the consumption of roast beef, plum-pudding, and port wine, and on the part of the children and maids by a picnic on shore, up by the signal station.

About 1 p.m. we all went to pay a visit to the 'Lancashire Witch,' a fine auxiliary-screw three-masted yacht, designed by Mr. St. Clare Byrne, and built on the Clyde. She is constructed very much on the lines of the 'Sunbeam,' was launched only about six weeks ago, and is now out here on a trial trip. There is a great deal to be done to her before she will be finished internally, but she is perfect in many respects, and her circular saloon is quite unique, and will be very effective if prettily decorated.

On board the yacht we happened to meet the English Vice-Consul for Siam, who showed us some beautiful specimens of Siamese gold-work, and a complete set of the old native coinage—little lumps of silver, pinched up on each side and stamped. When arranged in their proper gradation, they look just like the vertebræ of some animal. The new coinage, of which he also had some specimens, is very bright and handsome.

Thursday, October 10*th.*—Having had a good deal of trouble with our photographs, and not knowing exactly where the fault lay, we asked the General to allow the head of the photographic department here to come on board for a few hours to help us. He accordingly arrived at 7 a.m. while it was still cool and fresh, before the sun had come over the Rock, and gave us what I think will be some useful hints about the chemicals, exposure, &c.; but I much fear, from what he says, that there is something wrong with the plates themselves, in which case nothing remains but to hope that the next lot sent out from England may turn out better.

RECEPTION AT THE CONVENT.

After a visit to the 'Curlew,' a gunboat on her way back from China, we went to lunch with Lord and Lady Napier at the convent, and heard a good deal of interesting conversation about India and Afghanistan. The house has been thoroughly done up since we were here last. The old historical portraits of officers connected with the government and the various sieges of Gibraltar have been cleaned and brought up from the hall, and now form a very good and interesting collection in the dining-room, and several other improvements have been made. In the morning Lord Napier had held a levée, and in the afternoon Lady Napier had an afternoon reception. It was a pretty sight, in the semi-tropical garden, to see the people moving about, or sitting on the bright-coloured chairs and sofas under the trees, or enjoying lawn-tennis in the cool shady court. The children of the party, including our own, were entertained at the other end of the garden, where they amused themselves in their own way with Moorish swings and merry-go-rounds, toy tea-services, and all sorts of other things delightful to their juvenile hearts.

After leaving the Convent we went on board the 'Sunbeam' to receive the Governor, Lady Napier, and suite, who came to tea at 6 p.m. and paid us a long visit. They seem to be most deservedly popular here, everybody being delighted to have them back again, and wondering what they would do without them if the exigencies of war should call him away.

We had intended starting this evening, but it was late when our visitors left us, and quite calm; and so our departure was deferred until early to-morrow.

Friday, October 11*th.*—We set sail by 6 a.m., but, as

is so frequently the case when we are anxious to start, there was not a breath of wind, and we drifted about in the bay, sometimes going backwards with the tide, till nearly sunset. While thus detained we found ourselves surrounded by a shoal of porpoises, lazily disporting themselves on the surface of the water, slowly turning over or diving down. Suddenly they seemed to fall into the greatest possible state of excitement —rushing about, lashing the water with their tails, and making the most tremendous commotion. Out from the midst of them suddenly rose

A Water Party.

a shoal of bonitas, or flying-fish, three or four feet long, who, after taking leaps of four or five feet into the air, fell back into the very jaws of the porpoises. This scene lasted for some time, and was repeated in various parts of the bay, as the victims and their devourers surged backwards and forwards, while the gulls hovered and shrieked overhead, ready to swoop down and carry off any scraps that they could find. It looked as if the poor bonitas, having been driven from below by the sharks, had suddenly found themselves in the midst of other enemies, their escape from whom was prevented by the gulls hovering above, so that there was no safety for them anywhere. It is quite impossible to give any idea of the animated nature of the scene and of the noise and confusion caused by all this rapid rushing through the water.

By sunset we were only just outside Europa Point. The funnel, however, was not raised, as Tom kept hoping that a breeze from the right quarter might spring up before the morning.

Saturday, October 12*th.*—It was still almost calm early this morning, but a light easterly breeze sprang up later on and gradually freshened.

We tacked from Marbella (said to be a village of thieves) to Ceuta, the Spanish port in Morocco. The authorities at Gibraltar have just decided to enforce quarantine on all vessels arriving from this port, in consequence of the cholera now raging at Fez and in various other parts of Morocco. This may be regarded as a slight retaliation for the unnecessary restrictions now imposed at all the Spanish ports on vessels arriving from Gibraltar. Had it not been for the fear of quarantine, we should have gone to Malaga, and probably thence up to Granada, to meet some friends, and to see once more the unrivalled Alhambra. It is years since we were there, and just now its beauty would have been enhanced by the effulgence of the bright harvest moon.

At nightfall we saw the light on Cape Sacratif, near the small town of Motril. From early morning eight little pilot fish had been following, or rather leading us, swimming just in front of our bow, now fast, now slow, as the breeze freshened or died away. They would let the stem of the vessel almost touch them, and would then dart forward with great swiftness for a few feet. Sailors are very superstitious about them, and say they always come to warn a ship of danger, or to foretell the approach of sharks. Thinking that the latter idea might not be entirely groundless, we caused a very ugly-looking barbed iron hook and chain to be prepared for action; but no shark made his appearance. All day long we had been in the midst of a crowd of ships, both steamers and sailing vessels. Many of the former had passed us, and several of the latter had been left behind. At sunset we were still among quite a little fleet of barques and full-rigged ships, all of which had every stitch of canvas set; and as the sky became dark and the moon rose, their little red and green lights were to be seen on every side, shining like glowworms.

Tom and I had retired to rest, and were both fast asleep, when Mr. Bingham knocked at the door to tell us that Kindred wanted to see Tom on deck. This was by way of not alarming us, the fact being that we were in imminent risk of a collision, and that Kindred did not see his way to avoiding it. As there was no wind, I never thought of anything being amiss, and did not rouse myself, till I heard Kindred say to Tom, in an agonised voice, 'She *won't* come round, and we must be into her.' After our recent experience in Portsmouth Harbour, I lost no time in rushing up on deck, when I saw the huge black hull of a barque bearing slowly down upon us, with her red light showing, and her bowsprit pointed right amidships. As there was no breeze, we were both quite helpless, and, in spite of all we could do in the way of shifting sails, nothing seemed to succeed. Whether we tried to get ahead or astern of her, there appeared to be some force of attraction between the two ships that drove them slowly but surely towards each other, as they rose and sank on the heavy swell. After about half an hour's suspense, a breath of wind came, and we managed to draw slowly ahead, so as to allow her to pass astern of us. I

Colliding nearly.

never thought I should have been so glad to see any green light as I was to catch sight of hers. By the time midnight had arrived we were at a really safe distance, and retired to rest again.

At breakfast this morning we not unnaturally discussed the events of the night, and I asked Tom what would have happened had we really come into contact with the barque. 'Oh! we should have been bumped against, or have scrunched up and down against one another, till we went to the bottom. We should all have had to get on board of the barque, and take passage for any port to which she might be bound, and to which she would take us.' Rather a melancholy picture of all our little party, suddenly embarked on the deck of a strange and dirty vessel, to be carried we knew not whither, while our dearly beloved 'Sunbeam,' the precious floating home that has carried us so many thousand leagues in safety and comfort, lay quietly beneath the waters, on the surface of which she had thus far ridden so securely.

Sunday, October 13*th.*—At 2.30 a.m. we commenced steaming, and at 6 a.m. we were off Almeria, a large town situated in a plain of great luxuriance, on the shores of a noble bay of the same name. The big white houses with snowy fronts, facing the sea, looked quite like palaces, while the old brown Moorish castle and walls, surrounded as they are by orange groves and green foliage of all sorts, enhanced the picturesque appearance of the place.

At 8 a.m. there was a nice breeze, and at about 10 a.m. the yacht was off Cape Agate (Cape de Gat), so called from the mountain being composed almost entirely of spars and quartz, in which many amethysts are met with.

At a distance of about five miles from the cape we were hailed by a small sailing boat, manned by six men, who, to our surprise, offered us grapes, melons, pomegranates, potatoes, and all sorts of fruit and vegetables, which we were as glad to buy as they were to sell. Like the Fuegians in the Straits of Magellan, 'galleta' (biscuit) and 'tabaca' was their cry, and I believe some of our crew made far better bargains with them in exchange for those commodities than we did in exchange for coin, though of

TACKING.

the Spanish realm. I thought it was highly enterprising of them to set up this sort of village shop on the sea.

We had morning service at 11.30 a.m. and evening service at 3.30 p.m. In the afternoon the sea was quite rough, with a strong contrary wind, and at sunset we fancied we could still discern the Rock of Gibraltar. The light on Cape Falcon, on the coast of Africa, became visible later on. We tacked again towards Cartagena, and then back again, but seemed to make very little progress.

Spanish Market Boat.

Oran Harbour

CHAPTER III.

ORAN AND CAGLIARI.

*The golden lime and orange there were seen
On fragrant branches of perpetual green.*

Monday, October 14*th*.—The wind was still dead ahead, and as there seemed to be no prospect of a change we decided to alter our plans, put the ship about, and run before the breeze to the French town of Oran, in Algeria, where we had never yet been. Soon after the change was made, the wind dropped to a calm, fires were lighted, at 3.30 p.m. steam was up, two hours later the pilot came on board, and before 6 p.m. we were lying safely at anchor in the well-sheltered harbour of Oran.

The town stands prettily on a sloping hill, and the three branches of the river running through it cause the gardens and valleys to wear a most luxuriant aspect. It has been strongly fortified by Moors, by Spaniards, and by the French, two forts, built on high peaks, jealously guarding the entrance to the harbour. It fell dark soon after we arrived; but the civil *capitaine du port* made no difficulty about giving us *pratique*. He had descried the yacht from the race-course on the hills, and had hurried back on purpose to look after us. We therefore landed and found our way up a road running through gardens, where the perfume of the flowers was almost overpoweringly sweet, to the Hôtel de la Paix. Its windows look out over a sort of square with palm-trees in the centre, under which Moors, Arabs, negroes, and Zouaves were seated in the most picturesque groups. An Arab *fête* was going on, with its monotonous music, weird processions, and twirling lights, as the white-robed dancers, carrying a large circle of wood stuck with candles, slowly revolved in rhythmic measure to the sounds of dull drums and squeaky pipes, a spectacle which afforded intense delight to our children. The large coffee-room was crowded, this being the second day of the races. I am sorry we have just missed them, as I believe they were very good, the programme consisting of flat races and a few trotting matches, and finishing up with a grand Arab 'fantasia.' Arab chiefs from far and near had arrived for the occasion, mounted on their best horses, and each attended by numerous followers. After racing some of their horses against those of the French officers, they had some fun among themselves, and then gave a grand exhibition of their prowess in their native sports of firing, spearing, and manœuvring at full gallop. After dinner we sat for some time in the street, outside a *café*, observing the motley groups as they passed and re-passed, and reading the latest French newspapers, which, however, did not appear to contain the latest news.

Tuesday, October 15*th.*—At 9 a.m. we landed, started for a drive through the town and out at one of the gates to a fertile valley beyond, where every garden was ablaze with flowers and the trees were weighed down with fruit. So carefully has the system of irrigation been carried out by the Moors, that every drop of water does its appointed work, without stint and without waste, producing a thick mass of purple ipomœas, scarlet pomegranates, cytisus, passion-flowers, jasmine, hibiscus, &c., and bearing fruit in golden oranges, pomegranates, figs, pears, prickly pears, and melons. The view over the country from the hills behind the town, towards the Atlas mountains, is flat, dry, and burnt up.

Oran itself is a fine French town of 40,000 inhabitants, extending over several hills. The hotels and *cafés* are excellent, and very cheap. Despite these advantages, very few English people are to be met with, the exceptions consisting chiefly of people connected with the working of the mines in the neighbourhood and occasional travellers in search of health. Letters take only four days, and telegrams six hours, to reach London. Tlemcen, 120 kilomètres off, is a large town, standing in the middle of beautiful woods and forests containing magnificent timber, not far from the confines of the desert on one side and Morocco on the other. From Oran one may also go to Mansourah, a ruined Moorish town, with alabaster or onyx quarries, from which the large pillars in the grand Opera House at Paris were taken; and several other places of interest are not difficult of access. The railway is finished to Algiers, which may be reached in fourteen hours, unless the journey is broken at Orléansville, Relizane, or Blidah, all of which are interesting. Three kilomètres from Oran is Mars-el-Kibir, a safe anchorage for ships of any size in all weathers, and always accessible to vessels under sail alone. It is a pretty drive round the bay to it from Oran.

After breakfast at the hotel, we returned on board the yacht, in order to take advantage of the wind, which had chopped right round to the west, to make another start. Part of the French fleet, consisting of three ironclads and a despatch vessel, arrived this morning, and anchored off Mars-el-Kibir.

Moorish Girl.

We thought at one time of going to pay them a visit; but as the wind was so strong that it would have been a long business to beat back against it, the idea was abandoned. Having weighed anchor and got clear of the basin, an evolution which was accomplished with great dexterity, considering the length of the yacht, we proceeded on our course for two or three hours most merrily, when, alas! the wind dropped, and we were becalmed for the rest of the day and nearly the whole night.

Wednesday, October 16th.—We had steam up early this morning. Then came a fair wind, the engines were stopped, and sails set. We were close to the coast all day long, and could see the Atlas mountains, and at night the light on Cape Tenez. The sunset was very curious, the sky to the southward being of a lurid sand colour with light grey clouds floating in the foreground. It looked like, and doubtless was, a violent sandstorm from the Great Sahara driving the clouds before it. We were becalmed all night again, and it seemed as though we never should reach Cagliari or Naples, as Tom does not care to steam more than is absolutely necessary. Having heard at Oran that the eruption of Vesuvius has really commenced, I am very anxious to get there as soon as possible to witness it, though I do not expect it will be nearly so grand a sight as Kilauea.

Thursday, October 17th.—I was awakened at 6 a.m. by being almost thrown out of bed. I heard shrieks and a mixture of laughter and lamentation proceeding from the nursery, while crashes and noises of all kinds issued from the other cabins. A sudden squall had struck us, and for a few minutes all was bustle and hurry, while sails were lowered down on deck, halyards let go, &c. The usually tidy deck was soon a mass of ropes, spars, and sails, apparently in inextricable confusion, though in reality everybody knew exactly where to lay his hand on what was wanted. Before all these operations were completed, the first squall had passed over; but it was shortly succeeded by another and another, and this state of things continued throughout the day. A violent sirocco was blowing the whole time, covering the decks with sand; and each time that a fresh squall came it was just as if the door of a furnace had been opened, letting out a blast of hot air. Strong and fierce as the wind was, it heated rather than cooled one as it passed, and seemed to take all the strength and energy out of everybody. At midnight the squalls became so sudden and frequent that main and mizen sails had to be taken in and everything made snug. This atmospheric disturbance was undoubtedly connected with the great whirlwind from the desert which we saw yesterday, and which was now reaching us, slightly tempered by its contact with the sea.

We have had an enormous number of birds on board to-day, blown off shore doubtless by the force of the wind: starlings innumerable, four large hawks, an owl, linnet, robin-redbreast, thrush, redstart, tom-tit, water-wagtails, and a great many others. Poor little things!—they were quite done up, and in many cases lay panting and exhausted on the deck. I did so wish we could make them understand that they should have food, water, shelter, and rest, and be let go when we got near land. The sailors went crawling and creeping about all over the decks, rigging, and masts, to try and catch them, and succeeded in securing some by means of an ingenious sort of trap; but they are most of them too frightened to eat, and will, I fear, all die, except the starlings, who appear very bold and happy.

Friday, October 18*th.*—Nothing particular happened.

Saturday, October 19*th.*—At 8 a.m. we were abreast of Cape Spartivento, the southernmost point of the island of

Sardinia. It was curious to observe, in steaming along the rugged mountainous coast, that upon every little rocky point of special prominence a quaint-looking round tower was perched, very similar to those one sees in Ireland. About 10.30 a.m. we entered the bay of Cagliari. It is surrounded by hills, all of which are surmounted by ruined castles, and have picturesque little village nestling at their feet. In the bay were several ships at anchor, including the 'Vittorio Emanuele,' an Italian man-of-war, now used as a training-ship. We passed through them all, and anchored at noon close to the town, in four fathoms of water, just as the pilot came on board. The doctor immediately went ashore with him and the steward, to see about the bill of health, while we contented ourselves with observing and photographing the town from beneath the pleasant shade of the awning, regaling ourselves at the same time with delicious grapes, purchased at a penny a pound from the boats swarming alongside.

When the heat of the day had somewhat subsided, the children and I went ashore, whilst Tom turned in to take a much-needed nap after all the fatigues of navigation. A carriage had been ordered to be ready for us, but it turned out that there were only two in the place, kept by the same man, who is also the proprietor of two hearses, and that all four vehicles were unfortunately engaged this afternoon.

Salt appears to be one of the principal articles of export, as much as 175,000 tons having already been sent away this year. It can scarcely yield a large revenue, however, as the cost per ton, at the ship's side, is only eleven francs, and the expense of production by evaporation in salt-pans is not less than three and a half francs per ton.

For removing the salt from the boats into the ship's hold, a charge of fifty-five centimes per ton is made. The earnings of the labourers employed must be widely different from those of the stevedores in the London docks. We watched the process for some time. Two men in the boat

Our State-room.

shovel the salt into baskets, which are handed up by another man to a stage, halfway up the ship's side, whence they are again handed to a man on the bulwarks, who pitches the salt into the hold, and the empty basket into the boat, with almost incredible celerity.

We landed close to the Custom House, and proceeded along the quay to the residence of the English Consul, whose son kindly offered to accompany us on our tour of inspection. The streets of Cagliari are a little like those of Malta, very narrow and steep, consisting sometimes, as far as the roadway is concerned, of steps only. Every window had its balcony, some of handsome old Spanish iron-work, and all full of flowers. All the inhabitants appeared to be making preparations to present a clean appearance on Sunday, for between most of the balconies were stretched lines hung with diverse and strange garments. We climbed up and up, past some fine mediæval towers and walls, till we emerged from the mass of narrow streets on to what was once the site of the old ramparts, now converted into a charming promenade, commanding extensive views over sea and land. On the bastion are fine stone pines and pepper trees, planted among the square paving flags. There are several of these promenades on the heights above the town, and they add greatly to the attractions of the place. The cathedral, castle, and archbishop's and governor's palaces stand at the top of the hill, and all the best houses are clustered around them. As you descend, therefore, towards the shore, you get lower and lower in the social grade, until you reach the habitations of the poorest class, close to the water's edge.

At the hotel, where we had been warned that we must not expect great things in the way of accommodation, we were agreeably surprised to find a very pretty little *salle-à-manger*, decorated with flowers and looking-glasses, and to be excellently served by civil and attentive waiters. They certainly spoke a sort of Spanish *patois* which it was impossible to understand, and on our side it was equally impossible for us to make ourselves intelligible to them; but they managed to bring us what we wanted, which was the great thing after all. There were many officers dining in the room, belonging to the different Italian regiments quartered here. After dinner we descended a steep dirty street, a short cut to the post, stopping on our way several times to listen to the music issuing from the various houses.

The Sardinians bear traces of their mixed origin both in their dress and in their personal appearance. The men look and dress like modern Greeks, the dark-eyed women like Spaniards. The ladies, as a rule, wear mantillas, and the dresses of some of the peasants are really very beautiful and costly. The jewellery which they wear, made of pure gold, decorated with seed pearls or garnets, is often excellent in design and workmanship. The men wear handsome shirt and sleeve studs, and waistcoat buttons of thick worked gold or silver, set with garnets; the women have large earrings, some of them three inches square, set with pearls, besides finger-rings, hair-pins, and necklaces. We went this afternoon into a shop where nothing but this peasant jewellery is sold, and I was surprised both at its high price and at the great merit of the workmanship.

None of us were enterprising enough to go to the theatre, where 'L'Africaine'—as a play, not as an opera—was to be acted.

Sunday, October 20th.—Tom, the children, and I went ashore at 9 a.m. to hear mass at the cathedral. This time we succeeded in securing a carriage, in which we drove up a fine road, winding round and round the town, and having a promenade on either side, shaded by trees and well provided with seats. The cathedral is a handsome mediæval building. The marbles inside are beautiful, each chapel being constructed of a distinct colour and variety. The large altar, an admirable specimen of seventeenth century *repoussé* work, is of solid silver, and is furnished with silver statuettes and candelabras. These have as yet escaped the cupidity of the Government, which has already seized and sold much of the church plate, including a beautiful dish by Benvenuto Cellini, much to the indignation of both the clergy and the people, which I should have thought it was hardly worth their while to arouse. This celebrated dish was the pride alike of the town and the province; and yet the proceeds of its sale would not suffice to pay a single regiment or to maintain a man-of-war more than a very few days.

The service at the cathedral, which boasts a good organ and a fine stringed band, was imposing. The congregation included many smartly dressed people and numerous peasants from the surrounding villages in their picturesque costumes. The jackets of the women are, as a rule, of scarlet cloth, ornamented with silver buttons and trimmed with gold lace, and worn over a white linen chemise with open sleeves. On their heads they wear a piece of scarlet cloth, descending to the shoulders, while the lower part of the face is concealed by a veil. Some of the younger women wear tight-fitting bodices of satin, richly embroidered, and above this bodice a black velvet vest, also embroidered with gold and silver lace, and confined by a broad belt of the same material. Jewellery in profusion—chains, rings, and necklaces—is worn by all, and in many cases the costume is completed by a white satin apron and a scarlet petticoat. Among the men, the clothes-dealers have the character of being the most smartly dressed, and I believe the bakeresses occupy a similar position among the townswomen. On feast days the men wear scarlet waistcoats, blue jackets, embroidered in silver, very short white trousers, a short black stuck-out petticoat, black gaiters, and a scarlet cap.

The service over, we walked through the various chapels, which contain several handsome monuments to deceased bishops. Two recumbent figures under canopies specially attracted my attention. I never saw the expression and wrinkles of age more faithfully rendered than in the cold white marble representations of those mediæval prelates. From the sacristy there is an extensive view over the lower and surrounding country, and the sanctuary beneath contains some interesting tombs and delicate marblework.

On leaving the cathedral we walked to the museum, examining and admiring on our way the elephant tower, of mixed Pisan and Aragonese work. In the museum is an excellent collection of natural history specimens, minerals, and other things; but the most interesting objects were the antiquities which have been collected in the island at various times. There are many Etruscan, Roman, and Egyptian relics, glass vases, amphoræ, lamps, jewellery, &c., such as one sees in nearly every museum of the kind; but this establishment is specially fortunate in possessing an unrivalled collection of little bronze figures, ornaments, and arms, relics of the Phœnician rule. Some of the best specimens, which had been selected by a *savant* for exhibition at the Scientific Congress at Florence, had only just been returned from that place, and were still in the packages in which they had arrived; but the director of the museum most kindly caused them to be brought forth and displayed for our special benefit. They comprised three Phœnician inscriptions, engraved on narrow strips of very thin gold, about six inches long, and one inch broad, which had been found rolled up in small tubes with a figure on the top, something like old-fashioned seals. They have been carefully unrolled and copied, but I think not as yet interpreted. Only one other inscription of the same kind is known to exist, and that was discovered, I believe, somewhere in Malta. Busily engaged as the director was in superintending the unpacking and cataloguing, he found time to be kind and attentive to us, showing and explaining to us himself the most remarkable articles. Among them was a model of one of the round towers noticed on our voyage along the coast. They are built of a sort of black unburnt brick, with chambers inside, and are supposed to be of Phœnician origin, and probably two or three thousand years old. There are over three thousand of these towers, or *mithags*, as they are called, upon the island.

From the museum we returned on board, but found that, having been detained longer than we had expected, we were now too late for morning service. Soon afterwards the two consuls with their families paid us a visit, and appeared to be much interested in the yacht and in our curiosities, no doubt partly because yachts do not come very frequently to this port. I wonder that this should be the case, for there is a capital natural roadstead here, protected from the sea and most of the prevailing winds by the sand-banks across the mouth and by the mountains at the back. It would form an agreeable resting-place on the way up the Mediterranean, and there is much of interest to be seen in the island. Everywhere there are now excellent roads and fair inns. A railroad, constructed to carry the mineral wealth of the country, takes the traveller in a few hours to Sassari, Iglesias, or Oristano. Near the latter town is Milis, a place of which all who have seen it speak with such enthusiasm, that I cannot refrain from quoting the remarks of the traveller, Delessert, about this comparatively little known earthly Paradise :

'I had seen orange-trees growing in the open ground. I had even breakfasted one morning under these trees laden with fruit on the shores of Phœnicia, the most adorable spot of the earth, where the sea came murmuring upon golden sands at my feet ; but I had never experienced the bewilderment, the intoxication which accompanied my visit to the gardens of Milis. Here there is nothing but oranges —not, if you please, fruit placed at regular intervals along the branches, and encompassed by verdure, but huge clumps of thirty or forty oranges dragging the branch which bears them towards the earth. Do not imagine a group of orange-trees here and there, the perfume of which comes and goes as you approach and leave it ; but try to realise the idea of a wood—a veritable forest ! As far as the eye can reach under this balmy forest it meets with nothing but oranges. Oranges in the foreground, oranges in the half-distance ; oranges gild the horizon. . . . We were in this wood precisely at the time when the peasantry of Milis gather the oranges to sell them. A gathering is a very simple process. A cloth is spread under the tree, and a man, having climbed the branches, precipitates the golden harvest to the earth, whence an inconceivable aroma arises. To give a simple idea of the extent of this forest, as large as the Bois de Boulogne (I ask pardon for my comparison of those who do not know this wood), it took us two hours to trot round it at a smart pace on horseback. At the end of our journey we arrived before the king of the orange-trees. A man can hardly clasp the trunk of this old tree in his arms. The huge branches stretch boldly out, like those of an oak. It bears an inscription to commemorate a visit from Charles Albert on March 18, 1829. But orange-trees do not entirely monopolise these enchanted regions. Here and there you come upon glades where tall poplars protect their noble hosts from the violence of the winds, or upon clumps where the wild vine creeps round the trees to breathe the perfume of their fruit; and the clematis falls about in cascades, caressing the breeze with its sweet odour. The earth is sprinkled with violets, the periwinkle, and the forget-me-not. It is a fairy-land—something fabulous, heroic—which is alone worth a journey to Sardinia, and well rewards the trouble of travelling over the barren plains and desolate hills of the northern part of the island. The woods of Milis are, in their way, one of the wonders of the world; and I owe to this oasis, loved of the gods, the grateful remembrance of the wildest enjoyment. Of the forty-eight hours we gave ourselves at Milis, I spent at least thirty in the orange woods, gathering in a store of sweet perfume for less happy times, and envying Sardinia so great a treasure!'[1]

Cavias, not far from Oristano, is celebrated for the

[1] *Six Weeks in the Island of Sardinia.* By E. Delessert. Paris, 1850.

beauty of its inhabitants, a people of quite a different race from the islanders, and said to be descended from the shipwrecked crew of an English vessel stranded on these shores many years ago. At Tharras, too, any enterprising antiquarian can easily obtain permission to dig and delve on his own account, on the chance of bringing to light rare treasures of the most remote ages. The climate is delightful, except in November and March, when heavy rains fall.

Sardinia possesses many remains of antiquity, belonging to the period when it was a flourishing Carthaginian settlement, on which the Romans looked with longing eyes. Some of its monuments of the past belong to a still earlier period. The *horaghe* or stone towers which dot the island in various directions—there are upwards of three thousand of them in all—are of this description. Like the round towers of Ireland, they belong to a time and to a race of which we have no other record, and are a standing puzzle to the archæologist. The *horaghe* of Sardinia exhibit the appearance of a truncated cone, or tower, averaging from thirty to sixty feet in height, and from one to three hundred feet in circumference at the base. The materials of which they are built are the rocks of the adjacent locality, and they generally crown the summits of hills that command the neighbouring plains.

After luncheon evening service was held, with an excellent little sermon from Tom, and just about dusk we went ashore to the cemetery, which contains some beautiful modern marble monuments by Villa Giacobbe Cavalotta and other Roman and Italian artists. The designs are thoroughly free from conventionality, and are well executed. One, to the memory of Enrico Serpieri, who was associated with Garibaldi and Mazzini at the time of the taking of Rome by the French in 1849, is a splendid specimen of bas-relief. The cemetery itself is extensive, well kept, and planted with flowers.

In two of the public promenades excellent bands of music were playing. Besides these there are two other bands in the town, those of the fire brigade and of the civil service, a fact which is very creditable to the inhabitants, who support them. Two theatres are open here all the year round, besides an opera-house, at which performances are given throughout the winter months. The promenade this evening was so crowded that there was hardly room to move about. We sat down on one of the stone seats, and observed the people as they slowly strolled about. The women all appeared to have fine eyes, but as a rule were not otherwise good-looking.

To-day we let all our poor little feathered prisoners fly on shore, rested and refreshed, let us hope, by their stay on board the 'Sunbeam.' Wild as they were at first, they had become so tame that they would all eat out of my hand, and I half hoped that some might have taken a fancy to the ship and have remained on board; but after hopping about a little, and then flying up on to the rail and rigging, and getting gradually higher and higher, they all deserted us and flew to some high trees on the opposite shore.

Monday, October 21*st*.—Cagliari is built on the site of the ancient city of Caralis, and many interesting relics of the Greeks and Romans are frequently discovered here. Not long ago were found the remains of the house of Balbus, for some time proconsul here, containing mosaics as fine and as well preserved as any at Pompeii. This morning we landed early to go and see the amphitheatre, a short distance from the town. A carriage was to have been ready for us at the consul's house by 8 a.m., but, about five drops of rain having fallen two hours previously, the owner declined to expose his precious vehicle to the fury of the elements. However, after much persuasion,

Amphitheatre.

scolding, and delay, he was induced to bring it out. It was particularly annoying that this little difficulty should have occurred, as we had to return on board to breakfast at 9.30 a.m., the yacht in the meantime getting her anchor weighed and sails set, and lying to in readiness for an immediate start after our arrival.

At last we set out, and, after a steep up-and-down shake-bone little drive, reached the amphitheatre, which is hewn out of the solid rock. It is of great extent, with spacious subterranean galleries and passages leading even as far as the seashore, and though the rows of terraced seats are much broken, it is easy to trace the plan of the whole building as it existed in its perfection. After wandering about it for some time, I sat down on the highest seats, which commanded a fine view of the sea, and pictured to myself the scene which it must have presented when crowded with people decked for a Roman holiday, the *vela* spread over the top to shelter them from the sun, and the wild beasts fighting beneath.

We drove back to the town, refused the kind consul's hospitable offers, and with many good wishes started to rejoin the yacht. All her sails were set, and the anchor was just clear as we stepped on board, and Tom was in a great fidget to be off. Away we were sailing, when suddenly we noticed a boat coming off from the shore, the occupants of which were making frantic signals to us to stop. Tom was in despair, and would have liked to go on without stopping, so as to make a brilliant exit under sail among all the ships in the bay; but we persuaded him not to do so. 'Staysails a-weather!' was the order, and we waited, wondering what could be the matter. Presently we could make out the consul's clerk in the boat, waving my small bag, which had been left behind under the seat of the carriage. Sail was filled on her again, and we started away once more, past the ships at anchor waiting for their cargoes of salt. They are nearly all bound for Sweden and Norway, and on their return voyage they bring salt fish and Norwegian ice, both of which are in consequence excellent and abundant here. For just the same reason, one frequently meets with first-rate port wine in Newfoundland and Norway, in small villages and out-of-the-way places, where one would least expect to find it. It is brought back from Spain as a return cargo by the ships which sell salt cod fish in the various Roman Catholic countries.

The 'Vittorio Emanuele' started under steam about the same time as we did under sail, and we were hoping for a race with her, but in a very short time the wind fell light, and then died away to a calm. We drifted about in the bay for the rest of the day and all night, fortunately on a smooth sea.

Sardinian Clothes Dealer.

CHAPTER IV.

NAPLES, POMPEII, PÆSTUM, CAPRI, MESSINA, AND CYPRUS.

> *The semicircle*
> *Of dark blue waters, and the narrow fringe*
> *Of curving beach—its wreaths of dripping green—*
> *Its pale pink shells.*

Tuesday, October 22nd.—At 6 a.m. we were still between Capes Spartivento and Carbonara, and it was not until three hours later that a slight breeze sprang up and gradually increased to a strong wind, before which we sped gaily along until the evening, when it again fell light.

Wednesday, October 23rd.—A day of calms and variables, with heavy cross-swells from three directions at once. I suppose that this state of things is due to the fact that there has been a sirocco from the African coast, a strong westerly wind from the Atlantic through the Straits, and a gale in the Gulf of Lyons, so that we have the combined effects of all three. At sunset we could see the island of Ischia and the top of Vesuvius, and at 8 p.m. made out the light on the island of Ponza, just off Gaeta.

Thursday, October 24th.—A grey rather rainy morning, but even under these unfavourable circumstances the Bay of Naples, with its numerous promontories and islands, looked as lovely as ever. There is nothing really equal to it in the world, as far as my experience goes. There was hardly any wind, and as we crept slowly up the bay under our square canvas, there was ample time for the grandeur of the scene to sink into our minds.

About 10 a.m. we dropped anchor under shelter of the Military Mole, in a position which, though convenient in some respects, was rather too near the shore to be pleasant. The 'Himalaya' is here, waiting for the First Lord of the Admiralty and the Secretary for War, and our gangway was not even down before a large party in the 'Himalaya's' gig came alongside, followed soon afterwards by another party of friends. They did not, however, stay

Bay of Naples.

long, as all were anxious to make the most of their last day in Naples, where they seem to have had a pleasant time of it. The Italian naval authorities apparently do not agree with Tom's principle of not putting 'too many eggs in one basket.' The 'Duilio' and the 'Dandolo,' now building at Spezzia, and the 'Italia' at Castellamare, will be three of the largest ships of war in existence, with armour-plates and armament of proportionate magnitude. They would doubtless be most formidable antagonists in any naval engagement; but it must be remembered that a small torpedo might succeed in inflicting a blow which would at once sink the huge mass, and thus cause a loss of nearly three-quarters of a million sterling, to say nothing of the lives of the crew, whose loss would be far more severely felt by Italy than a like disaster would be by England, the number of trained seamen in the former being so very much smaller in proportion. I agree with Tom, and should prefer a great many fast strong little ships to a few big vessels.

About noon the weather cleared up, and we were soon surrounded by boats bringing all sorts of things for sale—coral, shells, pictures, fruit, flowers, &c.—besides commissioners and washerwomen, and a band of serenaders, with guitars, zithers, and flutes. It was rather amusing to have our own letters of recommendation, given in 1874, brought back to us again as vouchers for respectability. The proud owners, Luigi, a cicerone, and Berta Falsalta, a washerwoman, took charge of us and of our clothes with an air of rightful possession and of defiance to all comers, Luigi's first commission being to go off to the consulate and get our letters, which were a real treat after long privation.

We all landed to lunch at the Hôtel de Russie, which we found as comfortable as ever, and afterwards drove through the gay crowded streets to San Martino, renowned ever since the fourteenth century for the beauty of its situation and the richness of its convent. Like all other convents in this country, it has been broken up and despoiled of its moveable contents since the union of Italy; but the richly inlaid marble walls, wood carvings, and frescoes still remain to repay the trouble of a visit, the pictures by

Spagnoletto and Luini being specially beautiful. The white marble cloisters, in the centre of which the monks were buried, are very fine. The children were immensely interested in the curious trap-doors, through which the old Carthusian monks, who were shut off from all other communication with the outer world, used to have their food handed to them. But the glorious view is really the great feature of the place.

Friday, October 25*th.*—This morning Tom again went on board the 'Himalaya' to breakfast, and afterwards went over the 'Italia' and the dockyard at Castellamare, where all the officials were most civil to the Lords of the Admiralty, showing them everything of interest. The 'Himalaya' proceeded later on her voyage to Cyprus.

We started by the 8.15 a.m. train for Pompeii, and breakfasted at the Hôtel Diomède, opposite the railway station. The ruins of the buried city are now enclosed, and are under Government supervision. Two francs a head are paid on passing through the gates, and a very civil soldier is sent round as a guide with each party. No beggars are tolerated or tips allowed, which is a great comfort. Tom sent half of our crew and the servants thither to-day for a treat, and they seemed to enjoy themselves thoroughly.

The new excavations now in progress interested me immensely. The Government has been spending a great deal of money on these works, employing many men, and discovering a large number of interesting things; but the authorities are very strict about admitting strangers to the spot where these excavations are in progress. Our hope of seeing anything of the work was consequently slight.

Fortunately for us, however, one of the head officials chanced to travel down in the same train with us from Naples, and he very kindly gave us his card and permission to visit the works and see all there was to be seen. After we had inspected all the old excavations, therefore, the guides conducted us to the new part, where we found two very polite officials directing the work, and a number of men, with pickaxes and a sort of large hoe, clearing away the ashes and fine pumice-stone from a beautiful mosaic pavement in the centre of a large house. The small rooms had been cleared out the day before, and had contained many bronzes, statuettes, glass articles, &c. So we sat down to watch the proceedings with the deepest interest.

At first there was not much to be seen. The men picked and scraped away at the pumice-stone, but only uncovered some large tiles, evidently from the roof, and then some leaden piping and taps. What a curious thing it is that, while all the arrangements connected with the water supply are so deficient all over modern Italy, perfect pipes and taps and cisterns were in use at Pompeii! Presently a large amphora was uncovered, next some bronze-coloured glass bottles and cups of exquisite shape, then an entire set of leaden weights, like those one sees every day, and a steelyard. After this came another layer of ashes; but soon a shout of delight announced the discovery of a unique silver vase, several bronze vases, and a little store of copper and silver coins. Next came, mixed with decayed fragments of wood, several small lachrymatories and large glass bottles rendered iridescent by age, a pair of scissors, and a bunch of keys. Then, for a time, nothing but ashes, till the efforts of the searchers were again stimulated by the discovery of a necklace of gold and agate beads, unstrung of course, a lovely bronze vase full of coins, a rock-crystal ornament, and some tiny little crystal bottles tied together with a gold ribbon. But a glass vase, of the most graceful shape, could not bear being moved, and fell to pieces in the hands of the disappointed finder, careful as he had been to remove all the superincumbent ashes before attempting to change its position. After unearthing one or two large wine amphoræ and other unimportant objects, the wall of the building was reached, the room was cleared, and the work of excavation ceased for the present. I was sorry when it was over, for it was impossible not to feel the deepest interest in the proceedings. The men got quite excited occasionally, and seemed to know by instinct, or rather by the force of long experience, exactly when they were on the point of coming to anything good, and even to be able to tell, by the colour of the ashes immediately surrounding it, of what material the object would be composed. I should have liked to secure some trifle as a remembrance of the occasion; but this was impossible, as the Government strictly prohibit the purchase of any of the treasure-trove.

We said good-bye to the officials, and gave some money for wine to the workmen, with which they were much delighted. I stepped into the *portantina*, the dogs barked with joy that there was to be a move at last, and off we started through the silent streets to the railway station, to catch the 2 p.m. train.

We reached Vietri at about 4 p.m., and from the station door a glorious prospect lay before us—the blue sea of the Gulf of Salerno on one side, that of Amalfi on the other, with all the little bays, and the red cliffs clothed with orange-trees and verdure to the very edge. A steep road brought us to the long narrow street leading to the sea-shore ; and after passing beneath the stupendous works that here support the railway in its passage across the valley, we reached the town of Salerno itself. Here we found very good rooms, facing the sea, at the Hôtel Victoria, which boasts of a lovely garden full of beautiful flowers, just in their prime. We had proposed to ourselves to rest here for a time ; but Luigi determined otherwise, and carried us off to see the cathedral, built by Robert Guiscard, in 1084, from the ruins of Pæstum and other neighbouring temples.

After a long visit to the cathedral we drove back to the hotel, and, as we had the prospect of an early start tomorrow before us, went early to bed.

Saturday, October 26*th.*—Up before daylight, and after an early breakfast we bustled off to catch the 7.30 a.m. train at Salerno station, some distance from the town. All this haste turned out to have been unnecessary, for not only did times differ, but the train was late. Some bandits, who had just been captured, and were being taken off to Naples to be tried, were among the intending passengers at the station. They were fine-looking men, and did not appear to be at all cast down, but laughed and chatted with their guards and the bystanders most unconcernedly. At last the train arrived, and we were soon speeding on our way to Battipaglia. Here we found a carriage waiting for us, in which we drove through a flat campagna-like country for miles and miles.

We reached Pæstum in about two hours and a half, and, on arriving at the thick walls of the ancient city, were taken possession of by a Government official, who showed us all round. The three celebrated temples, which we have come all this way to see, present a splendid spectacle as one approaches them. The Temple of Ceres or Vesta is a perfect little bijou, but is far eclipsed in grandeur by that of Neptune, from which a splendid view stretches over sea and land. We walked across the plain to the Basilica.

We had a hasty lunch on the steps of what was once the scene of many a splendid ceremony, and, having gathered some flowers and bought some photographs, drove back to Battipaglia. The train was fairly punctual, and at about 6 p.m. we found ourselves once more at Naples, where Tom met us at the Hôtel de Russie.

Tom has had a very pleasant time, during our absence, with the Lords of the Admiralty and Captain Grenfell, visiting again the dockyard at Castellamare, where they saw the enormous new ship the Italians are building, and many other interesting things.

Sunday, October 27th.—This was a showery day, but very hot. Tom, Mabelle, and I went ashore to the English church, a convenient building, capable of holding a large number of persons, and curiously decorated with flags.

One or two friends came to lunch; and after their departure, and a short service on board, we again landed, Tom and I to go for a drive along the Chiaja, and then, skirting the shore of the bay, to Posilippo, and on towards the Island of Nisida. How beautiful it all was!

Vesuvius seems very active to-night, more so than at any other time since we have been here. Unfortunately the stream of lava is flowing down the other side of the mountain, so that it cannot be seen so well from the town as it otherwise would be.

At Naples there are what may be called manufactories of productions of art by the yard, of which our men have largely availed themselves, having had portraits painted of themselves from the original, and of their parents, wives, and sweethearts

'The image of him!'

from photographs. These are very damp, and are generally taken out, dried, and admired on Sunday, opinions being very freely expressed. This morning there was a special exhibition, and the whole fore part of the deck looked like an art gallery.

Monday, October 28th.—Started soon after 8 a.m., and drove through the villages of Resina and Portici to the

Hermitage, part of the way up Vesuvius. The road was very dreary and desolate in places, but wherever the lava had become at all decomposed, vegetation of all kinds had sprung up luxuriantly. A crowd of little *gamins* accompanied us, and kept running off into the gardens and bringing us fresh figs, crab-apples, and grapes. It was curious to trace, as one could distinctly, the whole course of the two recent overflows of lava, and distinguish plainly the roof of some house that had been overwhelmed and destroyed, or the ruins of another that had partially escaped as by a miracle.

On arriving at the Hermitage, we mounted on horseback and rode to the foot of the crater. I was carried up the cone in a *portantina*, while the others were dragged and hauled with straps, and pushed and helped with sticks, to the summit. It was a very windy day, and we were almost blinded and suffocated with the fumes of sulphur. My bearers slipped quickly over the edge, and proceeded to carry me backwards down the inside of the crater through a dense cloud of smoke, their feet sliding and the ground giving way beneath them at every step. Altogether I spent a *très-mauvais quart d'heure*, and was by no means sorry to be safely landed at the bottom, close to the edge of the new lava basin. We walked across the old bed to the spot whence the new supply was issuing, and gazed on the wonderful scene for some time in silence. From the top of the cone the descent was very amusing: some ran, some slid, some were dragged, and some tumbled through the soft deep ashes; but we all found ourselves at the bottom in ten minutes.

We rode back to the observatory, where we dismounted

to see the collection of minerals that have at various times been ejected from the mouth of the crater, including many specimens which are regarded as peculiar to far-distant parts of the globe. We also examined the seismometer, an instrument which, by a complicated yet simple system of electricity, rings a bell in order to attract attention to the smallest volcanic disturbance of the earth in the neighbourhood of the mountain, at the same time registering the hour, duration, force, direction, and other details of the event without the possibility of a mistake.

We were on board the yacht again at 7 p.m., and very soon after dinner were all glad to go to bed, pretty well tired out by our long day.

Tuesday, October 29th.—A pouring wet day. It is lucky that our expedition was made yesterday, and that we had arranged to spend this morning at the museum, where we enjoyed a rich treat in seeing all the beautiful sculptures and other works of art once again. In the afternoon we waded through the streets and looked at the shops, which were unusually bare of the pretty things generally to be seen in them. After dining on board the yacht, we went to a reception at the English consul's, where we met some very agreeable and interesting people. It was a lovely night when we returned to the yacht, and the mountain looked like a real pillar of flame.

Wednesday, October 30th.—After the rain and wind of yesterday, the weather looked quite promising when I went on deck this morning. Preparations were therefore promptly made, and at 8.15 a.m. we started in the cutter to catch the little Capri steamer at Santa Lucia. It was rather rough going round the mole, and the steamer rolled ominously at her moorings as we went on board. As soon as we got outside, our misgivings were justified, for we began to roll and pitch in a horrible manner, and the deck soon presented a most deplorable scene. I never saw people so ill and so frightened at sea before. The poor things shrieked, howled, and went into hysterics. At lovely Sorrento, where we stopped in the course of about two hours, all the passengers but ourselves deserted the steamer, preferring to sacrifice

Landing-place at Capri.

their passage money and the chance of seeing Capri to the certainty of undergoing further misery. From Sorrento to Capri the state of things was even worse. We shaved the shore so closely, and went so near to some pointed-looking rocks and islands, that, had anything gone wrong with the engine, we must have drifted on to the lee shore and been dashed to pieces in a few minutes. I began to be afraid we should not be able to land; but the captain ran the steamer in quite close to the shore, just off the Marina, and we were bundled into a boat which was rowed as near as possible to the mole. A rope was then thrown to us, and we were hauled in with considerable difficulty and some danger.

After lunch, Mabelle and I rode on donkeys up through the vineyards and orange gardens to the village or town of Capri, the capital of the island. Thence we climbed upwards and along a neck of land, commanding views on every side, to the Salto di Tiberio, a perpendicular precipice 700 feet above the sea. Not far from this spot are the ruins of the Pharos, and of the Villa Jovis built by the Emperor Tiberius. From the rock itself the prospect that lay before and around us was wide and grand, extending over a large portion of the island, the wide expanse of the Gulf of Sorrento, and the distant ruins of Pæstum, Amalfi, Sorrento, Mount Vesuvius, Monte Somma, Naples, Baiæ, Nisida, Ischia, and Procida.

Woman of Capri

A nice old Italian woman, who kept a sort of restaurant near the Salto, supplied us with some delicious Catawba grapes, which she called 'fragola' on account of their strawberry-like flavour.

After dinner this evening some peasants were sent for and asked to dance a tarantella, which they did with the greatest animation, the girls going through all the intricate figures in the most coquettish manner, to the sound of two tambourines. The dancers got quite excited, but were always graceful, though sometimes a little too vigorous. Five couples took part in the dance, relieving each other as, one by one, they fell out, utterly exhausted.

Vesuvius was magnificent to-night, a stream of burning lava flowing down its side, and a cloud of fire hovering above its head. I had my bed drawn close to the window, so that I could watch the mountain till I fell asleep: what wonder that I dreamt of the burning lake at Kilauea, Etna, Stromboli, Cotopaxi, and all the volcanoes I had ever seen or heard of?

Thursday, October 31*st.*—I closed my eyes, as I have said, on the volcano last night. I opened them this morning to see the 'Sunbeam's' white sails just gliding out of the harbour of Naples. Before we had done breakfast she had got across, and Tom had landed, without the children, however. It was still blowing hard, and from what he heard yesterday of the difficulty of landing, he had been afraid to attempt it with them; but finding how much matters had improved, he now sent the boat back for them.

In the meantime we all went up to Capri, and drove thence nearly to Anacapri, along a splendid new road, excavated in the face of the rock, in making which they have, I am sorry to say, cut through and partially destroyed the picturesque flight of steps that used to form the only means of communication between the lower and the upper parts of the island. After leaving the carriage I rode a donkey, and the rest walked, towards the top of Mount Solaro, where we enjoyed more beautiful views. We then descended to Anacapri, a small village with a large church, where a great religious ceremony was going on in consequence of its being All Saints Eve. We drove back to Capri, stopping occasionally on the way to gather myrtle and arbutus, narcissus, and other flowers, and, on our arrival at the inn, found that the children, with some of the crew and servants, had just come ashore, in high spirits, and were on the point of starting off for a donkey ride.

After luncheon we bargained with some of the donkey girls for black coral, which seems quite a speciality of the place, opercula, shells, and flowers, and finally, at about 4 p.m., we all started in the large cutter, with reefed sails —for it was blowing pretty fresh again—to rejoin the yacht. The sea was rough, and we were obliged to go right round the point of the island ere we could get alongside, and had some difficulty in scrambling on board. Luckily the wind was fair, and we were soon bowling along before it, and fast losing sight of Capri.

Steps at Anacapri. (Barclay.)

Friday, November 1st.—A fair wind in the morning, and a rough sea. In the afternoon, calm, with light airs, making us raise and lower our funnel more than once. All day long there was a cloud over Stromboli, and at night the flames shone out bright and strong against the dark sky.

Saturday, November 2nd.—At 3 a.m. we got up steam, and at daylight we were near the mouth of the beautiful Straits of Messina. About 8 a.m. we were off the Faro, and two hours later had passed Scylla and Charybdis, and dropped anchor in the harbour of Messina.

We had no sooner anchored than boats, as usual, flocked round us, containing all sorts of commodities; but the most welcome was the consul's boat, bringing a quantity of letters and newspapers, and a box from England. One must travel a good deal, and be short of news for a considerable period, before one can properly appreciate the luxury of receiving letters from home. After glancing at their contents, we hurried ashore to see the consul, visit the post-office, and give the children a donkey ride. We waited the distribution of the mail brought by the English boat at 2.30 p.m., but received only two newspapers, and then proceeded to get under way. The wind was fair, but the glass was falling. All down the Straits it was pleasant sailing, but outside Cape Spartivento it soon became far too rough to be agreeable. In fact, Tom had serious thoughts of turning back, as the barometer continued to fall rapidly; but, after a consultation on all the *pros* and *cons*, he ended by deciding to take advantage of the favourable wind, and a terrible night we had of it. I do not think anybody slept much on board, for it was blowing a hard gale.

Sunday, November 3rd.—Not quite so rough this morning; but I was too ill to get up. There were prayers at 11.30 a.m., and again at 4 p.m. At midday we had come

167 miles since 4 p.m. yesterday afternoon. Everybody turned in early, and we had another bad night.

Monday, November 4th.—Wind still strong and fair. At noon to-day we had gone 234 miles during the previous twenty-four hours, and were off the south-west coast of Cerigotto and could see Crete ahead. We made Khania light before dinner, and saw Suda Bay light afterwards. There had been some talk of stopping at the latter place,

Cape Spada.

but, the wind continuing fresh and fair, Tom determined to take advantage of it, and push straight on to Cyprus. I could not help regretting the necessity for this decision, as I should have much liked to visit the spot where our fleet so often lies, and to have seen a little of the island itself. On our way home in our voyage round the world, we had passed close along the south side of Crete, and had then an opportunity of admiring the beauty of its coast from the sea. Now we are going along the north coast, but unfortunately at night, when it is impossible to see anything of the shore.

Tuesday, November 5th.—A most perfect sailing day; strong wind and smooth sea; going through the water at the rate of 10½ or 11 knots, without any motion at all. In the morning we passed the barren-looking island of Naxos.

This being the 5th of November, everybody in the nursery was busy constructing a guy, which was dressed in Tab's clothes. At dusk this was marched all round the deck, accompanied by a band of music and a procession, till by a judicious manœuvre he disappeared into the deck-house on one side, while the children's attention was engaged on the other. A tar barrel, fastened to a raft, was then set alight and slipped overboard, so that when the children looked for their guy he was apparently seen sailing away in a blaze of fire, a surprise productive of great excitement.

Wednesday, November 6th.—Light winds all day; towards the afternoon we were obliged to get up steam, in order to ensure our reaching Cyprus at daybreak to-morrow. It was a lovely night, and our usual game of whist was played on deck by the light of the moon.

Earring from Curium.

Port Papho.

CHAPTER V.

ISLAND OF CYPRUS.—PORT PAPHO, LIMASOL, LARNAKA.

Nequicquam Veneris præsidio ferox.

Thursday, November 7th.—At 6 a.m. I came on deck, to find that we had already made Cape Arnauti, the western point of the island, two hours previously, and were rapidly approaching Cape Drepano, Port Papho, the small town of Ktima above, the ruins of ancient Paphos, where may still be traced the remains of the temple dedicated to the worship of the Paphian Venus. The coast is high, rocky, and at present very brown and bare-looking, though after the winter rains it will probably become green and bright. Both sky and sea were of the most lovely blue, as we crept along the shore before a light breeze, scarcely sufficient to ripple the water or to fill the sails of our own vessel and those of two or three small coasting schooners in our vicinity. Not far off was a large five-masted man-of-war, which proved to be the 'Minotaur,' Lord John Hay's flagship, lying to in order to send some boats on shore. We exchanged names with her, and the admiral then hoisted the signal, 'Will you come on board to breakfast?' to which Tom replied in the same manner, 'Very happy,' and in due time proceeded to avail himself of the invitation.

After our own breakfast we all paid a visit to the mighty monster, though it was not without difficulty that we got on board, as she was then under way. There was, of course, no accommodation-ladder down, and they wanted to lower a chair for me from the yard-arm; but I preferred mounting by the ordinary steps against the ship's side— not a very wonderful feat after all, as there were ropes to hold on to, and the ship was comparatively steady. She is certainly a magnificent vessel, with a charming stern gallery, first-rate officers' quarters, and two splendid decks, well furnished with guns of various sizes, all, it need hardly be said, in perfect order and as bright and clean as possible. She does not, however, show to advantage just at present, as the upper deck is encumbered with large boats inboard and some Indian ponies which are being sent back, while the main deck is curtained off into berths for the invalid officers returning from Cyprus. Yesterday all the big guns on board were fired for practice, and we were told that the vibration stove in the bulkheads in the admiral's cabin. What a treat for the poor invalids, who lie with their heads right against them! Two officers, one a Japanese, the other Chinese, learning their profession in our service, are very ill on board. The latter, who they fear is dying, is in great agony of mind because, though he is very well off, no one can promise to send his body home to rest in the sacred burying-place in the White Cloud Mountains near Canton. He, poor man, imagines he will in consequence be doomed to eternal torments. It is very sad for him, and he is killing himself with apprehension; but it is a contingency which he ought to have contemplated before taking service in the navy of a far-off country. Some people think that this is one of those cases where a departure from the truth would be pardonable. It would ease his dying moments, or possibly so relieve his mind as to give him a chance of

Mounting the 'Minotaur.'

recovery. Whether the end would justify the means is a point which I must leave my readers to decide.

Everyone on board the 'Minotaur' gives a bad account of the climate of Cyprus, and seems thoroughly glad to get away from it. The crew have always drunk distilled water during their stay, and though they have been much on shore they have enjoyed a comparative immunity from fever. Mr. Hepworth Dixon, who is on his way to Malta, after spending over three months in Cyprus, was among those on board the flagship. I was pleased to have the opportunity of meeting a man whose works I have enjoyed so much. We had an interesting conversation, in the course of which he gave us a great deal of valuable information about the island, and the things best worth seeing in it. He specially recommended us to beware of the horses, which are often extremely skittish—a fact of which he himself had had painful experience, having broken his collar-bone by a fall from one of them.

Getting down again into our boat was not quite so easy as getting up had been, for the 'Minotaur's' sides are high and steep ; but the sailors carried the children, and we all safely accomplished the descent. After the admiral had returned our call, he steamed away towards Malta, while we approached still closer to the shore, and at last anchored just outside the ruined fort and harbour of Paphos, which looked very pretty from the yacht. Over the square tower of the little fort the flag of old England drooped languidly in the breezeless air. Along the shore grew the trees of what were once the gardens of the Temple of Venus,[1] beyond which was a barren spot, covered by the ruins of the temple itself, with more groves of trees close at hand. On the hills at the back is perched the little village of Ktima, with its mosque and minaret, above which stood the white tents and brown huts of the 71st Regiment ; while the background of the whole scene was formed by the more distant

---

[1] See Note A, Appendix.

mountains, part of the chain to which Mount Olympus belongs.

We sent the steward ashore to try and get some fresh provisions, and to secure some mules or donkeys for us to ride; and in the afternoon, as soon as it had become a little cooler, we also landed, provided with our saddles and bridles, and found some bare-backed steeds waiting for us, with their Arab owners, at the landing-place. It took some time to mount so large a party, and to find suitable animals for the children, who were thoroughly happy at the prospect of a donkey ride. Very little of the ruins of Ktima now remains above ground. A few broken marble columns, sarcophagi, and slabs with inscriptions on them, some standing, some lying down, were all we saw, though even the fields and roads were strewn with fragments of white marble capitals and acanthus-leaf ornaments. Venus's bath still remains, with a stream of pure water flowing into it; and the column to which St. Paul was tied, that he might be scourged for preaching the Gospel in the island, was also pointed out to us.

It was quite a steep climb up the rocks to Ktima, a little Turkish village, surrounded by gardens full of fruit. Wherever there was the least sign of moisture, the ground seemed to produce in abundance. We went to the prison and the court of justice, and then rode through the bazaar, most of the shops in which were already closed, it being nearly the hour of sunset. A very short distance beyond the town is the camp of the 71st. Some of the huts were finished yesterday, and were already occupied. Hitherto the men have been crowded together in tents, without beds, sleeping on the bare ground, with one blanket under and another over them. No wonder, therefore, that out of 105 officers and men, 27 are still down with fever, while many of those who are convalescent show terrible traces of the disease, being hardly able to crawl about, and looking more like ghosts than men. The camp contained an imposing-looking surgery, but unfortunately no supply of proper fever medicine, and the poor doctor was consequently in despair. The site of the camp looks healthy, and the view from it, especially at sunset, when we saw it, is lovely.

From the camp we went to have tea with some friends in a Turkish house, which they have already made to look quite pretty and homelike by means of a few flowers and knick-knacks.

We rode back to the shore by moonlight, and, while waiting for the boat, had a long chat with 'Peter,' an Italian-speaking Greek, who keeps the canteen here, and is most useful to the troops. It seems that, as might have been expected, prices have gone up since the arrival of the English, but that living is still cheap. Fowls may be obtained for one shilling each, turkeys—and very fine ones too—for three shillings, a sheep for ten shillings, eggs at from fourpence to sixpence a dozen, and other things in proportion.

In the mountains, near at hand, are found the celebrated Paphian diamonds, which are really only a superior kind of rock-crystal, and also that curious incombustible mineral, asbestos.

Some of the officers of the 71st came on board to dinner. We had a cheery evening and plenty of talk about Cyprus, and we were all very sorry when it was time to separate and say good-bye.

Friday, November 8th.—Fires were lighted at 4.30 a.m., and we were under way by 7 a.m., steaming close along the coast, which looked very much like that of the other islands hereabouts at this time of the year—mountainous, rocky, and bare, with occasional groves and trees, and patches of verdure wherever there is a little water. Cape Blanco stands up boldly from the sea, and the chalky precipices on either side remind one of the white cliffs of old England. Close by is the modern town of Episkopi. Here it was that General Cesnola found his great treasure —three rooms, under the ruins of the ancient temple, quite full of gold and silver vases and other ornaments, necklaces, brooches, ear-rings, and all sorts of valuable things. The theory of their presence in this particular spot is that the inhabitants of the city, being threatened by invasion, hid their valuables in the temple, or rather beneath it, after which they were all either exterminated or else carried off into slavery, thus leaving no clue to the secret of their treasure-house.

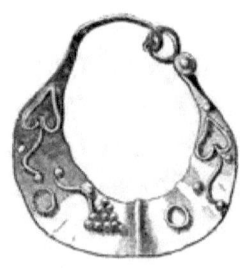
Earring from Curium.

We next passed Cape Zeogari and Cape de Gatto, the latter of which derives its name from a breed of wild cats which abound among the bushes, and which are said to be the descendants of some formerly imported by the monks inhabiting the Monastery of St. Nikola, which stands on the top of the hill, to kill the asps that then infested the island. These two capes form the southern extremities of a long low-lying promontory, enclosing a large salt lake, which, some say, would form an excellent well-sheltered harbour, if it were connected with the sea by means of a short canal. It is close to Limasol, which is in some respects the most important port of the island, as, although the steamers do not touch there, all the native wine is exported thence, principally to Egypt, in sailing ships. In the neighbourhood the best wine of Cyprus is produced, on what was formerly the Commanderia, or estate of the Knights of St. John. This is the most fertile district of Cyprus, and here one may ride for miles among highly productive but almost uncultivated vines, where sheep and goats stray at their will, browsing on the leaves, or trampling in the dust the grapes gathered by the peasants, which lie waiting removal. As soon as the owners find time or inclination to perform the operation, the grapes are crushed and placed, to stand and ferment, in large jars, well pitched inside, any one of which would certainly hold Ali Baba or any of his forty thieves. After this process has been gone through three times, the wine is fit for sale, at the price of about a penny for a measure equal to three quart bottles, at the vineyard. To my mind, however, and to that of most of our party, it is extremely nasty, being very strong and sweet, with a marked flavour of tar. It is said to be very wholesome; but as it takes a hundred years to develope its good qualities, it must by that time have increased considerably in value. The grape is the same as that grown in Madeira, and when the vines failed in that place some years ago, the Greek priests sent a fresh supply from this island.

Limasol, where we arrived at about 10 a.m., is a long low white town, stretching along the sea-shore, with domes and minarets interspersed among the houses and palm-trees. Never was anything so blue as were the sky and sea this morning; but if the colouring was beautiful, the heat was disagreeably intense. The very small landing-stage was decorated with vines and olive branches, the remains of a triumphal arch prepared two or three days ago on the occasion of the visit of the Governor and the Lords of the Admiralty. The mayor and the whole of the population came down to see us land, thinking probably that we were another party of distinguished English visitors, to whom more addresses ought to be presented. When they found we only wanted some mules for ourselves and the children to ride, their interest abated, though the mayor and a select body of followers accompanied us all round the town to the khan, the place where the market is to be, and to the old semi-Venetian, semi-Turkish fort, from which there is a fine view over the surrounding country.

While we were wandering about, a letter was brought to us from the Commissioner, Colonel Warren, with whom we had travelled some years ago in Russia, asking us to lunch with him. He soon found us out himself, and said that he had just returned from a three days' expedition into the mountains, that he had been much delighted with all he saw, and was amazed at the fertility of the land and the enormous acreage of the vineyards. We went with him to the Government House—which is also the post-office and court-house—where we found that the Assistant Commissioner was very ill with typhoid fever. The doctor, who had been sent for from Larnaka, was in despair, as he had arrived to find his patient almost dying, and he had no medicines to treat him with. Fortunately we were able to supply him with what he wanted, and also with port wine, beef-tea, turtle, and other medical comforts, of all of which he was absolutely destitute.

When it was time to embark the mayor saw us off, and gave me two or three specimens of old glass, of which great quantities are found in the tombs near here. Digging for antiquities is now forbidden, and I believe the Government intend to take the matter into their own hands.

Limasol is now a fairly clean town, without any pretension to a harbour. There are no troops here; but the fever seems to be very bad among both European and native residents. Colonel Warren has been here some time, and takes great interest in his work, which is of the most arduous and varied description, as his jurisdiction extends over several hundred square miles of country.

We had rather an amusing barter with the colonel, exchanging *new* newspapers for *old* pots and earthenware vases, some of beautiful shape, from the tombs; and after a few little delays we finally got under way again and proceeded on our voyage along the coast. Soon after leaving Limasol we passed the site of the ancient city of Amathus, and, later on, Carubio Point and Cape Kiti, where stood once the city of Citium, though some authors contend it was nearer the present town of Larnaka.

For dinner this evening we had some of the beccaficos, or preserved birds, which are so well known in these parts. Delicious fat little morsels they would be; but to my mind they are completely spoilt by being dipped, as soon as they are killed, feathers and all, into the strong vinegar made from the wine of the country, the taste of which spoils their own delicate flavour, though they are considered a great delicacy by most people. They are preserved in bottles for months, and thus sent away to other countries. Even in the classical ages they were famed, and at the time of the Crusades they were specially prized, no doubt owing to their having been preserved to greater perfection in the Commanderia wine made by the Knights of St. John.

About 9 p.m. we were off the port of Larnaka, steaming close by H.M.S. 'Raleigh' and 'Humber,' and several other steamers and sailing ships. We dropped anchor at 10 p.m. An officer from the 'Raleigh' soon boarded us, but had not much news to impart, except that war with Afghanistan was really declared, and that the 42nd Regiment was ordered away immediately for India.

Saturday, November 9th.—All the ships in port were dressed to-day in honour of the Prince of Wales's birthday. The harbour-master came on board at 6 p.m. to give us *pratique*, and soon afterwards Lord Lilford's agent, to whom he had given instructions, came to see what he could do for us. He gave a very bad account of the health of the place, which, considering the hot and steamy state of the atmosphere at the time, seemed by no means surprising.

A little later on a telegram arrived from Sir Garnet Wolseley, asking us to go up to the Monastery Camp near Nikosia, to stay with him, which we arranged to do as soon as mules and a conveyance could be procured. There was some talk of a diligence, but it ultimately proved to be a small tea-cart drawn by a horse and a mule. Horses for us to ride were also provided, as well as mules to carry the luggage.

While waiting to start, we had an opportunity of seeing

something of the town of Larnaka. I believe it has already considerably improved in appearance since the arrival of the English; but it is still a miserable-looking place, with half-a-dozen wretched little jetties and broken-down quays, in course of repair with stones from ancient Salamis, on the sea-shore. The sea itself washes almost up to the house-doors, and in many places it is necessary to make a detour by a back street in order to get into a house.

Larnaka.

There are some large stores, full of things not now required, the owners of which will, I fear, in many cases be ruined, owing to their having speculated to provide for a larger number of troops than have been sent to the island. The last of the Indian contingent embarked last week. They seem to have left a good impression behind them, as the best-behaved and most docile soldiers ever seen. Their surplus stores were sold off a day or two ago at a fearful loss, horses fetching from seventeen shillings to a pound each, and their provisions for the winter and other things being sold at equally low prices. Truefitt's establishment, of which we have heard so much in England, is rather a large affair, and does a good deal more business than merely haircutting and hairdressing. All the men engaged in it have been down with fever, most of the hairdressers are gone home, and neither the children nor I could have our hair cut by Truefitt in Cyprus, as we had intended doing. Some of the stores are really very well supplied, and almost any reasonable requirement can now be satisfied at Larnaka. But it is quite depressing to go into any of the shops or houses, or to speak to anyone residing here; they all have a more or less invalid look, and agree in giving a terrible account of the fever that has prevailed among them.

About 3 p.m. we started, passing through the narrow dusty streets of mud houses, by a Turkish mosque, where the wet-nurse of the Prophet Mohammed is supposed to have been buried, and a Roman Catholic convent of Oros Stavro, or Mountain of the Cross, the sisters of mercy belonging to which have behaved like angels all through the recent times of sickness and misery. On leaving the town, the road lies over sunburnt plains and between stony hills, all the way up to Nikosia, not a trace of cultivation being visible except in the gardens just round two or three wretched little villages, and in a few forsaken vineyards and cornfields. The road itself is bad, and we were just an hour and a half going the first eight miles, to the village of Furin, where we changed horses. Here an enterprising English blacksmith and a plumber and glazier, failing to obtain employment in their respective trades, have entered into partnership, and, pending the completion of a stone house they are building, have pitched a tent, which they call the 'Dewdrop Inn,' and from which they supply the thirsty traveller with beer, lemonade, and other refreshments. Another nine miles' ride brought us to Athienu, where we changed again. The proceedings of nearly all our horses and mules, being of a highly erratic character, made our journey occasionally rather a perilous one. Once we were as nearly as possible upset, owing to the horses shying at a dead donkey (a sight said to be as rare as that of a dead post-boy) lying in the middle of the road, which no one had thought it worth while to remove, though, as our driver informed us, it had been there for more than two days. We met the regular diligence during the afternoon, and between the last two stations passed the tents of the Eastern Telegraph Company's employés, who are busy replacing the present temporary wooden poles that support the wires by more substantial iron posts. We also met innumerable trains of heavily laden camels, bringing produce down from the interior, and long lines of empty bullock-carts, returning to fetch more things for the camp.

Gold Earring.

'Will they ever hear?'

CHAPTER VI.

NIKOSIA, MATHIATI, AND FAMAGOUSTA.

*The keeper's winking eyes began to fail,
And drowsy slumber on the lids to creep,
Till all the watchman was at length asleep.*

IT was now nearly dark, and the surrounding country was hardly visible. By the time we at last reached the gates of Nikosia we found them closely shut for the night, and it was only after waiting a long time, with much hammering and shouting on our part, that an old Turk made his appearance, with a lantern and the keys, to admit us. The air was rather cold, and we were quite glad of the wraps we had been recommended to bring with us. The walls of the city are high, thick, and machicolated, with many Venetian cannons lying about outside. In the bright moonlight the effect was very fine, and I think the gateway itself, through which we entered, cannot be better described than in the words of Ali Bey, a celebrated traveller between the years 1803 and 1807:

'The city has three gates, Paphos, Chirigua, and Famagousta. The last is magnificent. It is composed of a vast cylindric vault, which covers the whole slope or ascent from the level of the country below to the upper plain on which the city is built; halfway up the ascent there is an elliptical cupola, or a segment of a sphere, in the centre of which there is a circular opening for the admission of the

Asking for a Pilot.

light. The monument is entirely constructed of large hewn stone or rough marble, and the whole edifice is worthy of the ancient inhabitants.'

The narrow, dirty, and tortuous streets were deserted, the dogs howled and barked dismally, and the moonlight shone over the confused mass of Turkish, Greek, and Venetian palaces, mud houses, minarets, churches, and mosques. At last we drew up near what looked like a *café*, our coachman refusing to go any further, and proceeding forthwith to unharness his horses for the night. We were soon surrounded by a gesticulating crowd, who were very polite and brought us chairs to sit upon, but who all appeared to be desirous of taking us off in different directions. Unfortunately not a single word of any language we could speak to them was understood, and their remarks were equally unintelligible to us. 'The Governor,' 'the Pasha,' 'Sir Garnet Wolseley,' 'the Camp,' 'the Monastery,' 'Government House,' were all tried; but as each name was pronounced it seemed to have no other effect than that of puzzling them more and more. At last one man, evidently struck with an idea, flew off, and returned in a few minutes accompanied by the German-speaking landlord of the 'Albert Hotel, Restaurant, and Lodging,' as it was described on the card he gave us, who, evidently taking in the situation at a glance, endeavoured to persuade us to pass the night at his hotel, throwing all sorts of difficulties in the way of our proceeding further, and asserting that the camp, our destination, was still a matter of an hour and a half's journey. A waiter or friend who was with him, however, informed us that Government House was not so far off, and offered to show us the way. Tom put me on one of the horses, the rest followed on foot through more narrow streets, till at last, to our joy, we beheld the red uniform of a soldier of the Royal Engineers. He had been sent to meet us at a point where there was a short cut into the town, but had somehow missed us, and hence all our difficulty and delay. He told us we had still two miles to go, and at once proceeded to take us out through another gate and across some ground by the side of an aqueduct, over the dry bed of the river, till at last we arrived at the Monastery Camp, Sir Garnet Wolseley's head-quarters. Here we were warmly welcomed by friends, both old and new, including Sir Garnet himself, Colonel Brackenbury, Colonel Greaves, Colonel Dormer, Captain Wood, Lord Gifford, Mr. Herbert, and several others. Three huts, opening into one another, and comfortably furnished with impromptu sofas, easy chairs, writing tables, rugs, and mats, for which we learned afterwards that nearly every tent in the camp had been ransacked, were placed at our disposal. We are the first ladies to pass a night in

Arrival in Camp.

the camp, and as our arrival had taken place rather sooner than was expected, everybody had been busy all the afternoon, after the receipt of our telegram, trying to make things as comfortable as possible for us; and most thoroughly they had succeeded.

It was now past 10 p.m., and as we had eaten nothing since a light and early luncheon before leaving the yacht at 1 p.m., we were quite prepared to do justice to the excellent dinner that had been provided for us in the new mess-hut, which had only been completed this morning, and had not yet been used. We had much news to hear and tell, and it was late before we retired to rest in our cosiest of little beds.

Sunday, November 10*th*.—To sleep under six blankets, and yet to wake up feeling very cold at 5 a.m., was a new sensation to us after our recent experiences of heat. The air continued to be quite cool until 9 a.m., and then all at once became intensely hot. Such sudden changes of temperature must be very trying to those constantly exposed to them.

Our luggage had not arrived by the time we had to dress for 8 a.m. breakfast. Two hours later it was brought into the camp, Lord Gifford having kindly visited every khan in Nikosia to look for it, and finally discovered it at an inn a little way out of the town, where the muleteers in whose charge it was were quietly reposing, instead of bringing the luggage straight on, as they had promised most faithfully to do.

After breakfast we strolled through the camp to the Greek monastery from which it takes its name, a large ancient building, containing a church and many cells, some of which are now used by Sir Garnet for office purposes during the daytime, when the tents are unbearably hot. The pretty little garden attached is full of jasmine, verbena, and oleander, and we were invited to take a stroll in it till the Archimandrite, or Archbishop of Cyprus, was ready to receive us himself, with all his attendant priests, and to show us the church. He is a fine-looking old man, about seventy years of age, with piercing black eyes, a long grey beard, and a polite but dignified manner—altogether quite one's *beau idéal* of a Greek patriarch. In the church, to which he conducted us, there is a fine gilt carved wood screen, containing three pictures in the Byzantine style, of considerable merit, and surmounted by some lifesize figures of the apostles. The pulpit is most curiously arranged. A little carved and gilt lantern is fixed against the wall, close to an arch, on the opposite side of which is suspended a ladder by means of ropes, which, when lowered, forms the only means of communication between the pulpit and the floor of the church; so that when once the priest has ascended, and the ladder has been removed, he cannot get down again without assistance. After our visit to the church, the Archimandrite invited us to his own apartments, where we were entertained with sweetmeats, cold water, and Turkish coffee. The view from his balcony was very pretty, looking first over the camp with its now nearly empty white tents, and its huts fast approaching completion, to the town of Nikosia, which from the distance looks a most delightful place, its white churches, belfries, and mosques rising towards the blue sky from what appears to be a mass of verdure. Over the plain beyond we could see the Pentadactylon, or five-fingered mountain, in the northern range, which forms a conspicuous landmark in most parts of the island. Nikosia, the capital, possessed at one time some fine buildings, now in ruins, or replaced by the miserable mud houses of the modern Turk. The Archimandrite is the chief spiritual authority in the island, and though the principal convent, Kikko, is situated high up in the mountains, near the Troödos, he generally resides here, as being more convenient. His behaviour to us was most polite and courteous, though our conversation, being carried on entirely through an interpreter, was rather a tedious affair. He begged us to go and see his head establishment at Kikko, and at parting presented me with a beautiful sponge from Kyrenia, where the best specimens are procured. The British flag now waves over the monastery. The patriarch made a great ceremony of blessing it before allowing it to be hoisted, and had to send all the way to Kikko for his state robes, in which to officiate on the occasion.

It had by this time become intensely hot, and we therefore retired to our huts, to read and write, and look at the most recent English newspapers, brought by last night's mail. We were soon driven, however, to seek some cooler spot, which we at last found under the shade of some olive-trees, where we were fanned by a pleasant breeze.

There are not many soldiers in this camp now that the Indians are gone, but the percentage of sickness still remains very high. The state of things in the summer months, with the thermometer in the daytime at 120° and during the night at 80° (a great contrast), and the men dropping off like sheep, must have been terrible. The poor fellows had to sleep eight together in a bell tent, on the ground, without any comforts, with but few duties to perform, and no amusements to distract their attention from thinking who might next be seized by the fever. The Indians suffered just as much as the British. The difficulties of interment were great among men of so many different religions. Caste had to be considered. Some burned their dead; the rest buried them, with various peculiar ceremonies. Even among the Europeans there were Greek, Mohammedan, Catholic, and Protestant ideas on the subject to be taken into consideration.

The men remaining here are only just now being moved

into the huts as each one is finished. I fear, however, that these will not afford much protection against the cold and wet weather when it comes; for though they are well ventilated at each end and round the eaves, the boards of which they are constructed do not fit well, the spaces between them rendering it quite unnecessary to go to the windows in order to see what is going on outside. This morning, for instance, I watched from my bed, through the cracks in the wall, the sun rise over the distant plain.

The thermometer at 2 p.m., in the mess-hut, was very high; but by 3.30 p.m., when we all started for a ride into Nikosia, the air was beginning to get somewhat cooler. A large number of Greek women living at Nikosia, having heard of our arrival, had walked all the way up to the camp —a rather long journey for them—for the purpose of seeing us, and were now waiting quietly and respectfully under the olive-trees, at a short distance from our huts, in order to see us pass. We were quite a large party, attended by several zaptiehs, interpreters, &c. On our way we were met by the Commissioner of Nikosia, Colonel Biddulph, who kindly invited us all to go and have tea with him.

The town is disappointing inside, although there are some fine buildings still left. The old cathedral of St. Sophia, now used as a mosque, is superb in the richness of its design and tracery, and the purity of its Gothic architecture. Opposite the cathedral is the church of St. Nicholas, now used as a granary. The three Gothic portals are among the finest I have ever seen. Every house in Nikosia possesses a luxuriant garden, and the bazaars are festooned with vines; but the whole place wears, notwithstanding, an air of desolation, ruin, and dirt.

Government House is one of the best of the old Turkish residences.

From the Turkish prison we passed through a narrow dirty street, with ruined houses and wasted gardens on either side, out into the open country again, when a sharp canter over the plain and through a small village brought us to the place where the new Government House is in course of erection. This spot is called Snake Hill, from two snakes having once been discovered and killed there, a fact which shows how idle are the rumours of the prevalence of poisonous reptiles in the island. It is a rare thing to meet with them, and I have seen one or two collectors who had abandoned in despair the idea of doing so. The site selected for Government House is a commanding one, looking over river, plain, town, mountains, and what were once forests.

Having stopped to watch the glorious sunset, we had a capital gallop back into the camp, through another village, situated in the midst of fertile gardens and fields. We saw the place where the Ghoorkas had been quartered, with the rows of stone troughs from which their horses had been fed. The Indian paat tents they have left behind have been found both useful and comfortable; for being very thick, and lined with a dark blue material, they keep out the heat better than any of those furnished by the English commissariat department.

It was dark before we got back, and the air was quite cool. We had a pleasant dinner in the mess-hut, a party of eight.

Monday, November 11*th.*—The night was again cold, and even at 8 a.m. breakfast, by which time the sun was high and bright, the air was still chilly. About 10 a.m. we started to ride to Kythræa, a village situated in a lovely valley, about ten miles off. Our road at first was by way of the bridge over the river Pedæus. Close by is a precipice, down which are thrown the carcases of all the animals that die or are killed in the town; consequently there was a pack of hungry half-starved dogs hanging about, who barked at us most vociferously as we disturbed them. We passed a corner of the town, and rode along under the massive walls to the Kyrenia gate, which forms the entrance to a fortress, and is very like the Famagousta gate, already described. Here it was that, on August 25, 1878, a curious scene was enacted. The Turkish prisoners confined at Nikosia were all brought out, bound together in threes, made up into parties of about fifty, and marched in detachments to Kyrenia to embark on board the 'Black Prince' for the opposite coast. The walls of the town were covered with Turkish women, weeping, howling, and lamenting. Some of the men broke down, others behaved like Stoics; but it must have been a sad sight as they were marched off, and the women were left weeping round the three camel-loads of chains that had been removed from the prisoners. The men had previously been informed of what was going to be done with them; but it seems that they were under the impression that they were to be set free on arriving at their destination, and they therefore marched bravely along to Kyrenia, fifteen miles distant, without one of their number breaking down or attempting to offer the slightest resistance. It was well that this was the case; for the guard in whose charge they were, both English and Indian, were so much affected by the heat of the sun that they kept falling out by the way, and could have done little to resist any attempt of their prisoners to escape, more especially as the latter helped the tired soldiers by carrying their guns. They all reached Kyrenia at 4 p.m., having started at 7 a.m., and were handed over to the care of the commissioner, by whom they were put into the old fort, under the guard of some men of the 42nd Regiment. During the night two of them managed to escape through a hole in the wall, but the remainder were safely embarked on board the 'Black Prince' the next morning; and right glad was everybody in the island to be rid of them, for they were a set of desperate ruffians.

Leaving the walls of the city behind, we crossed a sandy stony plain. For about two hours we saw no signs of fertility, but we then began to pass through vineyards, cotton-fields, and pomegranate, olive, and orange-tree plantations, till we reached the house of a rich Armenian, whose brother is one of the interpreters at the camp. His wife and daughters came out to receive us, and conducted us along a passage full of girls picking cotton, and through two floors stored with sesame, grain of various kinds, cotton, melons, gourds, &c., to a suite of spacious rooms on the upper floor, opening into one another, with windows looking over a valley. Oh, the delight of reposing on a Turkish divan, in a cool stone-built house, after that long ride in the burning heat! Truly the sun of Cyprus is as a raging lion, even in this month of November; what then must it be in the height of summer? The officers all agree in saying that they have never felt anything like it, even in the hottest parts of India or the tropics. The lady of the house brought us sweetmeats, cold water, coffee, and lemonade, and after a little rest we were able to do full justice to the lunch which Sir Garnet had previously sent on for us by a couple of servants.

After that, we mounted fresh mules, and rode up the valley, by the running water, to the point where it gushes from the hill, or rather mountain, side, a clear stream of considerable power. It rises suddenly from the limestone rock at the foot of Pentadactylon, nearly 3,000 feet high, in the northern range of mountains. No one knows whence it springs; but from the earliest times it has been celebrated, and some writers have asserted that it comes all the way, under the sea, from the mountains of Karamania, in Asia Minor. The effect produced is magical, trees and crops of all kinds flourishing luxuriantly under its fertilising influence. The village of Kythræa itself nestles in fruit-trees and flowering shrubs, and every wall is covered with maidenhair fern, the fronds of which are frequently four and five feet long. The current of the stream is used to turn many mills, some of the most primitive character, but all doing their work well, though the strong water-power is capable of much fuller development.

On returning to the house of the Armenian, I chose and bought some fine large pure white turkeys, of a breed for which Cyprus is famed, to be sent into the camp and thence to Larnaka, where they will be shipped to England. It is curious that the proprietor of a large estate, including acres of the richest land in this most fertile valley, should, like his brother, be willing to earn 7s. 6d. a day as an interpreter in the camp, and even offer to act as private servant to one of the officers, and to perform the most menial duties. But the Armenians are, as a rule, a money-getting race, and will do anything for the love of gain, even to the sacrifice of their personal pride.

It was nearly dark when we started to return, and it was with many a stumble, but never a tumble, that we galloped across the stony plain, and reached the camp about 7 p.m. Here we found a silk merchant from Nikosia waiting to see us, with a collection of the soft silks of the country, celebrated since the days of Boccaccio. They look rather like poplin, but are really made entirely of silk, three-quarters of a yard in width, and costing about three shillings a yard, the price being actually reckoned in piastres for price and pics for measurement. The prettiest, I think, are those which are undyed, and retain the natural colour of the cocoon, from creamy white to the darkest gold. Some prefer a sort of slaty grey, of which a great quantity is made ; but I think it is very ugly. We bought a few specimens, and also some pretty crinkly stuff, made by hand by the native women, and worn in the shape of long chemises or shirts, trimmed with lace. Sir Garnet Wolseley sent one over to the Queen as a speciality of the country, and she liked it so much that she has sent for two more. The young lady who made the specimen chemise is the daughter of one of the richest men in Nikosia, a member of the council, and the holder of other important offices. She did not perform her task as a matter of sentiment, but purely as one of £ s. d. ; and when it was completed she sent her servant with the garment to the camp, giving her strict orders not to part with her parcel until she had received the money.

The clouds to-night look dark and lowering, and very

unpromising for our proposed mountain expedition. The rain has been due for more than six weeks, and is much wanted for the good of the island; but I do hope it will wait another day or two.

Tuesday, November 12*th.*—The night has been bitterly cold; not the clear crisp cold one sometimes feels on a mountain top, but a damp, clammy, penetrating cold, that made the teeth chatter and the bones shake, in spite of any amount of bedclothes. Dressing and a tub were a real trial, and I was positively too frozen to eat any breakfast at 7 a.m.; in fact, it was not until after a good gallop in the bright sun that my blood began to circulate freely again. I do not think the thermometer was below 40°, but even that implies a difference of more than forty degrees from the temperature of the middle of the day.

We felt very sorry to say good-bye to the camp, where everybody had been so kind to us, and where we have been made so comfortable. Sir Garnet Wolseley and Mr. Herbert rode with us nearly to the village of Zered, where we parted, with expressions of mutual regret, and a promise to meet again at Kikko on Friday. They returned to the Monastery camp, while we went on with a zaptieh to the camp at Mathiati, to lunch, and to see what there was to be seen there. It was a hot and dreary ride. Our zaptieh did not know the way very well; but at last we perceived some white tents in the distance, under the shade of a few carob-trees. It proved to be the camp of the Royal Engineers, who informed us that the camp of the 71st Regiment was not very far off. Tom stopped to have a chat with them. They looked miserably ill, and said they had suffered and were still suffering much from fever, though they seemed to think that if they had been properly fed and sheltered they might have escaped many of the miseries they have had to endure. Some people say that this island is not specially unhealthy, and that if the same number of troops had been landed at Malta under precisely similar conditions, they would have suffered just as much. It is difficult to understand why fever should be so prevalent here. Some of the doctors say that there is water all over the island very near the surface of the soil, though it does not actually appear; and in support of this theory they point to the ease with which water is obtained by sinking wells. Others say that the prevalence of disease, especially among the native inhabitants—who suffer nearly as much as the foreigners—is owing to the fact that almost every well is dug within ten feet of a Turkish or Greek cemetery. Others again are of opinion that the disintegration of the granite and sandstone, of which the island is largely composed, is the cause of the fever. Certainly it seems to be almost as bad five hundred or a thousand feet above the sea, on rocky soil, as it is on the plains near the sea-shore.

We rode through the camp until we met a soldier who took us to our friend's cool shady little tent, where everything had been charmingly arranged for our reception, and where we sat in the shade and chatted and lunched. Then we went all round the camp, admired the distant views of the mountains above Kyrenia and of the sea towards Larnaka, and visited the hospital tents, where we heard the usual sad tale that above twenty per cent. of the men were ill. This looks a perfectly healthy spot, the ground being rocky and sloping, the trees shady, and the water supply apparently good; and yet the men have suffered greatly, though not so severely as at Kyrenia.

In the course of our visit to the camp we had noticed a small square hut, looking exceedingly like a large packing-case, standing apart from the others on an adjacent knoll. From this presently emerged an old Gibraltar friend, who used to act as whip to the Calpe hounds. He has not yet thought it worth while to make himself comfortable, as he is awaiting the arrival of his wife and his hounds, now on their way out from England. All the soldiers are looking forward eagerly to the hunting, as there are plenty of hares and foxes about, and the country is not at all bad to ride over, though there are no fences.

Having indulged in a short rest after our expedition, we started to ride down to Dali, the ancient Idalium, where the carriage was to meet us. It was an interesting ride alongside the new road which the English are making from Dali to Mathiati. The whole population of the neighbourhood is employed on this work, so that we had every opportunity of observing the inhabitants. The men earn one shilling, the women ninepence a day, and even the little children get fivepence a day for filling baskets with stones and bringing them down from the hillside. When we reached Dali, neither zaptieh nor carriage could we find, and we were beginning to despair; for a Turkish village with windowless mud houses, doors tightly shut, and very few inhabitants, whose language is incomprehensible, is not at all a pleasant place in which to search for anything, especially when the shades of night are falling fast, and one is already tolerably tired. I was sorry that our visit to the place had not been made under more advantageous circumstances, as it was here that General Cesnola lived for several summers, almost in the open air, and in this neighbourhood that he made some of his most interesting discoveries, which cannot be better described than in his own words :

'On the eastern side of the river Pedæus, I discovered as many as five different ancient burying-grounds, all containing terra-cotta vases like those of the Phœnician Idalium, to which town they appear to have belonged, as I met with no traces of foundations of buildings, or broken pottery, or such other indications as to lead me to believe that there had been ancient habitations there.

'Farther to the south-east of these cemeteries there is a curiously shaped mound in the form of a sugar-loaf, which attracted my attention. I dug there, and though on its summit there are no indications of buildings, I discovered on its slopes several tombs deeply excavated in the calcareous rock, and made to contain a single body. In one of them I found two bowls of a green glazed terra-cotta, decorated inside with Egyptian representations painted in black, and a curiously shaped vase, representing a female figure, with movable terra-cotta earrings ; the stopper, also of earthenware, represented a crown, which, when placed on the aperture at the top of the head, completes the figure. The figure was seated on an earthenware chair. This curious vase holds a quart of water. The other tombs contained vases in the forms of quadrupeds and aquatic birds, some highly ornamented with geometric patterns ; also round-bottom vases with long necks, whorls and tripods in serpentine and terra-cotta. Some of these vases are identical in character with those found by Dr. Schliemann in his excavations at Hissarlik. These tombs are, in my opinion, among the oldest found in Idalium.'

At last we succeeded in finding zaptieh, carriage, coachman, and all, not a moment too soon, for just at this point one of the horses we were riding, who had not been well all day, refused absolutely to move a step further, and we were obliged to leave him behind to be sent on to Larnaka, which he never reached, poor beast, having died at the house where we left him. He was a cast-off from the Ghoorkas, and was bought only a week ago for seventeen shillings; but the poor beast had rare good pluck of his own, and could outgallop any of the others until to-day. While the horses were being put to, a civil Turk brought us out chairs, and offered us the usual sweetmeats and cold water. The manners of these people, even of the lowest class, are really quite charming, and make one feel that one's own ways are brusque by comparison.

The drive from this point to the main road from Nikosia to Larnaka was through a more fertile country, and Larnaka was finally reached at about 7 p.m., the Commissioner and another friend being engaged to dine with us on board at 7.30 p.m. The diligence, due at 4.30 p.m., had not arrived, nor the mules with the baggage. The muleteers, who almost all live at Athienu, halfway between Nikosia and Larnaka, are obliging and honest, but unpunctual and slow. It was 10 p.m. before the first lot of luggage arrived, and 8 a.m. the following day before the remainder reached us.

Colonel White showed us a great many interesting things during our few minutes' stay at his office—talc in large slabs, yellow ochre, lead, gold, copper, plumbago, and other mineral products of the island. Lastly he showed us a room full of vases and glassware, which General Cesnola's brother had dug up, and was taking away when stopped by the English officials. Unfortunately he had already succeeded in smuggling off a good many things before they knew what he was about.

On board we found bad news awaiting us. One of our men, named Bonner, had been taken ill with dysentery on the way from Messina to Cyprus, but had seemed to be getting better. The doctor now told us that a change for the worse had taken place, and that he feared he was dying. Another of the crew was also seriously ill, and the head steward was down with what at the time was supposed to be fever; while, to make matters worse, a telegram had arrived from England, announcing the death of the wife of poor Kindred, the mate. The news was a terrible blow to him, the more so as she was quite well when last he heard from her. It was rather hard work to entertain one's guests with all this on one's mind. We were to have sailed at 5 a.m. to-morrow, but this is now impossible.

Wednesday, November 13th.—Up very early, making arrangements for poor Bonner to be taken on shore. He was terribly weak, and some one had been sitting up all night giving him nourishment constantly. Still, I hope the change from his berth on board to a nice large airy room on shore may be beneficial, though I am sorry to say our doctor is very desponding about him. The moving was managed better than we could have expected. He was placed on my long cushioned basket-chair, landed at the nearest spot to the hospital[1]—or rather convent—and

---

[1] There is no regular hospital here, but the kind Sisters of Mercy have done their best to supply the want of one.

carried by relays of ten of our men right into his new quarters, a spacious room, of which the only tenant was a Frenchman, who speaks a little English, and who, I hope, will be a cheerful companion for him. It is strange that so strong a man should have been taken suddenly ill on a voyage from Messina to Crete, with a fresh invigorating breeze blowing all the time, after having braved the heats of the tropics and of the Red Sea. A gold medal was presented to him by the French Government for saving lives on the Arabian coast when the French mail-steamer, some of whose passengers were rescued by the crew of the 'Glen Eagle,' ran ashore. Bonner, then one of her crew, carried one woman seven miles across the burning sand, in the heat of the day, without shoes, and yet now he breaks down under what are apparently the healthiest conditions.

Bills had next to be settled, and the washing, which was of course not forthcoming, had to be sought for. One man had a portion of it, and, as no one knew where he lived, we had first to go and find him out, and then to get our linen away by main force, wet or rough-dried, just as it was. Then the doctor had broken his medical thermometer, and we had to get another, as a great favour, from the head physician here. But at last all these little difficulties were surmounted, and we found ourselves once more on board, really ready for a start, at 10 a.m., and the 'Sunbeam' steamed out of the open roadstead of Larnaka, along the barren coast, past some uninteresting towns and villages, to Famagousta, where we arrived at about 2 p.m.

H.M.S. 'Foxhound,' which had anchored shortly before our arrival, hoisted the signal, 'Take care—great caution required;' so we proceeded very slowly, until the officer in command, Lieutenant Noel, kindly came on board and showed us the way in. The channel is not really very intricate, but the mole is all broken down, and it is not easy to see where the reef ends. The walls of the town, from which there is a fine view over the surrounding country, are very massive, though in ruins in many places. The cathedral

Ruins of Famagousta.

and churches stand out grandly from amid the surrounding palm-trees, and give the place rather an imposing appearance; but there is an air of desolation about the whole city such as I never saw elsewhere, and the picture of ruin and decay was completed by an adjacent marsh. Famagousta is one of four cities founded by Ptolemy Philadelphus in honour of his sister Arsinoë, whose name it bore until after the battle of Actium, when it was renamed Fama

Augusti by the victor, Augustus, in his own honour. The city has been built, rebuilt, and fortified by Lusignans, Genoese, and Venetians, successively, always with stones from the ancient Salamis, four miles distant, across the plain by the sea-shore. The original of Shakespeare's Othello was at one time governor here.

On the way to the shore we met the doctor coming off in his boat to give us *pratique*; he turned round, and we all landed together. The inner harbour was full of small caïques, and on the shore stood a long team of camels, laden with pomegranates in sacks. Some civil but ragged Turks met us, offered the children and me some pomegranates, and showed us the way to the Latin cathedral of St. Nicholas. As in the case of St. Sophia at Nikosia, its Gothic arches are filled in with Turkish wooden tracery, and the building is now used as a mosque.

If Famagousta presents a melancholy appearance from the outside, the spectacle within is still more depressing. In the midst of the dust and ruins of houses and palaces, once containing a population of three hundred thousand souls, are now to be found a few miserable mud huts, the habitations of some three hundred people. Three churches remain standing where once there were two hundred; and in the streets only a few cadaverous-looking creatures may be seen gliding about like ghosts.

At the Government House we went to see some officers whose servants are all down with fever, including even the groom, a once celebrated Syrian highwayman, rather in the Dick Turpin style, whose history is decidedly interesting. This man was originally a groom in the employ of a wealthy Turk near Smyrna; but having eloped with his master's daughter, he found it necessary to flee to the mountains, where he became a brigand of the romantic type, robbing only the rich and assisting the poor. It is even said that at various times he gave dowries to as many as two thousand Greek girls. Every effort was made by the Turkish authorities to capture him; but as he had a friend in every peasant, he invariably succeeded in evading the soldiers sent after him. During the Crimean war, some British troops assisted the Turks in one of their expeditions in search of Kattirdji-Janni (which was the brigand's name), but with the same result. On one occasion it is related that he suddenly entered a house near Smyrna at the head of a dozen followers, all armed to the teeth. The family were at supper, and Kattirdji-Janni, quietly seating himself, remarked that as soon as they had finished he and his men would take the opportunity of refreshing themselves. His involuntary hosts at once rose and proceeded to supply him with all that he desired, whereupon, as a proof of his gratitude, he promised them his protection, and assured them that if they should happen to be travelling and to fall in with any of his band, they might rely on not being molested by them. At last, either tiring of his adventurous life, or being hard-pressed, he gave himself up to the Turkish authorities, upon their promise that he should be exiled to Cyprus. He was taken to Constantinople, and would probably have been sent thence to the spot he had chosen, had not a Frenchman connected with the consulate, who had formerly been robbed by Kattirdji-Janni and his followers, demanded that he should be severely punished. Thereupon he was imprisoned and kept closely confined in a small cell, where he was chained to the wall, for seven years. Later on he was removed to Famagousta, still heavily chained; and though the severity of his punishment was somewhat mitigated in 1875, owing to the intercession of Madame Cesnola on his behalf, it is only quite recently that he has entirely regained his liberty, and even now he is not allowed to leave the town of Famagousta.

Captain Bolton lives a little way off, at Varoshia, a

Ancient Guns

thriving village, surrounded by orchards and gardens—not an over-healthy place, I dare say, though the living there is cheap and good. The other three gentlemen live in this fearful town; and most sincerely I pity them. Close at hand is an extensive marsh, which abounds with woodcock, snipe, teal, and wild fowl of every description; but the story goes that should any sportsman venture there to shoot, he is certain to be down with fever before the birds he has killed can be cooked. These officers have not yet tried the experiment themselves, but the 'Foxhound' landed a shooting party to-day, and I shall be anxious to hear the result.

Notwithstanding the fact that the Turks have removed several shiploads of them, many of the fine old Venetian cannon still remain here, with tons of iron and marble shot. We brought away a specimen of the latter, as a remembrance of the ancient city that has withstood so many attacks from foreign invaders, but which is now left to moulder in silence and solitude in the midst of malaria. If the harbour could ever be restored, and the marshes drained, she might once again rise to comfort and prosperity.

On the way back to the yacht we paid a visit to the 'Foxhound,' a smart little gunboat, to see the officer in command. He gave me some pieces of armour which had formerly belonged to the old Knights of St. John, and which he had found at Famagousta a few months previously. By 6 p.m. we were once more on board the 'Sunbeam,' and continuing our voyage round the island. The visit to Famagousta had depressed us all, and we agreed that we had never been so affected by melancholy at the sight of any place.

It was a lovely clear night, and as our course lay close to the shore, the low mountains a short distance from the coast could plainly be distinguished. The shape of Cyprus has been compared by some to the head of a horned animal, and by others to the outstretched fleece of a deer. Accepting the latter comparison, we may now be said to be sailing along by the side of his tail, past the town of Karpas. On reaching Cape Andreas, the most easterly point of the island, we shall turn to the west, and, passing Capes Plakoli and Mandraleki, we ought to arrive at Kyrenia early to-morrow morning, and so keep our appointment with Mr. Herbert and other friends.

> And each may believe that now, as hansel
> Thereof, do Nikosia and Famagousta
> Lament and rage.

Mr. Bingham does not sometimes get up very early, and the children, who are always awake at cock-crow, are very fond of the opportunity for a bolstering match. One occurred this morning, of which I enclose a sketch.

'Get up, you lazy man!'

CHAPTER VII.

KYRENIA, MORFU, KIKKO, AND KARAVASTASIA.

While you in this isle are biding,
You shall feast without providing,
Every dainty you can think of,
Every wine which you would drink of,
Shall be yours; all want shall shun you,
Ceres' blessing so is on you.

Thursday, November 14th.—At daybreak the scene was very pretty. The sun, rising to the eastward of the island, right behind us, touched the tops of the northern range of mountains, and caused our old friend Pentadactylon and the beautiful ruins of Buffavento and St. Hilarion to show forth to great advantage.

About 10 a.m. we anchored off Kyrenia. The water is deep quite close to the shore, but there is no harbour except for small boats. It is really a lovely spot. Scarcely was our anchor down, when I heard a cheery voice calling out, 'Welcome to Kyrenia, Mrs. Brassey; I am so glad to see you again.' It was our old friend, Mr. Holbech, of the 60th Rifles, who has lately been appointed commissioner here, and who is evidently quite the right man in the right place. He at once took possession of us, and carried us off to shore. On the landing-place we found Mr. Herbert, and Captain M'Calmont, of the 7th Hussars, who had returned from Constantinople since we left Nikosia, and had ridden down to meet us.

KYRENIA

H.M.S. 'Humber' arrived an hour after we did, to embark the 42nd Regiment, and to take them away this evening. She has not come an hour too soon, for the men look terribly white and sickly, and thirteen fresh cases of fever are reported this morning. And yet it is a nice, cool, comfortable day, with a pleasant little breeze blowing, and the place feels to us as healthy as possible.

Mr. Holbech took us to his residence, at Government House, an old Turkish mansion, beautifully situated, with thick walls to keep out the heat of summer and the damp of winter. On one side the view extends over the fort to the bright blue sea beyond, on another over a large garden planted with groves of oranges and lemons—not one or two miserable little trees, but real woods of them, now laden with fruit. Yet even in this delightful spot, sheltered as they have been from the sun, with a pleasant breeze always blowing, and with comparatively light duties to perform, an average of one out of the three men composing the ever-changing guard has been struck down with fever every other day and carried away on a stretcher.

As our steward is still an invalid, I did the marketing to-day, and was surprised at the cheapness of everything. I bought a quantity of spinach, artichokes, capsicums, tomatoes, onions, and grinjals (a kind of egg-plant), amply sufficient for ourselves and the crew (a party of something like forty), for 2s.! After this business was transacted, we all went to pay a visit to the camp of the 42nd, calling on our way at the Konak, where we were introduced to the Kaimakam, or chief of the district, the Mudir, or head of the village, and the Cadi, or judge. I never saw anything so perfect in the shape of a camp before. It looked quite like a little Paradise. The tents are now nearly all empty, for most of the huts have arrived, but they had been pitched beneath large carob-trees, which afford a really thick shelter from the sun, and make it unnecessary for the men to remain altogether beneath the canvas. The officers of the 42nd have hardly used their mess-tent at all, but have breakfasted and lunched under the shade of an enormous carob-tree during the whole of their stay here. Two or three little streets of huts have already been erected; they looked comfortable beneath the shady trees, with a stream of fresh sparkling water gushing from the rocks above, and running close by. We peeped into several huts, built to contain ten men each, and thought they seemed very spacious and snug. In two of the huts we saw two men who had just been struck down with fever. These attacks come on without any apparent cause, and so suddenly that nobody feels safe for a single hour. The order to move was communicated to the regiment only a day or two ago, and it was not until this morning that they knew they were to depart to-day. It seems almost impossible that the arrangement can be carried out; but the confusion and bustle which have been caused by the suddenness of the order can easily be imagined.

After purchasing a nice fat sheep from the 42nd's mess for the sum of 13s., we returned to the village, and then went on to the fort, a large and strong structure in a very dilapidated condition, but supposed to be of great antiquity. It is now being repaired, in order to be made use of as a barrack, prison, magazine, storehouse, &c.

It was now luncheon time; and a large, merry, hungry party we were. Afterwards we landed again, and rode

CONVENT OF LA PAIS

across the fertile valley, under big carob and olive trees, up to the convent of La Pais, built by Hugh III., and destroyed by the Turks in 1570. Although all the fine sculpture and tracery of the Gothic cloisters have been defaced, enough still remains to give one some idea of what they have been. One room is nearly 150 feet long by 50 wide, and two stories high; two others are equally large, but not so lofty. Our Engineers had been repairing the floors, and putting windows and shutters into some of the best apartments, in order that they might be made available for the reception of invalids; but after a trial it was found that the place was of no use as a hospital. The men became worse there than even in their hot stuffy huts. It seems altogether unaccountable that a thick stone building like this, surrounded by cloisters, and with a comparatively equable temperature, standing five or six hundred feet above the sea, with plenty of fresh air on every side, should be so unhealthy. But we have been told that even at a height of 3,000 feet above the sea level the fever asserts its sway.

Sir Garnet Wolseley started yesterday on an expedition to the Troödos, to try and find a sanatorium. He was to go by way of Peristerona (the Place of Doves) to Lithodonda (or Stony Tooth) along the side of Mount Adelphi, 5,380 feet high, to Pasha Learthi and the summit of the Troödos, 6,590 feet above the sea, and thence *viâ* Prodromos to Kikko, where we hope to meet him.

We spent a long time at the monastery, looking at the fine church, now used as a mosque, the ruins, and the beautiful cloisters. The sun was setting before we left, and after the first half-hour our ride was dark and dangerous, for the path was rocky, and the branches of the carob-trees hung low. But the zaptieh knew the way well, and we reached the village safely soon after 6 p.m.

Ponies here are both cheap and hardy, surefooted and clever, but rather skittish, and always fighting with one another. I never before saw such quarrelsome little beasts. They cost from 7*l.* to 12*l.* each.

I have been rather tired and done up all day, and, not feeling very well this evening, am rather afraid about to-morrow's expedition, though I hope I shall be all right.

A heavy Load

Friday, November 15*th.*— We were off and steaming along close to the charming coast soon after 5 a.m., and, having rounded Cape Kormakiti, entered the Bay of Morfu, passed the town of the same name, and anchored off Karavastasia (or Stopping-place for Ships) at 9 a.m. As soon as the interpreter and mules which were to have been sent from the camp at Nikosia to meet us could be distinguished through a telescope, some of the party went ashore. We followed in due course, and found that our little expedition had attracted a crowd of curious villagers, headed by the Mudir, who informed us that he expected Sir Garnet Wolseley to arrive here in the course of the afternoon. The people were, as usual, very polite, offering us chairs during our short detention. At last, about 10 a.m., we effected a start; Captain de Lancey, who could manage to get only a very small donkey, on which he had great difficulty in finding room for all his miscellaneous kit, proceeding to Mathiati, *via* Lefka and Tamasos, while the rest of the party, consisting of Captain M'Calmont, Mr. Herbert, Mr. Bingham, Tom, Mabelle, and myself, with an interpreter, two muleteers, and two boys, were bound for Kikko, *via* Kampos. Captain de Lancey had a long ride before him —about fifty miles—but with a zaptieh to lead the way, a Turkish dictionary in one pocket and a Greek dictionary in the other, a packet of sandwiches, a pot of jam, and a bottle of cold tea, he started off as cheery as possible.

Our road, over the stony dusty plain, crossing and re-crossing the now dry bed of a river, was not very interesting at first, and was rendered still less agreeable by the heat; but soon we got into a valley among the hills, where the water began to trickle and the forest trees to grow. After rather more than an hour's ride we met Sir Garnet and his staff, on their way down to Morfu. Having found a place where the path was not quite so narrow, we all dismounted, and had a long chat and drank claret and soda-water in the shade. Sir Garnet seems to have been well pleased with his ride and with the country he passed through, though he had come to the conclusion that the forests and the game with which it was said to abound were alike a myth. There are fine trees, but they are few and far between, and in no place do they grow close enough together to form a real forest, or anything more than occasional patches. As for the game, I believe that there is hardly any in the island. The best bag I have heard of was six brace of partridges to two guns, after a hard day's work. There is very little cover, the birds are all redlegs, and they run for miles. In the mountains hares are still to be met with, but we saw only two all the time we were on the island. It has also been said that horses and ponies, bulls and cows, descended from those let loose by the Venetians in the olden time, are still seen in the interior; but all enquiries on the subject have convinced us that they are now quite extinct.

Sir Garnet told us that the air was delightful early this morning up among the hills—bright, clear, and bracing, with ice half an inch thick on the ground in some places. It sounded very delightful to us after our hot ride in the sun, but by no means improbable, as even where we were the air in the shade was tolerably cool, and it was necessary to be careful to avoid getting a chill.

Having rested and refreshed ourselves, we proceeded on our respective ways, Sir Garnet Wolseley to Lefka and Karavastasia (where he intended to pay a visit to the yacht), and thence, by way of the convent of Xeropotamos, to Nikosia, while we continued our course through the valley, climbing gradually higher and higher up the mountain side. In another hour we met Sir Garnet's train of baggage-mules, tents, &c., and half an hour later we thought we were entitled to another rest, in a delightful, cool, shady spot, under some Scotch firs, with fragrant herbs growing at their feet. Our path increased in beauty at every step, running by the side of a brawling stream. Wherever there was a little more space, the way was shadowed by magnificent plane-trees, spreading their branches far and wide, while delicate little cyclamens poked their tiny heads through the stones beneath. We passed the village of

MEETING SIR GARNET WOLSELEY

Kampos, where we saw the operation of making 'mastic,' a much-prized liqueur, the best of which comes from the island of Chios. A large wood fire had been lighted beneath some spreading plane-trees, and on stones placed above it stood a huge iron cauldron, filled with refuse skins and stalks of grapes, which were in course of distillation. The spirit produced is flavoured with gum-mastic, brought from the other islands, and makes a wholesome but medicinal-tasting liqueur. The wife of the head man of the village came out and sprinkled us with rose-water, and a large crowd assembled to observe us when the mules' bridles were taken off to let them enjoy a drink at the cold, clear, crystal fountain gushing out of the rock.

We were now fairly, not among, but on the mountains, and a steep rocky road (a water-course, I suppose, in winter, but now almost like an English lane) led upwards to the village of Izachastra (or Coquette). Here again we were sprinkled with rose-water. Venus certainly has not left behind her much of her beauty as a legacy to this her favourite isle. The women have almost all good eyes and features, but bad complexions, teeth, and figures. Those in the towns never stir out of doors, and look white and delicate; those living in the country are burnt brown as berries by constant exposure to the sun while working in the fields. They all have a slovenly gait, and look as if they were tumbling to pieces. Their clothes are generally dirty and of dingy colours, so that the effect is not even picturesque.

Soon after leaving Izachastra, we came out on the neck of the ridge, and had a beautiful view on either side. The landscape changed at every step, and the sea at every point of the island was from time to time visible, as we rounded peak after peak, covered with straggling pines.

There is not much twilight here, and it soon became dark, when we had to trust to our mules to find their way to the convent. Notwithstanding our faith in their powers, however, we were all glad when we saw the hospitable lights shining through the trees. We first alighted at the back door, much to the horror of the subordinate priests, who came out and showed us the way to the proper entrance, to which we scrambled round as best we could. Here more priests met us and led us across the courtyard, up staircases and along passages, to a little room with a beautifully carved cedar-wood ceiling. The head priest, accompanied by his attendants, paid us a visit here, and said that as we had not arrived before sunset they had quite given us up, and dinner could not now be served in less than an hour and a half. This was rather a blow, for we had not lunched at all substantially; but kindly they at once proposed that we should have a little luncheon now, it being past 6 p.m., and promptly produced the usual uneatable sweetmeats, water, and coffee, and then bread, grapes, cheese, mastic, and Cyprus wine. About twelve monks waited on us, watching with great earnestness for the slightest indication of our wishes, though they did not know a word of our language, nor we one of theirs.

Mabelle's and my bed-room was a small vaulted chamber, with walls four feet thick, grated windows, and a silver lamp suspended from the roof. The furniture consisted of two large divans, covered with Turkey rugs, and eight chairs, arranged in two rows against the wall—absolutely nothing else. When we expressed a wish to wash our hands, one monk appeared with a tin wash-hand basin, another with soap, a third with a towel, while a fourth held a candle. It was with great difficulty that I persuaded them to leave the things for us to perform our ablutions. They politely insisted on holding the basin till we had dipped our faces and hands in it, and then merely waited outside the door till we had completed our toilette.

Kind Attentions.

Saturday, November 16th.—We were up very early, and after a partial toilette Tom, Mabelle, and I went out for a walk, to enjoy the beautiful lights and shades of the early morning on the mountains. But the Archimandrite, who had come up from Nikosia on purpose to receive the Governor and ourselves, was before us, even though he had been suffering from fever the previous evening. He met us as we were going out, and was full of regrets that, owing to our late arrival last night, our reception had been of so informal a character. Had the rules of his order not forbidden his being out after sunset, he would have met us part of the way down the mountain, and would have taken us into a church and blessed us before we entered the convent, and rung peals of bells in our honour. I am not sure that we were sorry to have missed all these attentions, kindly meant as they were.

We climbed up a little hill above the convent, from the summit of which stretches a fine view over the whole length and breadth of the Troödos, and Mounts Adelphi and Olympus. It was rather like looking at one of the raised model maps one sometimes sees, so numerous were the spurs of the mountain, stretching in every direction, and so endless the ramifications of the valleys. Below us were vineyards, now all dry and barren, for the grapes have long since been gathered. We looked over the farm buildings attached to the convent, and saw through the windows the large jars of wine, and the stone press in which the grapes, ripe and unripe, sound and rotten, stalks and leaves, are all crushed together under the feet of the peasants. It is a rough process, but the place seemed cleaner than many others I have seen, where the wine has been kept in a room or storehouse, together with all sorts of nastiness.

We returned to the convent at 8 a.m. to breakfast, after which the Archimandrite again paid us a visit, to conduct us to the church. It is a fine building, much like that at the Nikosia convent, containing an altar screen ornamented with Byzantine pictures, some handsome books and candlesticks, and the same funny little gilt lantern-like pulpit, with its shifting ladder. There is a portrait of the Virgin Mary, said to be by St. Luke; at all events it bears his name. They showed us his signature, which is all anyone is allowed to see, except on one particular day in the year, when thousands of people flock to his shrine.

From the church we went to the Archimandrite's private apartments, and were entertained with sweetmeats, cold water, and coffee. He seemed very ill, poor old man (he is nearly eighty), and could hardly stand, but insisted on showing us round the place, leaning on his staff, or supported by two of his attendant priests. He took us to the library, which contains some choice editions of the old Fathers and of the classics, and afterwards passed through many passages and quaint cloisters. We were shown the piece of wood which used to be struck as a summons to prayer when bells were prohibited by the Turks, and the piece of bronze which was afterwards allowed as a substitute as a special mark of favour. Finally the splendid peal of bells from Moscow, presented by a Russian family, were rung, in order that we might hear their several tones.[1]

The Archimandrite expressed a wish to accompany us to Lefka or Karavastasia; but as the state of his health rendered this absolutely impossible, he sent his private secretary, who carried a gun, rode a good mule, and spoke a few—a very few words of English. While waiting for the mules to be loaded and saddled, I had a chat with two Englishmen who are staying here, but had only just made their appearance; and who are collecting specimens of natural history for Lord Lilford. They do not seem

[1] See Note B, Appendix.

to think much of the country as a collecting ground, or to have made much progress in their undertaking. I was interested in seeing some of their specimens, which included two francolins, handsome birds, rather bigger than a partridge, and very like the African painted quail; two mouflons, a species of sheep with a skin like a deer, and horns like those of an ibex, but coarse and abbreviated; a real asp, such as that by which Cleopatra, it is said, allowed herself to be killed; a chameleon, and some warblers, believed to be unknown to naturalists.

We had a choice of several routes by which to return to the yacht. From the Kikko Monastery there is a road across the mountains, leading, after an eight hours' ride, to another monastery, whence the road runs through delightful groves of oleander and myrtle to Ktima and Paphos. Or we could have gone to the top of the Troödos, and thence down to Lefka and Karavastasia, a ten hours' ride, exclusive of halts. But as Tom was afraid that either of these plans would be too fatiguing for me, we decided to retrace our steps by the way we had come.

Halfway down, a halt was called under the shade of some widespreading plane-trees, near a stream, in a valley whose name was Chaos, and a couple of hours passed very agreeably in chatting and resting and collecting roots of the lovely mauve cyclamens with which the valley is carpeted. Captain M'Calmont related to us some of his adventures last autumn with the Turkish army in Asia Minor, where he was for several weeks, and where he had a narrow escape of being taken prisoner by the Russians, when the Turkish rear-guard were cut off as they were entering Erzeroum. He has only just left Constantinople, and seems to think we shall find our proposed visit there most interesting just now. The remainder of the journey to the sea-shore at Karavastasia was completed more quickly and agreeably than could have been expected from our previous experience, the temperature being much cooler, and therefore less exhausting. The shadows looked long as we left the narrow valleys and emerged on to the thirsty stony plain, and by the time we had commenced the descent of the last hill, leading to the shore, and caught sight of the 'Sunbeam' lying at anchor, and of the boat putting off from her to fetch us, darkness was fast approaching. Our monkish friend, the Archimandrite's secretary, had been anxious to go on board the yacht with us, and we should much have liked him to see what I am sure would have both pleased and astonished him after his fifteen years' residence in the convents of Cyprus; but unfortunately the sun had set before we reached Karavastasia, and he was constrained to go on to the convent of Xeropotamos, accompanied by the interpreter. Captain M'Calmont and Mr. Herbert went on board with us to dinner before going on to Xeropotamos, where they also are to pass the night.

The doctor, children, servants, and crew seem to have thoroughly enjoyed themselves during our absence, and were almost sorry to see us back again, as it involved sailing to-night, instead of not until Monday, as they had hoped would be the case. Yesterday Sir Garnet Wolseley and staff lunched on board. The doctor and John Walford went out shooting, and killed one woodcock and some pigeons. To-day a whole party of them went on an expedition to Lefka on donkeys, taking with them some cold provisions. The Mudir found them out, took them into his house, entertained them with sweetmeats, bread, coffee, and fruit, got up some native dancing and music for them, and finally sent them home laden with fruit and other good things—all this, too, without their having been able to speak or to understand a word of each other's language. I never saw the children in such exuberant spirits about anything, and they were wild to repeat their visit to the kind Mudir to-morrow, instead of going to sea to-night.

At 8 p.m. we parted from our friends; in half an hour the boat that took them ashore had returned, steam was up, the anchor was hove short, and we soon afterwards bade farewell to Cyprus, where the last ten days have been so agreeably spent.

The doctor reports that the whole ship's company are a great deal better for their stay at Cyprus, and no one on board has had the slightest touch of fever, I am thankful to say. There were several false alarms, however; for whenever anybody's little finger ached he went with a long face to the doctor, who carefully took the temperature and diagnosed each case, so as to be able to express a confident opinion about it. The general result seems to be that the climate has agreed with us all, though we have led very different lives, some remaining altogether on board, some landing only at the ports and on the sea coast, and some travelling inland, exposed to the full heat of the sun and to the disadvantages of irregular hours and meals. Personally I am much better for my visit to Cyprus. In fact, I never felt really any improvement in my health till I landed here, and began to ride about. The 'Raleigh' attributes the exemption of her crew from fever, both ashore and afloat, to their having been supplied with condensed water while on board and also whenever they landed. We unfortunately had to fill up our tanks twice during our stay in the island, happily thus far without any ill effects. The natives say that this has been a most exceptional year, and that the very dogs have died in the streets from fever. It certainly is extraordinary that the rain, due early in October, has not yet begun to fall. The long drought and the continuance of the fierce heat of summer are beginning to be severely felt. There have been years when no rain has fallen, and when, to avoid starvation, the inhabitants have been shipped off in large numbers to the opposite coast, the remainder being fed, or rather just kept alive, by means of the biscuits supplied by the Turkish Government.

The terms of the Convention entered into by Great Britain and Turkey on the subject of Cyprus are a source of great difficulty in the effective administration of justice, the sale and transfer of land, &c., as no one seems to know precisely how long our sway is to last, or what are the exact conditions of our tenure of the place. Some people seem to think the sooner we give it up the better, as it is not likely to become anything more than a coaling station, unless the climate greatly changes. The other day a great scare was caused by a *canard* that the Sultan had objected to our flag being hoisted on the forts and public buildings, as he considered that Cyprus still belonged to him, and that his flag ought to be hoisted above ours.

Cyprus has been successively ruled by the Phœnicians, the Greeks, the Persians, the Egyptians, the Romans, the Byzantines, the Saracens, the Franks (under the Lusignans), the Venetians, and the Turks. She has enjoyed great distinction, and has suffered many troubles; and for the last three hundred years her condition has been a sad one. Let us hope that brighter prospects are opening before her; that, under our beneficent rule, oppression may be removed, the burdens of taxation lightened, and justice more evenly administered. Let us hope too that she may become healthier and happier under her latest, and—as they ought to prove—her best masters, than she has ever been before.

Prison at Rhodes.

Rhodes. (Müller.)

CHAPTER VIII.

RHODES, BESIKA BAY, THE DARDANELLES.

> *How reverend is the face of this tall pile,*
> *Whose ancient pillars rear their marble heads,*
> *To bear aloft its arch'd and pond'rous roof,*
> *By its own weight made steadfast and immoveable,*
> *Looking tranquillity.*

Sunday, November 17th.—The night was calm; ceased steaming at 8 a.m., and lay tranquilly becalmed all day. Litany and hymns—the latter conducted by Mabelle—at 11.30 a.m.; evening service at 4 p.m.

Monday, November 18th.—Still a flat, oily calm. Got up steam at noon. The coast-line of the mountains of Karamania looked very beautiful. We kept at half-speed—$6\frac{1}{2}$ knots an hour—as our coal is running short, and it is not desirable to put in for a fresh supply before Constantinople. The evening was so warm and bright that we played cards on deck by moonlight. The atmosphere felt very different from that of Cyprus, but later on a heavy dew began to fall.

Tuesday, November 19*th.*—The island of Rhodes could be made out at the earliest dawn, and by 8 a.m. we had dropped anchor off the town. As a homeward-bound 'Messageries' was just leaving the harbour, all letters which happened to be ready were hastily sent on board. We had no sooner stopped than we were surrounded by boats full of all sorts of things for sale, including fresh bread, tobacco, sponges, inlaid wooden clogs, and boxes made from olive-wood in the form of little birds and fishes. The inevitable *proveidor* soon made his appearance, armed with letters of recommendation from other yachts, and under his guidance we started for the shore.

Rhodes is even now a picturesque-looking town from the sea, though its chief attraction, the palace of the grand master of the Order of the Knights of St. John, was partly destroyed by an earthquake in 1856, and partly by an explosion of gunpowder which occurred later in the same year. The two harbours are more or less choked up, and on the piers that separate them, and all along the water's edge, are built innumerable windmills for grinding corn. Like Cyprus, Rhodes has had many masters, beginning with the Phœnicians, and ending with its present rulers, the Turks. The capital, Rhodes, was founded in 408 B.C. Strabo says that in his time it was the finest city in the world—finer even than Rome. The remains of the celebrated Colossus, erected 280 B.C. and destroyed by an earthquake fifty-six years later, lay for nearly a thousand years on the spot where they fell when the bronze was sold by Caliph Othman IV. to a Jew, who carried away the fragments on the backs of nine hundred camels. The history of the island acquires perhaps its greatest interest from the time of its presentation by the Emperor Emmanuel to the Knights of St. John of Jerusalem (A.D. 1308) to the time when, after much suffering from the attacks of the Turks, the knights were finally driven out, being allowed to depart with all the honours of war. The Turks showed their respect for the memory of their gallant enemies by carefully preserving all the inscriptions, carvings, armorial bearings, &c., which they found in the island. The Christians have not behaved so well, and all the Portuguese and Spanish and many of the French and English coats-of-arms have been torn down, taken away, or broken.

The landing-place is not grand, and our first steps on shore took us into a very dirty market and thence to a sort of bazaar, where curious little wooden objects, made by prisoners, were exposed for sale. We rode along outside the city walls to the arsenal, where Tom made arrangements about supplying the yacht with water, whilst we looked at some handsome, though broken, bronze cannon lying on the sea-shore. They were beautifully carved, in high relief, and ornamented with various armorial designs and bearings. No doubt they had belonged to the Knights of St. John. Our guide informed us that they had been brought to the shore by a French admiral, who had intended to convey them away in his ship, but was abruptly stopped by the Turkish authorities. The next visit was to the English consul, who showed us some fine Rhodian plates. His son also was kind enough to accompany us round the town, pointing out all the objects of interest. Under his guidance we all went to a loft over a carpenter's shop, smelling deliciously of cedar-wood, where we bought some good specimens of plates, collected at various times in different parts of the island. These plates have been so much bought up lately that they are now getting very scarce.

After passing through a Gothic gateway into the old

Street of the Knights.

city, we walked up the Street of the Knights, where all the old *auberges* used to stand, and where many of the buildings still bear the coats-of-arms of their former owners. The street reminded us very much of Malta. The Grand Hospital of the Knights, a fine building, is now used as a barrack for Turkish and Egyptian soldiers. In the central court were sixteen heavily ironed prisoners, who had recently attempted to escape and had been recaptured. The clanking of the chains with which they were laden had a most melancholy sound. They carried a large iron girdle round their waists, from which hung enormous chains, fastened to other fetters round their ankles, so that they could not walk without holding them up with both hands. In many cases their legs were rubbed and sore, and bound up with dirty rags. It was just dinner-time when we arrived, and we were invited to taste the soup, which we found excellent.

From the hospital we were taken to see the church of St. John and the ruins of the palace, where some beautiful tombs and fine monuments still remain. Some members of the order in England propose, I believe, to found a museum here, and to make a collection of objects of interest, before they are all dispersed. It was well worth the climb to the top of the hill, over the fortifications and ramparts, bristling with cannon and piled with heaps of balls, to enjoy the beautiful view over mosques, minarets, palm-trees, and orange-groves below. After this we went to the prison, where all the ordinary prisoners were assembled in a large courtyard, some in heavy irons, but all occupying themselves as they liked, working for their own profit, buying and selling, and evidently much interested in the strangers who had come to see them.

Passing through another fort or gateway, and over a drawbridge across a dry moat, we walked through many streets to a clean little inn, where we all felt that we could have spent a week very comfortably. It was a quaintly arranged place, with a mosaic pavement, kitchen in the yard, bed-room in a verandah, everything where it was least expected to be, and charming little peeps of scenery from every corner.

Everything had been arranged for sailing this afternoon, but there was no wind, and as Tom was not very well, he thought he would have a good night's rest and wait till the morning. The evening was again fine, and the difference between the air here and that of Cyprus was very perceptible. The climate of Rhodes is reputed to be the healthiest in the Mediterranean, as it is never either too hot or too cold, and it is always free from fever.

'Ma's Donkey Man.'

Wednesday, November 20th.— Tom is still unwell. I went on deck at 3.30 a.m. and again at 6.30, but it was always a flat calm; instead, therefore, of getting under way at 5 a.m., it was 10 a.m. before the sails were hoisted. The slight sea-breeze that was then blowing soon died away, and we finally had to get up steam at noon, and to steam all day and night.

Thursday, November 21st.—Still calm. At daybreak we were off Nikaria. At 8 a.m. we passed Patmos, where the cavern in which St. John wrote the Apocalypse is still shown. Nikaria—or Icaria—is a large island, with no good harbour, and containing about eight thousand inhabitants. It is supposed to take its name from Icarus, the son of Dædalus, who, to escape the wrath of Minos, King of Crete, is said to have made for himself and his son wings of feathers fastened by wax. Icarus imprudently approached too near the sun, the wax melted, and he here fell into the sea and was drowned.

At Lefka the doctor had shot a little owl and broken its wing. The poor little creature was then easily caught and brought on board, where the wing was successfully set. He would not eat at first, but I coaxed him with a dead bird and some bits of meat with feathers on, until at last he became quite tame. He was a funny little fellow—rather like those that guard the bizcacho holes in South America—and he had the drollest way of hopping about, as grave as a judge, catching insects. To-day Mabelle and the doctor were playing with him on the steam-chest, when suddenly he tumbled down a hole into the bunkers, and then ran along behind the boilers, where he must, I fear, have been scalded to death. I am sorry for the poor little thing, and should have liked much to bring him home to England as a curiosity.

Friday, November 22nd.—A fair breeze at daybreak, gradually freshening. At 7 a.m. we were off the Kaloyera Rocks, with Chios and Ipsara ahead. The wind had increased almost to a gale. Chios is a large fertile island, among the orange groves of which we spent a day four years ago. It was here that the French consul, thinking the 'Sunbeam' was a trading vessel, asked us to take his daughter and himself to Tenos. Like almost all the other Greek islands, Chios has a very ancient history; but the most important and terrible of its misfortunes took place in 1822, when, having been persuaded by the Samians to aid them in a revolt against the Turks, the island was invaded, and 45,000 of its inhabitants were carried off as slaves. Of the remainder, no less than 25,000 perished by the sword, while 15,000 escaped penniless to other countries. At the end of that disastrous year there were not two thousand Greeks left in the whole island. The islet of Ipsara, not far from Chios, has also been conquered and cruelly ravaged by the Turks. Nothing is left there now to repay the trouble of a visit.

The wind kept fresh and fair as we rushed on, past Mitylene with its three excellent land-locked harbours, until in due time we found ourselves off the island of Tenedos, better known than its intrinsic importance deserves from its standing so near the entrance to the Dardanelles. On the eastern side it has a good town, which was quite brilliantly lighted, when we passed it, late in the afternoon, on our way to anchor at Besika for the night. By the time we arrived it was very dark, and somewhat difficult to pick up an anchorage; but the bright lights of two men-of-war guided us to a safe spot. On the shore close by is the place where the kennels of the celebrated 'Fleet Hounds' are kept. This pack forms an important item among the amusements of the naval officers stationed here, and they must have great fun, hunting foxes and hares with them. They also get up races, paper-chases, and all kinds of similar sports. There is a large marsh, too, in the neighbourhood abounding in game, so that it is really not at all a bad station as far as healthy amusements on shore are concerned. Only the 'Pallas' and 'Research' are here at present, but the 'Thunderer' is expected to arrive tomorrow on her way up to Artaki.

Saturday, November 23rd.—Under way by 7 a.m., but with only a light breeze in our favour, and with the strong current from the Dardanelles to contend with, our progress was by no means rapid. The yacht lay quite still for some time, and then drifted slowly backwards, till at last I began to think we never should get into the mouth of the channel, for as fast as we succeeded in getting her head in the right direction the current caught it, and swung it round, rushing through the opening between the screw and the rudder, and we found ourselves worse off than ever. Under these circumstances it was mortifying to be passed, slowly but steadily, by an old trading brig, bound the same way as ourselves, but evidently better informed as to the tricks of the tide. At last, just as we were in despair, a stronger puff of wind came and carried us over the most difficult part into a wider channel where the current was less powerful. The morning was bright, and the Dardanelles looked beautiful. The gracefully shaped hills along the shore were covered with trees or cultivated to the water's edge. Curious old forts, tumbling to pieces, but armed with fine new cannon, mud villages with tiny minarets, and the white tents of the various camps pitched among the trees, added to the general picturesqueness of the scene. The air was so calm and clear that we could hear the soldiers singing at their work, or as they walked along the shore, driving their donkeys, sheep, or oxen before them from village to camp.

About 3 p.m. we reached the two forts, stationed one on either side of the Dardanelles, and called respectively Chanak-Kalesi (or Earthenware Castle) on the Asiatic, and Khilid-Bahri (or Lock of the Sea) on the European shore. These forts are also known to the Turks as Boghaz-hissarlari, and to Europeans as the Castles of Roumelia and

Anatolia. We landed, to procure the firman and to get our bill of health properly visaed. This was quickly done, and then a polite old Turk took us through the town to the residence of the English consul. As the 'Sunbeam' was hove-to, waiting for us, we could not stay long on shore. The breeze freshened, and by 9.30 p.m. we were anchored off Gallipoli.

On our way thither we had an accident which might have been serious, but which ultimately proved to be ludicrous. It was a very dark night. Tom and Kindred were both on the bridge, trying to pick up a good berth for the yacht, when Tom suddenly made a step backwards just where there was no hand-rail, turned a somersault, and disappeared into the abyss of darkness below. Kindred uttered a piercing cry when he saw his master disappear; but, hurrying to his aid, we found Tom standing by Kindred's side again. His muscles being very strong just now from much exercise, he had managed to save himself by clutching hold of something with one hand just as he was turning head over heels, and had succeeded in pulling himself up again. The men stared in astonishment, which was not diminished

Upside down.

when Kindred, to account, I suppose, for his shriek, merely said, 'Pick up the governor's cigar.' I heard much discussion going on, and no doubt their heads were sorely puzzled till the watch was relieved and the matter explained.

While we were at Cadiz a white pigeon had flown on board and been captured. It became a great favourite with everyone and the pet of poor Bonner, whom we had to leave behind so ill at Cyprus. He was always talking and dreaming about it when delirious at night, and when he left us I promised to take the greatest care of the bird, and to bring it home safely to England if possible. To-day the pigeon has disappeared, having no doubt flown overboard, owing to his wings having been insufficiently clipped. It is like an ill omen, and makes me feel quite nervous about receiving bad news at Constantinople.

Sunday, November 24*th.*—Captain Seymour, of the 'Téméraire,' sent a message early this morning to invite us to go to church on board his ship; but as we had already made arrangements to have a service of our own, we declined, and went afterwards. She is a splendid ship, and her taut masts and light airy cabins contrast favourably with those of the ugly but useful ironclads. Lord Henry Thynne's son was on board, much pleased to meet us again after our old experiences at Rio. Captain Murray, too, had just come down from Constantinople, where he had been staying at intervals with Sir Henry Layard. He had been engaged on a special mission with reference to the Roumelian frontier, and was full of interesting information.

Captain Seymour had borrowed some horses for us from the pasha, and directly after luncheon we went on shore for a long ride, through the town and on to the Turkish lines towards Boulair, which occupies an important position on a narrow neck of land, with a harbour on each side of it. It is a large town still, with well-supplied bazaars, though its population has fallen from 85,000, in 1875, to 15,000. Boulair was the first place occupied by the French and English in 1854, at the beginning of the Crimean war, and the fortifications then constructed, after being allowed to fall into decay, were last year repaired and strengthened by the Turks, who now hold them with a force of 10,000 men, which is said to be insufficient for their defence.

Our way lay through the town, which is exactly like all other Turkish towns, and then by a sandy road to the beach, past the building where the Stafford House Committee was established, and on to a large building still used as a Turkish hospital, though happily not containing many patients at the present time. Not far from the hospital was an enclosure with several open graves and a party of soldiers waiting to receive and inter the bodies. Sometimes we rode across the marshes, sometimes along the sea-shore, till at last we reached the first line of sentries, and soon afterwards a small camp of Turkish soldiers, who were cooking their one daily meal—a mess of flour and water—in large tin dishes. They are a fine sturdy-looking set of fellows, in spite of their ragged appearance and want of uniformity of costume. Their food, we found, consisted of a daily ration of flour and water, and five pounds of meat among eight men three times a week. They have nothing to drink but water, and they have not received a farthing of pay for nineteen months! Last week they were short of provisions, but yesterday a supply for twenty days arrived. They have to trudge wearily over the country to fetch water and to seek fuel, and we saw several of them, at a distance of seven or eight miles from the camp, cutting down the scanty brushwood which was to be the reward of their toil. They must really be wonderful men, for, in spite of all this privation and hardship, they look merely brown and weather-beaten, not miserable and sickly, like our poor soldiers at Cyprus. Many of them stood six feet high, and would weigh down and over-measure in breadth and depth any one even of our guardsmen. Under English officers no better troops could be wished for, but they have little or no confidence in their own leaders. The Russians themselves confess that if Osman Pasha had pushed on after the first victory at Plevna they would have been driven back beyond the Danube; and even after the fall of that place the Turks might have retired on Adrianople, and thus have saved the misery of the evacuation and all the horrors attending the flight of the wretched peasants.

We rode among the soldiers, and along the huts they were building of mud and straw, with the addition of a little wood for beams and doorways. I should like to see how English soldiers would manage in such a plight, with no conveyance for materials except their own backs, or at best those of a few horses. During our twenty miles' ride we continually met, and could see with our glasses for miles around, lines of soldiers slowly wending their way over hill and dale, carrying firewood, mud, bricks, and provisions, while their tiny ponies were quite hidden beneath the planks with which they were laden.

It is the universal custom in the Turkish army for the men to be summoned at sunrise and sunset to offer a prayer for the Padishah or Sultan; it is an impressive ceremony, and occurred this evening just as we reached Fort Sultan, as the sun was setting. Such a ragged crew the men looked, some even being apparently dressed in old sacks! When the bands struck up, and the whole army gave three hearty cheers, it was quite touching to hear the shouts echoing from hill to hill and from camp to camp, some of the men being perched on the top, and some hidden among the undulations of the ground.

Bonner's Pigeon

Although we rode quickly in order to reach the town before dark, Captain Seymour and I managed to lose our way among the narrow tortuous streets. Not a light was to be seen, and the whole place seemed deserted, except by the ubiquitous and miserable dogs, the inhabitants having no doubt gone to bed.

Just when the men lowered the staysail this morning, Bonner's pigeon stepped out from amid its folds, as fresh and happy-looking as if nothing had happened, little knowing the sorrow that had been felt for his supposed loss. His reappearance gave great pleasure to all on board, and is considered by some a good omen for Bonner's recovery and the success of our own voyage.

Monday, November 25th.—Off early under canvas, and after exchanging parting flag salutations with the men-of-war, we slowly made our way up to the Sea of Marmora. Our large chart of the Dardanelles had been sent up to London for reference in the spring, and had unfortunately been left behind. Tom, therefore, has nothing to guide him except a small scale chart; and as this does not show the nature of the shore or the depth of the water, the task of beating up against the wind has been one of considerable difficulty. Once, while he was below for a few minutes, we were so near the shore that when he came on deck he could not bear to look, and really turned his back, as he feared every moment to hear the grate and the crash of our contact with the rocks. Not long after this most unpleasant little episode the 'Thunderer' passed us, steaming up to join the fleet in Artaki Bay. She looked bigger than ever in her solitary grandeur, more like a fort than a ship, and as unlike the old idea of a man-of-war—'a thing of life,' with 'canvas filling to the breeze'—as possible.

The progress throughout the day has been slow, but after dark the wind changed and became dead fair. It was annoying to have to heave-to for the night, and thus to lose the favourable breeze; but it was impossible to see anything, and Tom did not like the idea of going ahead in a strange land-locked sea, where the native and Greek craft hardly ever carry lights.

Tuesday, November 26th.—We were off again at 7 a.m., and came in for light airs and calms all day. Tom was anxious to go the few miles (fifteen) from Cape Kum Burgas to Artaki Bay under sail, and our progress was vexatiously slow. Still the day was a very pleasant one, the weather throughout being delightful. In one tack the yacht was allowed to go too far, and as there was not enough wind to enable her to come round sharply, she ran hard aground on a low sandbank at the mouth of a river on the south shore. The officer of the watch, who made this mistake, showed great promptitude in rectifying it. The anchor was dropped, boats were lowered, the kedge was got out, and in half an hour we were afloat again. There was a large marsh close by, where wild ducks and

'Sunbeam' Aground.

geese abounded, and where wild swans were to be seen in considerable numbers.

I dare say you remember I told you that the poor little Cyprus owl tumbled into the steam-chest some days since. Fancy our astonishment and delight at finding him to-day in the screw tunnel, where he was discovered just as they were getting up steam, as black as a coal, as thin as a skeleton, and covered with grease. Kirkham was in the act of turning the screw lever, when his hand came in contact with the little feathery mass. One second more, the shaft would have revolved, and he would have been a dead owl. The marvel is that he did not die instantly when he fell, and how he got where he was and how he has passed the week must remain a mystery. At any rate, here he is, ravenously hungry, and as tame and pert as ever. And now I only hope that the poor bird will not be killed with over-kindness and stuffing.

The weather continuing calm, steam was at last got up. At 9.30 p.m. the 'Sunbeam' was safely anchored in Artaki Bay, in company with the fleet, consisting, at the present time, of the 'Alexandra,' 'Invincible,' 'Monarch,' 'Achilles,' 'Thunderer,' 'Salamis,' 'Helicon,' and 'Cygnet.' The boarding-officer from the 'Invincible' was soon alongside, and not long after him came our old friend, Captain Tryon, from the 'Monarch.' We had mutually much to hear and tell, and it was past midnight before we separated.

'Why, here's the Owl!'

CHAPTER IX.

ARTAKI BAY, ENGLISH FLEET, AND CONSTANTINOPLE.

He recks not, though proud glory's shout may be the knell of death;
The triumph won, without a sigh he yields his parting breath.
He's Britain's boast, and claims a toast! ' In peace, my boys, or war,
Here's to the brave upon the wave, the gallant English tar.'

Wednesday, November 27th.—The air was very cold early this morning, and, after the recent hot weather, made me feel far from well, but as the sun rose the temperature improved.

Soon after breakfast Admiral Hornby came on board for a long chat. I was glad to find that he seems to have been more favourably impressed with Cyprus than most people, particularly with the capabilities of the harbour of Famagousta, to which the first survey did not do justice. It appears from a careful examination, made subsequently, that at a comparatively small expense the mole might be repaired, and the harbour dredged and made capable of containing more ships than the whole area of the grand harbour at Malta, including Dockyard Creek and Bighi Bay. The fact of the sailors having, as compared with the soldiers, suffered so little from sickness, was doubtless owing to the greater amount of care with which they were looked after, though it is quite certain that they were much harder worked; and this, perhaps, was one reason why they kept in such good health. From almost everybody in the island we heard that much of the suffering was due to the attempt to effect an instantaneous occupation, instead of making a slower but surer arrangement; and this is, I fear, only too true. I believe it is a fact that the head of the commissariat department at Malta, having been asked how long it would take to ship and send off certain quantities of stores to Cyprus, replied that a week would be necessary, though the work might possibly be accomplished, after a fashion, in five days; and that the answer to this was, 'It *must* be done in two days.' The task was actually accomplished in three days, but in such a way that many of the most important stores could not be found again for three months after their arrival, and the poor soldiers consequently had to sleep on the bare ground in the most unhealthy spots, there being no means available for transporting them or their baggage to more healthy localities. Melancholy as this is from one point of view, it is encouraging from another; for it seems to imply that with proper precautions the island may, after all, not be so unsuited to ordinary European constitutions as it has hitherto appeared to be. There has been a talk of sending some of the poor wretched Turkish refugees there, furnishing them with sufficient money to purchase seeds and tools to cultivate the land, or, better still, with the articles themselves. It seems an excellent way of providing for the poor creatures, with their wives and their families. They are a steady, industrious, hard-working, but not a money-making people. The introduction of a large Mussulman population into the island would be a great thing, especially if it ever became a really permanent possession of England. If the Greek element should once prevail, it would be a perpetual thorn in our side, and the end would probably be that we should be requested to move out when we had done everything possible in the way of administrative reforms, the construction of harbours, railways, and improvements of all kinds, just as in the case of the Ionian Islands. The Turks, on the other hand, would suit the climate as well as the natives, and would be always contented with our rule. The matter has, however, dropped through somehow—I don't know why, except that I believe Sir Garnet was afraid of having too many women and children on the island, unable to support themselves.

Tom went back with Admiral Hornby to lunch, and to see his ship, the 'Alexandra,' which we had visited several times at Chatham, while she was in course of construction, but which we had not seen since the day she was launched.

After luncheon we all went for a slow ride on shore, the children on donkeys, we on horses. There was quite a collection of animals at the landing-place. The clever Greeks, as usual, have learned to supply the demand, and have scoured the surrounding country and villages in search of the means of affording the British officer his afternoon ride. The view from the top of the cliff near the little landing-place is very pretty, over the British fleet at anchor in Artaki Bay on one side, and the village of Artaki, on the shores of the Sea of Marmora, on the other. The whole country is fertile, and the town nestles among olive groves and vineyards.

The vintage is over now, but some of the grapes are still on the vines, and are excellent. The olive harvest is in full force, and we saw many a picturesque group as we wandered about. Up the old grey-foliaged trees boys and men beat the ripe black and the unripe green berries down on to the ground below, which was covered with mats, cloths, and carpets, to receive them. Brightly dressed women and girls, with large dark eyes and clear complexions, were busily engaged in picking up the berries and filling the panniers of the patient donkeys; and at each entrance to the town sat the tax-gatherers, with their wooden troughs, baskets, measures, and scales. Very sad and rather sulky some of the poor people looked, as a 'dime,' or tenth, of their freshly gathered produce was taken from them, and put into the great wooden troughs on the ground.

After riding some distance along the sea-shore, we returned through the town, which is rather large, with streets cleaner than might be expected. Some pretty Greek girls sat embroidering at the doors of their houses; but the streets were remarkable chiefly for a great many grog-shops, kept by the followers of the fleet, and for innumerable cocks and hens, as well as numbers of *lavender*-coloured cats. The best public-house in the place is called 'The Duke of Wellington,' and is kept by an Italian gentleman with quite a romantic history. He was a clerk in a bank at Liverpool, ran away with a pretty milliner, was dismissed from his employment, and left penniless. They have followed the fleet about, turning their hands to anything, and are making quite a little fortune. As soon as they have accumulated capital enough they intend to set up at home in a more comfortable and less vagrant way of life, though not a more respectable one, for everyone who knows them likes them and speaks well of them. They did a great stroke of business the other day, when all the other houses in the town were shut up by order of the Kaimakam for a fortnight, as a punishment for selling bad spirits, and they had the sole monopoly of the trade. The wife, who is really very nice-looking, has a pony and side-saddle, which she has kindly lent me for use during our stay here.

We dined with the admiral on board his flagship, the 'Alexandra,' where we met several friends, and enjoyed listening to a charming selection of music played by an excellent band. Afterwards we had much interesting conversation about the events that have taken place in these parts lately. The description of the passage of the fleet through the Dardanelles in a dense fog last February was specially exciting—everything ready for action, and no one knowing when the first shot might be fired. The three fruitless expeditions to the Dardanelles, when the fleet was recalled by telegram each time as soon as it arrived, were so disheartening, that the officers quite feared the effect on the seamen, who were inclined to think they were being made fools of.

Thursday, November 28th.—Another cold, bright morning. The children went for a donkey ride on shore. A crowd had assembled to see them, and it was a great business to get them off. The admiral's steward had procured one beautiful white donkey, with a scarlet velvet saddle-cloth. Of course both little ones wanted to ride him; but as he was said to be very spirited, he was ultimately given up to Emma, the nurse, in consideration of her greater strength and heavier weight. Mr. Bingham and the doctor went off shooting, Tom went with Captain Tryon to see some of the ships, whilst I remained on board and received visits from all the captains and officers of the ships whom we had known before. Yesterday most of them had been detained by a court-martial on board the 'Monarch.'

Admiral Hornby came to luncheon, and afterwards took us for a delightful ride to Cyzicus. We had sent on the horses and an interpreter some three miles along the shore, so that we landed at quite a different spot from yesterday's landing-place. There was some doubt about the safety of the road, and the Turkish governor had sent out two detachments of zaptiehs, to meet us at intervals; but there were so many English officers about, that I do not think we ran much risk. Some were shooting in parties of two and three, while many were on horseback, surveying and marking out the ground, and making the jumps for the steeple-chases on Monday next. There are to be athletic sports and two steeple-chases, one for the officers and one for the men. The road wound through brushwood and vineyards, olive groves and plantations of small trees, until at the end of about five miles we came to a river. This had to be crossed and recrossed many times in climbing up the valley to the ruins of the ancient amphitheatre of Cyzicus. The amphitheatre is beautifully situated, and is one of the very few where the ancients could have held really large *naumachiæ*, or mimic naval battles between galleys of war. The valley used to be dammed up, as the ruins of the vast dam still show, and these aquatic combats took place on the water that was allowed to accumulate. The scale on which they were organised may be imagined when one hears that in the time of Claudius no less than 19,000 persons took part in one of these representations, the combatants being gladiators, criminals, and slaves.

Cyzicus, in the days of Alexander, was one of the most

important cities of Asia Minor. It was besieged by Mithridates, but resisted his attack successfully, and prospered under the Roman rule. The ruins of the Roman amphitheatre, the theatre, the temple, and various other buildings may still be traced for miles among the vineyards and olive groves.

It was very cold, in fact a clear, bright, frosty evening, by the time we got on board again. The doctor and Mr. Bingham returned from their sporting expedition soon after, with an empty bag, not having even seen a bird. They had no dog, and did not know the right way to go. Some of the officers here manage to get very fair, though not wonderful, sport; but this cold weather and the bright nights will soon drive the woodcock down and make them abundant everywhere.

Lunch with a Turk.

Friday, November 29th.—A clear, cold, frosty morning, with a sharp wind and a bright sun—just the weather I hate, for it always makes me feel cross and ill. The doctor and Mr. Bingham went off to Cyzicus, where the latter wanted to make a sketch. They spent a very pleasant day. Mr. Bingham succeeded in making a pretty sketch, and they had luncheon with a civil old Turk, off bread and figs, by the side of a running stream full of watercresses. Mabelle went ashore to collect green stuff for the table, flowers

NAUMACHIA AT CYZICUS

being an impossibility. The arbutus bushes here cover the hills, and are a mass of scarlet and orange berries, not only well suited for table decoration, but sweet and pleasant to eat. There is also a good deal of terebinth and myrtle, besides other flowering shrubs.

Later on, I took the children ashore to a spot where their donkeys were to meet them, which turned out to be close to the corral into which all the cattle are driven as they arrive from the surrounding country; and, what was worse, just by the slaughter-house where they are killed for the use of the fleet. Another large white donkey had been sent for the children's use to-day, and as it had come from a place fifteen or sixteen miles distant, the poor beast arrived laden with prayer-carpets and saddle-cloths, embroidered on camels' hair at Kona and in the interior. They were very well done, and I bought several specimens. I also discovered on the beach part of a piece of statuary, a draped figure, evidently belonging to the finest period of Greek art. It had been brought from Cyzicus as ballast in a boat, and pitched ashore when room was required for the return cargo.

Captain Lindesay Brine, Commanders Holland and Hammick, Mr. Napier, and Mr. Daniel,[1] of the 'Thunderer,' came to luncheon. Captain Fitzroy would also have accepted our invitation, but was busily engaged with some torpedo experiments. He came afterwards and took us to see the explosion of some countermines, which were laid down by boats in a line for a distance of about a thousand yards, and buoyed with what looked like red barrels. After they had all exploded in succession, the channel was supposed to be clear for the passage of a large ship.

[1] Since unhappily killed by the explosion on board the 'Thunderer.'

Having announced our intention of being 'at home' this afternoon, we had quite a large reception of officers, in spite of the fact that a good many were engaged on shore in completing the arrangements for their athletic sports. I should think, from the programme, a copy of which I annex, that they will be great fun,[1] and I only wish we could stay for them.

ARTAKI BAY, 1878.

There will be Athletic Sports on Monday, December 2, the anniversary of the Princess Alexandra's birthday, when prizes will be given by Vice-Admiral Sir Geoffrey Phipps Hornby, K.C.B., Captain Robert O'B. FitzRoy, and the officers of H.M.S. 'Alexandra.' The officers and men of the Squadron are invited. The ground will be decided on later.

PROGRAMME.

Races			Prizes		
			First	Second	Third
1. Boys	100 yards		5/	2/6	—
2. Stokers	250 ,,		10/	5/	—
3. Petty and non-commissioned officers	250 ,,		15/	5/	2/6
4. Officers	100 ,,		One Prize		
5. All comers	440 ,,		10/	5/	—
6. Tug of war (15 a side)			2/6 per man		
7. Hurdle race (all comers)	120 ,,	8 flights	10/	5/	—
8. Hurdle race (officers)	120 ,,	8 ,,	One Prize		
9. Marines	250 ,,		10/	5/	—
10. Seamen	100 ,,		10/	5/	—
11. Subordinate officers	250 ,,		One Prize		
12. Long jump (all comers)			10/	5/	—
13. Tug of war (final)					
14. One mile (all comers)			15/	5/	2/6
15. One mile (officers)			Two Prizes		

16. '*Alexandra Stakes*' for any horse. To carry 12 stone—over a fair hunting country. Distance 1 to 2 miles. Two Prizes. Winner in addition takes stakes of five shillings each. Articles 32 and 33 of the Jockey Club Rules. To be ridden in colours.

The sports will commence at 11 a.m. All entries to be sent on board the Flagship not later than 6 p.m. on Saturday, November 30, addressed to the Committee.

N.B. The Committee reserve to themselves the right of any alteration in the Programme.

---

[1] We afterwards heard that nothing could have been more successful than the way the sports went off, and that everybody enjoyed them.

Saturday, November 30th.—We got under way and under sail, with a light wind, about 9.30 a.m. Soon the wind came ahead and fell very light, so that we had to tack pretty often and to use great care to avoid the island of Pergamos. Our progress was therefore slow, and we might easily have rowed back to lunch with Admiral Hornby, as he had asked us to do. Later on, he passed us in his steam-launch, going out to shoot.

The children had great excitement this morning in finding a tortoise on board. I suppose it must have come with the vegetables, as no one knows how it arrived.[1] Tortoises abound in these parts, and are frequently used for wedging up cargoes of barrels and cases on board ship. I believe that is the explanation of the barrow-loads of tortoises for sale to be seen in the London streets, more particularly in the neighbourhood of the docks.

'You are not a tennis ball!'

Ultimately we got up steam, passed into the Sea of Marmora, between the peninsula of Kizik or Artaki and the island of Liman, and held on towards Constantinople. The night was beautifully calm, and, to my great comfort, considerably warmer than it has been lately.

Sunday, December 1st.—The thick fog of the early morning cleared off just as we were passing Seraglio Point,

---

[1] Many weeks afterwards we heard from Captain Holland that one of the officers, after playing lawn tennis, had packed the tortoise up with the balls, for a bit of fun, in order to surprise the children.

and the atmosphere in the Golden Horn seemed to be particularly clear. I quite agree with those who declare that there is nothing finer in the world than the approach to Constantinople, with its numerous towers separated by noble sheets of water, with the low mountains of Asia Minor and the high chain of the real Olympus as a background to the scene. A man calling himself a pilot, but really only a runner to a grocer, boarded us; but as it soon appeared that he knew nothing about the anchorage, Tom took the matter into his own hands, and anchored, as in 1874, at Fundukli. During our six weeks' stay in that year we had made several moves, to the Black Sea, Therapia and back, Broussa and back, &c., and tried several anchorages, and had at last decided that we liked this position the best. We dropped anchor at about 8 a.m., and were quickly surrounded by boats containing Jews, touts, and dragomans, who had known us on the occasion of our previous visit. Our old servant George, however, who was delighted to see us again, took possession of us at once, and soon sent the rest away. We had scarcely finished breakfast before some old friends arrived to welcome us, and to insist on our going on shore to lunch and dine with them. We accordingly all landed together, and forthwith went to the Embassy. Finding there was no service there, we went on to the Memorial Church, a fine building, erected to the memory of the English who fell in the Crimean war.

Our host was good enough to lend me a horse; Tom, Mabelle, and Mr. Bingham had 'sowajees,' or street horses, and after luncheon we all went for a ride. The ' sowajees,' in fact, take the place of cabs in Constantinople, and are really the most suitable means of conveyance through the steep and badly paved streets. They may be regarded as supplementary to the caïque. They stand about for hire by casual passers-by, and are very quiet, yet with plenty of spirit. We had a capital ride across country, at a pretty good pace, as we wanted to make the most of our time. First we went to the Sweet Waters of Europe, crowded throughout the summer months with all the Turkish rank

Mosque of Sultan Achmed.

and fashion of Stamboul and Pera. Here the poor Sultan Abdul Aziz used to keep hundreds of peacocks; but they are now all gone, and the place has altogether a deserted, melancholy look, enhanced by the falling leaves and the changing autumnal tints. The day was as warm as summer, and roses, heliotropes, carnations, &c., were all ablow in the open air. Never has such a season been known in

Constantinople and its neighbourhood—summer, with its beauty, warmth, and fragrance, prolonging itself far into the winter months. From the Sweet Waters we rode across country nearly to the forest of Belgrade, where the Russians still have some encampments. Then we came back, through Turkish villages, to Mashleck, and by the Sultan's model farm to Yildiz Kiosk, where the present Sultan, Abdul Hamid, always resides. A new sultan never occupies the residence of his predecessor, and must always be building, or he would die immediately. Such, at least, is the Turkish belief. Hence the crowd of splendid palaces on the Bosphorus, most of them uninhabited, while the Sultan lives in a comparatively small building, outside the gates of which he scarcely ever shows himself, except to go to a mosque, not a hundred yards from the entrance, every Friday. Abdul Aziz lived at Dolmabagtcheh, Murad V. at Tcheragan,[1] and now Abdul Hamid at Yildiz Kiosk. On the way from Yildiz Kiosk we passed an entirely new street of buildings, like large shops. Some people say that they are dependencies of Dolmabagtcheh, others that they were designed to lay the spirit of the old dervish at Tcheragan. Anyhow, they have been put to a good use, for they serve as shelter to thousands of the poor refugees from Roumelia, Bulgaria, &c., who are supplied by the Government with one meal a day. This is better than nothing, and their condition is a happy one compared with what many of their compatriots are suffering, shipped away as they are by thousands in wretched unseaworthy vessels, to be landed at ports in districts governed by corrupt pashas, who, appropriating to themselves the money confided to them to

---

[1] See Note C (2), Appendix.

supply the refugees with food and seeds, tools and houses, leave the poor wretches to starve and die.

Monday, December 2nd.—A rainy morning. I was called at 5 a.m., and was busy all the morning with my letters. A telegram from Cyprus announces the death of poor Bonner. He was a great favourite with his shipmates, who are one and all greatly cut up by the sad tidings. Colonel White and Mr. and Mrs. Williamson appear to have been very kind to him, and to have fully carried out our wish that he should have every comfort and attention. The description of his last moments, and a letter dictated on his death-bed, full of gratitude to us and all on board, and praying for forgiveness for unintentional neglect of duty, were most touching. I have heard of some one making a collection of the records of the last words that fall from the lips of dying men. Poor Bonner's last words, as he raised himself for a moment and imitated the act of rowing, were, ' Pull all together, boys ;' then he fell back—dead. If the precept of that unconscious sermon could always be carried out, how much happier would many a ship's company, many a family, and many a nation too, be for it! Poor Kindred has received further particulars as to the death of his wife ; another man learns that he has lost a child ; so that altogether our news is of a melancholy character, and everybody on board feels more or less depressed by sad and sympathetic feeling for the suffering and sorrow of others. But I am thankful to say our own belongings at home appear to be well and happy.

About 11 a.m. we went ashore to the mosque of St. Sophia, described by Fergusson as the finest building in the world. I had seen it several times during our former visit, but to-day I thought it looked more striking than ever, with its magnificent span of roof, its huge vacant centre, its exquisite mosaics, and its perfect proportions. What a contrast must its grandeur have presented to the misery of its occupants, when, last winter, five thousand refugees— men, women, and children—in every stage of starvation and disease, were encamped under its vast roof! Lady Strangford was indeed a ministering angel there, and with her coadjutors did all in her power to alleviate their sufferings, and to administer to the best advantage the funds committed to her care. Everyone speaks well of her administrative talents, as well as of her kindness and devotion, although some may think that in certain respects her arrangements might have been more judicious.

From St. Sophia we drove to the Hippodrome and the mosque of Achmed, with its six beautiful minarets. We did not go inside this time, but contented ourselves with admiring the exterior. Then we looked at the Egyptian obelisk, the most perfect that exists, and very deeply cut, though not so large as Cleopatra's Needle. We also examined the twisted bronze column of the Three Serpents which supported, it is said, the golden tripod of the priestess of Apollo at Delphi, as well as the obelisk constructed of brick, which is not, however, very interesting. There are the Thousand and One Columns just below, in what was once an enormous reservoir, from which the city used to be supplied, though whence the water came nobody seems to know.

We lunched at the Hôtel de Byzance, a far more comfortable place than Misseri's old Hôtel d'Angleterre, now completely gone to ruin, I believe. Poor George was in a great way at our defection, feeling in honour bound to defend and recommend his old master's establishment. Afterwards we paddled about in the mud, looking at the shops, but were hardly rewarded for our trouble. Constantinople has lost much of its glitter and glory, but the mud, squalor, and misery remain, and are increased tenfold. At Lady Thomas's, where I called, I met the Princess Nazli, who was delighted to see me again, and with whom

Refugees at the Princess Nazli's door.

I had a most interesting conversation on the events which have happened since we were last here. She has sold almost everything she possessed to feed the sick and poor, and to maintain her own household. She has worked hard in the hospitals, and just outside her palace door, at Fundukli, where we land every day, there is a little square place literally filled with poor refugees, who find an imperfect shelter beneath improvised tents or under projecting doorways, and who are in great measure dependent upon her bounty. Now that the weather is turning cold and rainy, I do not know what they will do, for their numbers include many women and babies. I saw them drying their scanty bedding this morning, and cooking their miserable meal. The princess had been reading 'Tancred' lately, and was much interested in some of the utterances that the author had put into the mouth of the Emir, and which she regarded in the light of a prophecy, especially the following:

'"I'll tell you," said the Emir, springing from his divan, and flinging the tube of his nargilly to the other end of the tent : "the game is in our hands, if we have energy. There is a combination which would entirely change the whole face of the world, and bring back empire to the East. Though you are not the brother of the Queen of the English, you are nevertheless a great English prince, and the Queen will listen to what you say, especially if you talk to her as you talk to me, and say such fine things in such a beautiful voice. Nobody ever opened my mind like you. You will magnetise the Queen, as you have magnetised me. Go back to England and arrange this. You see, gloze it over as they may, one thing is clear : it is finished with England. There are three things which alone must destroy it. Primo, O'Connell appropriating to himself the revenues of half of her Majesty's dominions. Secondo, the cottons ; the world begins to get a little disgusted with those cottons ; naturally everybody prefers silk ; I am sure that the Lebanon in time could supply the whole world with silk, if it were properly administered. Thirdly, steam ; with this steam your great ships have become a respectable Noah's ark. The game is up. Louis-

Philippe can take Windsor Castle whenever he pleases, as you took Acre, with the wind in his teeth. It is all over, then. Now, see a *coup d'état* that saves all. You must perform the Portuguese scheme on a great scale; quit a petty and exhausted position for a vast and prolific empire. Let the Queen of the English collect a great fleet, let her stow away all her treasure, bullion, gold plate, and precious arms; be accompanied by all her court and chief people, and transfer the seat of her empire from London to Delhi. There she will find an immense empire ready made, a first-rate army, and a large revenue. In the meantime I will arrange with Mehemet Ali. He shall have Bagdad and Mesopotamia, and pour the Bedoueen cavalry into Persia. I will take care of Syria and Asia Minor. The only way to manage the Afghans is by Persia and by the Arabs. We will acknowledge the Empress of India as our suzerain, and secure for her the Levantine coast. If she like, she shall have Alexandria, as she now has Malta; it could be arranged. Your Queen is young; she has an *avenir*. Aberdeen and Sir Peel will never give her this advice; their habits are formed. They are too old, too *rusés*. But, you see, the greatest empire that ever existed; besides which she gets rid of the embarrassment of her Chambers! And quite practicable; for the only difficult part, the conquest of India, which baffled Alexander, is all done!"'

Perhaps you may like to know how the princess was dressed. She wore a rich dark ruby velvet *princesse* dress, with filigree buttons down the front, and trimmed with reversible ribbon, bows of velvet to match, and the palest blue satin. The wide pockets and sleeves were also trimmed with gold Smyrna lace. A charming bonnet, to match the costume, was partly hidden by a very fine muslin yashmak. She wore no jewels except diamond earrings and a wedding-ring.

We were to have had some friends to dine on board to-night, but it was blowing a hurricane and pouring with rain, so that only two of the expected guests appeared, and they had the greatest difficulty in reaching us. They are here to examine into, and to endeavour to regulate, the Sultan's finances—rather a difficult undertaking, I should imagine.

Tuesday, December 3rd.—This morning dawned beautifully bright and sunny after the rain, and we debated between an expedition up the Bosphorus and one to the bazaars; but the latter finally carried the day, and about 10 a.m. we started—all except Tom, who stayed on board to have a chat with Hobart Pasha.

The bazaars have very much gone off since 1874. The Russians, it is said, have bought up nearly everything, and what they left has now been sent up to Adrianople, in the hope that they may purchase even the wretched remains. There are a few exceptions, however. In the Bezistan, or place of arms, a central bazaar, where all sorts of things are sold by auction, great treasures may occasionally be picked up in these bad times. But one must be on the spot when they are first brought there for sale. Everybody in Turkey—certainly in Constantinople—from the highest to the lowest, appears to be more or less hard up. The slaves from the harems are constantly bringing valuable jewels and plate to be disposed of for a little money, not having themselves the least idea of their value. In this way we picked up some beautifully inlaid turquoise belts, carved ivory cups, old silver, and other things, by the merest chance. A friend of mine saw five splendid hoop gem rings, each worth nearly a hundred pounds, sold by a slave to a Jew for one pound each; and, on another occasion, some superb coffee-cup holders, a mass of rubies and diamonds, disposed of for next to nothing. These must have belonged to some of the princesses, or to ladies of the highest rank, for no one else would be likely to possess such things. The bazaars themselves are picturesque, dirty, and dark, as of old, but the gay part of the crowd has departed. No more gorgeous silk-lined carriages, drawn by white horses, and guarded and attended by eunuchs, slaves, and soldiers; no more less pretentious equipages, from which step ladies, attired in silk and satin and sparkling with jewels, their bright eyes imperfectly concealed by their yashmaks and feridjees. All these are past and gone, and all that can now be seen are a few poorly dressed ladies making their small household purchases.

From the bazaars we went to the Pigeon Mosque, and paid a few piastres to see the birds fed. It was a wonderful, and to the children a delightful, sight when they came flocking down in thousands and tens of thousands. The pigeons actually trampled one another on the ground, so thickly were they packed. At one moment their heads were all hidden, as they picked up the food from the ground, and nothing was visible except a mass of little grey tails, fluttering and wagging; then some slight noise would disturb them, and their soft innocent little heads would all be lifted up, causing a shimmer of emerald and ruby tints as their beautiful throats glittered in the sun. Then the children went off to see the dancing dervishes, while we proceeded to the Amber Bazaar, where the prices seem to have increased more, in proportion, than anywhere else. Such a necklace as was worth from ten to twenty pounds four years ago could not now be bought for less than sixty.

After lunching at the Hôtel de Byzance, and looking

Pigeons at the Mosque

through the latest newspapers, we again separated, Mabelle and I going to call on some old friends; but we found only Madame Ikbal Kiasim at home. She is like a very charming Frenchwoman, and it is difficult to believe that she was originally a Circassian slave. She still lives with her son, Izzet Bey, who is married to the Princess Azizieh, niece of the Viceroy of Egypt, and half-sister to the Princess Nazli.

We went through the usual hospitalities of sweetmeats and coffee, and had a long chat about people and things in general. She looks younger than ever, and was dressed in a beautiful blue Cashmere shawl, cut into a *princesse* robe, trimmed with lovely old lace, and ornamented with diamonds.

It was dark before I returned on board, where I found a great treat awaiting me in the shape of a large basket of delicious sweet-smelling flowers—roses, carnations, heliotropes, geraniums, &c.—a special luxury after having had so few lately.

During dinner we discussed with our guests the trip to Constantinople, and heard a good deal of news. It seems quite impossible to visit the lines of Tchekmedje, as General Baker Pasha has already been obliged to refuse an immense number of applications for permission to do so. Even Turkish officers are not admitted, except when on duty.

Wednesday, December 4th.—A very wet morning, of which we all took advantage to write our letters until luncheon time. Then, in macintoshes and thick boots, we paid another visit to the bazaars and bought some more treasures.

To-morrow will be the Kourban Bairam, and just as we landed the guns were firing from ships and citadels to announce to all Mussulmans the pleasing fact that at sunset to-night their fast would be at an end, and feasting and revelry might begin. It is a different feast from the other Bairam, and has evidently some connection with the Jewish Passover; and as every family makes it a point to sacrifice, if possible, a sheep or a lamb on the occasion, the city has been full of flocks of all colours, sizes, and breeds, for some days past. The most ridiculous sights are constantly to be witnessed of great big-horned rams being carried pick-a-back by a hamal, or Constantinople porter. Sometimes ten or a dozen of these men may be seen, each carrying a big sheep in a different attitude, some of the poor animals looking about them as if, like children, they really enjoyed the ride, while others, with their heads hanging mournfully down, appear fully to realise their position, and to have ceased to take an interest in any-

Pick-a-back.

thing. The hamals are said to carry anything, from a packet of needles to a grand piano, up and down the steep streets. Personally, I have never seen one man carry more than a *cottage* piano on his back at one time.

The weather cleared up, and the afternoon turned out very fine. I went to call on Sir Henry and Lady Layard, who seemed full of interest in our voyages and visit to Cyprus. Several people dropped in during my visit, all more or less *bouleversés* by the sudden change which has taken place in the ministry. Tom had been spending the afternoon with H.B.M.'s Consul-General, who painted a

dreary picture of the horrors of our intended journey to
Adrianople, dwelling on the misery of the accommodation to be met with, or rather of the want of it. But others
tell a different tale, and it is rather puzzling to decide which
is the correct version.

It was so rough in the evening that it was quite a
matter of difficulty to return on board the yacht. The
seas were breaking over the Princess Nazli's steps, and
Mabelle and I had to embark at a small harbour higher up
the Bosphorus.

Thursday, December 5th.—A friend kindly sent his
cavass on board at 7.30 a.m. to take us to see the Sultan
going in state to the mosque. He ought, according to immemorial custom, to have gone to the mosque of Achmet,
in Stamboul, but settled to go to Fundukli instead, and
preparations had accordingly been made. Finally he decided to go to a mosque near Dolmabagtcheh, close to the
palace of the same name. Our interpreter, George, had
not expected so early a start, and as we had to wait some
time for horses for ourselves and a carriage for the children, the Sultan was already in the mosque when we
arrived. A considerable crowd, but not nearly so numerous
as in 1874, was waiting to see him come out. We were
specially interested in watching various little broughams,
mostly hired, all seedy and shabby, and full of ladies
and children from the harems, this being one of their few
outings in the course of the year. The soldiers did not
look nearly so smart and clean as they used to do, the
uniforms being of various colours, some new, some ragged,
and some in middling condition, the best-looking being
placed in front. The men themselves were all well armed,

and looked well fed and in good condition. At last the playing of the bands and the cheers of the people announced the Sultan's approach. First came two lines of ministers—present and to come ; the past are as completely wiped out as writing from a slate by a wet sponge. Some of their faces struck me as being fine, without good expression ; and their gorgeous ill-fitting uniforms, a mass of gold and jewels, made one inclined to believe the story that all the tailors of Stamboul and Galata had been sitting up the whole of last night in order to complete them for the unexpected holders of power to-day. The Sultan himself was mounted on a pure white Arab steed, whose pedigree, I believe, dates back for many thousand years. Behind him were led five other splendid chargers. I never saw such horses anywhere in my life, and could not help desperately coveting a young iron-grey and a chestnut with four white legs. The Sultan did not sit his horse badly, but appeared to be in a great fright. He is thin, cadaverous, and melancholy-looking, with great sleepy eyes, rather inviting affection than commanding respect. It was an interesting pageant, but soon over, as the Sultan was in haste to get safely inside the gates of his palace, and to complete the ceremonies of the Bairam. We lingered about some time, looking at the crowd, the horses, and the soldiers, and thinking of the contrast between this and the gorgeous pageant of 1874, and then rode back to the quay and went on board to breakfast.

We had a busy morning on board. Several friends came to luncheon, and others arrived soon afterwards. Then came Princess Nazli, Princess Azizieh, and Madame Ikbal Kiasim, each with her suite, and by appointment, to see the yacht and to have tea with me. Their costumes were more Parisian and their yashmaks thinner than ever, and the slaves, having forsaken their beautiful Eastern costumes since we were here before, looked more fashionable, but not half so pretty. Some had visited the yacht previously,[1] some had not, but all were interested in seeing our curios from various parts of the world. They drank tea and coffee, smoked innumerable cigarettes, and stayed until nearly 6 p.m., though some of them were rather overcome by the motion of the vessel as it was anything but a smooth day. The last four years seem to have added

Princesses Embarking

greatly to the amount of liberty they enjoy. They are now much less particular about seeing gentlemen, and, once in the cabin, laughed and talked with the greatest freedom and enjoyment. Some of the princesses had been on board the 'Antelope' and the 'Alexandra,' to see some torpedo experiments, and were quite pleased to meet Admiral Hornby (who was on board the yacht) again. A few months ago Princess Nazli went to Egypt, and was not allowed to return to Constantinople. She put on a thick

[1] See Note C (1), Appendix.

yashmak and feridjee, borrowed a thousand francs, and travelled back with her English maid, who has now been with her for five years. As soon as they had made a clear start they threw off yashmak and feridjee and travelled as two English ladies, until they reached Constantinople, when they again assumed the Oriental costume. Within comparatively recent years such a proceeding on the part of a Turkish married lady would have been rewarded by the bowstring, the sack, and the Bosphorus. Not so very long ago six hundred women of the Imperial harem actually suffered this fate, their bodies being sunk in sacks in the Gulf of Ismid, close to where our fleet has been lying recently. In some of the numerous intrigues and conspiracies, these unfortunate women were supposed to have aided and abetted the usurper in his pretensions to the throne, and they were thus treated by the successor when his turn came shortly after. The ladies of the harem of the late Abdul Aziz have fared better than that, as many as possible having been sold, married, or otherwise provided for, whilst the rest were pensioned off. The once proud, vindictive, all-powerful Sultan Valideh, who really governed Turkey, and who, as I have mentioned before, washed her face, and refused to eat for twelve hours, because the Empress of the French condescended to give her the kiss of a sister sovereign, is now living in the strictest retirement at Kandili, with plenty of time to think over her extraordinary career. The present Sultan has four children, all by one acknowledged wife, but even she dares not sit down in the presence of the Sultan's mother, but remains meekly standing before her when lady visitors are there. Sultan Abdul Hamid has always been a nervous man, with the constitutional family dread of plots, conspiracies, and assassinations. Since the horrible affair at Tcheragan he has never been himself, and lives in a state of perpetual dread. The man who now possesses the most influence in Turkey is, we are told, the Cafidje, or maker and hander of the Imperial cups of coffee. The Sultan trusts and believes in him more than in anybody else. He is always afraid of some attempt being made to restore poor Murad,[1] who is said to be quite mad, and whom he has had confined in a kiosk in his own park, with high railings all round, so that nobody can by any possibility gain access to him.

The present Sultan appears to be much liked by all

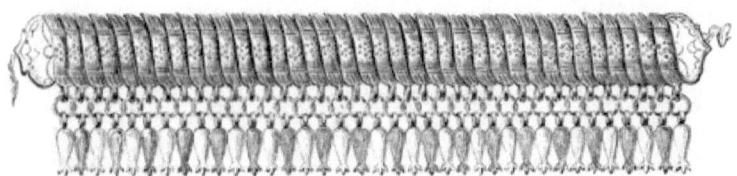

Turkish Bracelet.

who come in personal contact with him, and to have an earnest desire to do what is right, though he is easily influenced by others. Sir Henry and Lady Layard are never tired of praising him, and Hobart Pasha, Sir Collingwood Dickson, and many others who have occasion to see him continually, seem to be equally fascinated. It was the Sultan himself who suggested sending for Baker Pasha to carry out the idea of the lines which are now being so ably executed under his active superintendence. He dines

---

[1] This is the young man to whom I alluded, in the account of my previous visit, as the eldest nephew of Abdul Aziz (p. 71). He succeeded to the throne on his uncle's deposition, but, as is well known, was himself deposed a few weeks afterwards, in favour of his next younger brother, the present Sultan.

in European fashion every day, and in all his ways is much more civilised than his predecessors. He is very fond of pets of all kinds; and when he gave Lady Layard a small white cockatoo the other day, it arrived at the Embassy in great state in a two-oared caïque, with a full-uniformed and medaled aide-de-camp in attendance, to the intense interest of the people of Therapia.

Before the princesses left, many other visitors arrived, and I was nearly tired out when the last departed. Tom, in the meantime, had been to see what he described to me as 'one of the most terrible scenes of human misery that can be imagined.' The 'Asia,' a ship of 900 tons burden, was laden with two thousand refugees—men, women, and children—all bound for Chanak, Smyrna, Beyrout, and Larnaka. It was impossible to move on either of the decks without treading on some one. The poor creatures had no covering, no food, no room to move, and the ship itself was without ballast. The captain seemed half an idiot; the crew could understand no language but their own, which was unintelligible to everybody else. The first and second mates put their heads together and determined to lay the case before the British consul; so the 'Asia' has been detained for a day or two, the result of which will, I hope, be some mitigation in the sufferings of her passengers. Several died last night, and Tom said he felt sure many more deaths must shortly follow.

The expedition to Tchekmedje, which we had some faint hope of being able to make, seems to be an impossibility; but we were told that every facility would be granted us by the minister of war for a visit to the other lines at San Stefano. I fear, however, we shall not have time to avail ourselves of the opportunity if we go to Adrianople.

After dinner we went to the Austrian ambassador's, where we met all the diplomatic circle and a good many Turks, and the evening ended with a pleasant little dance.

Bulgarian Earring.

CHAPTER X.

ADRIANOPLE.

Famine is in thy cheeks,
Need and oppression starveth in thine eyes,
Contempt and beggary hangs upon thy back ;
The world is not thy friend, nor the world's law.

Friday, December 6th.—We were called at 4.30 a.m. The elements certainly seemed to have conspired against our expedition to Adrianople, for the wind howled, and the rain came down not in torrents but in sheets. However, all arrangements had been made, so we determined to start—Mr. Bingham, Mabelle, and I ; for Tom could not get away, having much business to attend to and much writing to do. George was late in coming off, and we nearly missed the train, having to row right across the harbour to Stamboul, and then to wade through a sea of mud, followed by a line of porters, to the station. There we found that there was some mistake about the saloon carriage ; but we managed to make ourselves comfortable in a first-class carriage, in company with a gentlemanly Turk who spoke English, and a French lady who appeared to be in the habit of making frequent journeys between Adrianople and Constantinople, and consequently knew all the places on the road. We passed slowly through the town of Stamboul and its old walls, on to San Stefano, where one set of lines branches off to Tchekmedje.

Every station was crowded with Turkish soldiers, and was surrounded by a large encampment and many stores awaiting transport. The line meandered along near the edge of the sea and over salt marshes nearly all the way, by Baksais and Cattaldza. Some of the little gulfs were quite black with wild fowl and wild geese, which rose from the reeds and marshes in whirring flocks. At Tchorlou the train stopped to allow the passengers to dine. Sometimes there is not enough food for everybody, and as we had been warned of this we brought our own provisions and consumed them *en route*. This gave us time to walk about and see what there was to be seen, which was not much. The rain still continued to pour down, as if it would never stop. A long dreary road stretched away from the station to a distant town, while in different directions were several camps, hundreds of soldiers, and tons and tons of stores. It was here that, during the war, the Stafford House Committee did so much good by visiting the trains of wounded and sick soldiers, binding up their wounds, and giving them soup, wine, and water. What angels of mercy they must have appeared to the poor suffering wretches, who had been jolted and knocked about for days, untended and uncared for! There are no railway officials except the station-masters and those attached to the train: all the porters' work is done by soldiers, and they appear to perform their task well and civilly, though the stations are filthy beyond description. The carriages themselves look clean and comfortable, and run smoothly, so that the journey, though slow and monotonous, is not really fatiguing. The contract for making the line from Constantinople was taken at so much a mile, and its execution was not carefully looked after. The contractor consequently wandered about all round the country, in order to be paid for as many miles as possible, as well as to avoid bridges, viaducts, cuttings, earthworks, tunnels, or other expensive labour. In this way he contrived to add over fifty miles to the distance, besides making a very bad line, which is washed away whenever there is a heavy rainfall. It was a French *Christian* who did this for a Turkish *Mohammedan!*

We passed a great many villages that had been sacked, burnt, and destroyed by the Russians. At Lilli Bourgas we left the Turkish camps and soldiers behind, and passed through the Russian lines. The Russians seemed to take to porters' work just as handily as the Turks, only that they were a little more stolid and stupid. From this point it was quite dark, and I think we all slept till we reached Adrianople, soon after 9 p.m., where a friend kindly met us at the station. While we were talking to him at one door, a Russian soldier crept in at the other and tried to steal one of our bags. Luckily James, our new servant, saw him, and made him drop it, but the man escaped.

All round the station was a sea of mud; but as our friend had thoughtfully brought his carriage, we accomplished the few hundred yards' journey to the hotel in comfort. It was not a very inviting-looking place at the first glance. There were two large rooms full of Russians eating and drinking, a dirty stone hall, a staircase leading to a large square wooden upper hall full of Russian soldiers (officers' servants) making tea and smoking. Round it were about twenty little rooms, with thick walls and strongly barred doors, each containing a bed, washstand, and chair, and all scrupulously clean, well carpeted, and curtained. One bedroom had been turned into a sitting-room for us, and the table was prepared for dinner quite nicely.

From our windows we could see nothing but Russian soldiers, tents, and huts. All night long there was a constant rumble of forage, ammunition, and provision carts, fetching stores from the station. They say they have enough here for six or seven years—which does not look much like an immediate evacuation.

Saturday, December 7th.—A lovely morning after the rain. Even the poor street dogs, which appear to be more abundant than ever here, wagged their apologies for tails, shook their starved bodies, and licked one another in congratulation at once more seeing the sun shine.

We breakfasted at 8.30 a.m., and were ready for the carriage at 10 a.m. But it did not appear, and at last James got us a wretched little country vehicle, called a telika, very high, without springs, and with a sort of tilted roof, like that of a wagon, over all. There was one high step about two feet from the ground and two openings for doors, through which one was obliged to precipitate oneself head foremost on to the floor, trusting to be able to get right again when once fairly inside. There was no room to sit upright, and, with noses and knees touching, we were jolted over the most awful roads, sometimes with one wheel up in the air and the other in a deep hole, always in a sea of mud, which came over the steps. There were crowds of people, chiefly soldiers, besides carts and horses, all the way. We crossed the Maritza and Tunja rivers—two out of the three that meet here—by two fine bridges, and on reaching the town, which is about three miles from the station, we dismissed our uncomfortable cart-like conveyance, and procured a better carriage before proceeding to our friend's house, which was fitted up half in Oriental, half in European style, but very comfortably. Here we found his wife, son, and daughter, all waiting and wondering what had become of us, and they were greatly annoyed when they heard of the failure of the carriage.

First we drove to the bazaar Ali Pasha, the most celebrated and the most Eastern-looking of all Oriental bazaars. It is 300 feet long, very lofty, and has rows of little shops on the ground floor, occupied by the regular shopkeepers. Besides these there were merchants from Persia, selling turquoises, carpets, and embroidered shawls; merchants from the Balkans, offering carpets, curtains, and embroideries; merchants from all sorts of places, wandering about to sell their wares. There were a few little stalls for the sale of French jewellery and watches, which looked rather incongruous. The crowd was a motley one, and I could have stayed all day watching it, but there was much more to see.

After leaving the bazaar, we had a most shaky drive through the streets of the town, past several mosques, till we came to a beautiful forest, once the favourite resort of the people of Adrianople, and adorned with little *cafés* and kiosks, now all destroyed by the Russians. At the end of the principal walk is a square tower, partly in ruins, and a bridge, crossing which we arrived at the gate of the Old Seraglio, or Eske Serai, which, until last year, was one of the most interesting places in Turkey. It was built in the zenith of the Ottoman empire, and is the only establishment of its kind remaining. Unfortunately, on January 17,

ADRIANOPLE (BRIDGE OVER THE TUNJA)

1878, it was accidentally destroyed by the Turks, in their attempt to blow up some ammunition stored close by, to prevent its falling into the hands of the Bulgarians. The Old Seraglio tower is now a heap of ruins, and has only the outer staircase and the marble doorway remaining.

The Sultan Valideh's bath has been utterly destroyed; the Sublime Porte remains standing, but the little pavilion close by, where the Sultan used to receive all important visitors, has been quite destroyed internally, though a few fragments remain to show how exquisite the decorations must have been.

We wandered about and picked up some broken tiles, bits of charming colour, wonderful light and dark blues and greens. In driving back there is a good view of the city, which stands well, and with its splendid mosques and minarets presents a striking *coup d'œil*. Farther on are the remains of a building originally a large barrack, and afterwards occupied as a hospital by the Stafford House Committee, but since blown up and destroyed by the Bulgarians. Inside the walls many excellent large Turkish tents were pitched, and used as hospital tents by the Russians. On our way back we saw Lady Strangford's hospital. Both of these excellent institutions did immense good in the time of need.

Bulgarian Earring.

The mosque of Selim II., to which we were next taken, is the finest in the world, the span of the dome being even larger than that of St. Sophia, though it lacks its rich mosaics. To make up for this, however, it possesses beautiful Persian tiles, texts of the Koran printed on dark blue or light blue ground in the very best style of Eastern writing, with Persian borderings of exquisite design. In the centre there is a curious tulip carved in stone, the only ornament on every one of the numerous columns, and one specially stipulated for by the original owner of the land as his sole remuneration when he parted with his favourite tulip garden to the then Caliph, as the site for the future mosque.

As it was the feast of Kourban Bairam, amusements of every kind were going on in the courtyard of the mosque; merry-go-rounds, swings, and all sorts of diversions; sellers of sweetmeats, eatables, and drinkables abounded; the people were gaily dressed, and it seemed as bright and happy a crowd as anyone could wish to see. Big Russian soldiers in uniform were swinging alongside tiny Turkish betrousered infants. Outside, sitting patiently in rows against the walls or shop-fronts, were crowds of refugees waiting for their miserable little daily doles of food. Even the children seemed too gentle and patient to cry and complain, but sat quiet, stolid, and indifferent. I have particularly noticed how well the various nationalities appear to get along together in the crowded, narrow, filthy streets. There are representatives of every nation under the sun here, and crowds of Russian soldiers; and yet, when most pressed for room, I have observed how patient and gentle they all seemed, even in pushing their way past the Turkish women or children, who were making their little purchases quite alone and unprotected. There are

Circassians, Cossacks, Finns, and, in fact, soldiers from every part of the vast Muscovite empire. Some are fine, handsome, intelligent-looking men, while others appear fitted to hold a position in the social scale but little higher than that of the inhabitants of Tierra del Fuego. All looked more or less stolid and indifferent.

Having brought our sight-seeing to an end, we went to call on the consul, whose acquaintance we had made in Constantinople in 1874. We found him engaged in an earnest consultation with the Austrian, French, and other consuls, as to an occurrence which appeared likely at the time to lead to somewhat serious consequences. It seemed that an Englishman, named Stock, had been buying up some old cartridges with the object of melting down the lead they contained. Having separated the bullets from the powder, he had collected the latter, and had conveyed it by the train, a proceeding which was contrary to the regulations enforced by the Russian authorities. They had found this out, had arrested him, and had kept him a close prisoner for two or three days. A rumour of the affair having reached his ears, the consul sent to enquire into the facts of the case, and offered to take charge of the prisoner pending further investigations. Mr. Stock was accordingly sent to the consulate; but the next morning the Russians changed their minds, for they made a demand that he should be re-delivered to them, and on the refusal of the consul to comply with their request they despatched some soldiers to take him by force. The consul fastened his door; the soldiers tried to force it open with their shoulders, and, failing in this attempt, they broke their way in with a hatchet, and carried off Mr. Stock. An hour later he was sent back, with an apology from the Russian commandant, but the violation of British territory (*i.e.* the consulate) was considered *une affaire très-grave* by all the consuls.[1] Under these circumstances, it may be imagined that we found some amount of excitement prevailing. Mr. Calvert, the consul, seemed to consider our visit rather opportune, as he was desirous of sending some important despatches to Constantinople, which he requested us to take charge of in order to ensure their safe arrival. The Russians exercise a strict supervision over all letters and telegrams sent to and from Adrianople. Even our own message from Constantinople, although it only referred to the rooms we required, had been detained for a couple of days.

After leaving the consulate, we drove quickly back through the suburb of Tchergatasch, where many of the diplomats and rich people of Adrianople live, though all have a summer residence. After this came dinner, and then 'early to bed.' It proved a noisy night, for artillery and troops were moving constantly, nobody knows why or where. There has been a great exodus from Adrianople of Russian troops during the last few days.

It was impossible to sleep, and I lay and looked out of the window in the moonlight, and pictured to myself all the scenes of misery that had taken place at the station close by. Men, women, and children used to sit there for days in long lines extending nearly a mile on either side of the station, waiting for a passage by one of the few passing trains, clinging frantically to steps and buffers when carriages

---

[1] This transaction attracted a good deal of attention in England at the time, and was referred to in all the papers.

and cattle-trucks were full, only to be dragged away and left behind, or thrown off and killed at the first curve or sudden jerk. Carts went round every morning to carry a little coarse food, and to bring away the dead. One morning, after a severe frost and heavy snow, six cartloads of little children were carried away from among the crowds of refugees.

Sunday, December 8th.—We were called at 4 a.m., and found it very cold and dark. After a cup of hot coffee we went to the station, which was crowded with Russian soldiers. The country near Adrianople, which we had before passed in the dark, is much more interesting than that near Constantinople, which consists of nothing but bare marsh and moor land, with a few scattered villages, now, alas! burnt and abandoned. The train was very long, and full of Russian soldiers. At every station there were crowds of refugees waiting in the hope of obtaining a passage. At Koulleli-Bourgas, where we crossed a wide river, there is a branch line running up into the hills to Durcos, in the Balkans, through a country that looked quite pretty.

At Sidler-Tchiflik three men sprang on to the train just as it was starting, and clung to the carriage-doors. The guard saw them, but dared not push them off for fear of killing them, yet could not venture to stop the train on account of the delay this would have caused. He therefore beckoned to the men to creep slowly along the side of the carriages after him. It was a terrible walk, and made my blood run cold to see it. The poor men were wet, benumbed, and awkward. Each had a bundle on his shoulder—one on a stick, one on a gun, one on a sword. As they crept slowly along, hanging on for their lives, first one bundle, then another, dropped off, till at last, after an agony of suspense, they were safely landed in a cattle-truck, having lost the very little all that they possessed. A similar scene with but little variation was repeated several times in the course of our journey. At Tchorlou, where we stopped three-quarters of an hour, the other passengers seemed to be enjoying a very good lunch. In two adjoining first-class compartments, sitting alone in solitary grandeur, were a

Refugees on the Train.

Russian and a Turkish general officer, each on his way to inspect the troops under his command.

Constantinople was reached about 7 p.m., and we were met at the station by servants and sailors, who took our luggage straight on board. We had to go up to Pera to deliver our letters, as promised, at the Embassy and Mr. Whittaker's. At the latter place we found that Tom was dining, and as soon as our friends heard we were at the door, they insisted on our going in, dirty and dishevelled as we felt after our long tiring journey, and spending the rest of the evening with them, instead of carrying out our original intention of proceeding direct to the yacht. When once we had settled down and got over the first embarrassment of so sudden and unexpected an arrival, we spent a very pleasant evening in the company of many interesting people, including the Servian and Swiss ministers, both clever men; Izzet Bey, the husband of the Princess Azizieh, Major A., one of the Bulgarian commissioners; and Djamil Pasha, who was governor of Adrianople at the time of the evacuation in January. We naturally felt the greatest interest in hearing many of the details of the latter event from one who had taken so prominent a part therein, particularly as we had just returned from the scene of the occurrences described. One gentleman who had been expected to be present that evening (Raouf Pasha) had excused himself at the last moment on the plea of illness. We afterwards heard that the real cause of his absence was the fact that he had been arrested by order of the Sultan, and had received instructions that he was not to leave his house previous to his departure for Tripoli. Many other arrests were made the same evening, the unfortunate pashas being sent off into exile without the slightest warning.

Our host was for many years the editor of the 'Levant Herald,' and was liked and respected by all in Constantinople, both Europeans and Turks. Unfortunately he offended the government of the country by some remarks in his paper, and the result was that he had to fly for his life, only escaping with great difficulty. He waited until the affair had blown over, and then returned to Constantinople, where he now edits his paper again, though under another title.

We did not reach the yacht until nearly midnight, when we were all glad to get to bed.

Earrings and Necklet in one.

CHAPTER XI.

CONSTANTINOPLE AGAIN, GALLIPOLI, SYRA, AND MILO.

The more a man denies himself, the more he shall obtain from God.

Monday, December 9th.—We had an appointment at 8.30 a.m. with the new Grand Vizier, Khaireddin Pasha, and accordingly presented ourselves punctually at the palace on one side of the gate of Dolmabagtcheh. His suite were waiting to receive us, and beautiful Turkey carpets had been laid across the muddy garden to the gateway. Inside the building a blazing fire burned in a common cheap grate, set in a lovely alabaster mantelpiece. The silk divans were superbly embroidered, and the carpets were all hand-made. Cigarettes in jewelled holders were handed round, as well as coffee in cups with stands thickly encrusted with large diamonds, which must have been worth many hundreds of pounds. We waited and waited, but the great man did not come; so, in spite of the entreaties of his suite, we took our departure and returned to the yacht to breakfast. About midday we received a message expressing the Vizier's deep regret at not having kept his appointment, and explaining that the Sultan had sent for him at twelve last night, having been frightened by the rumour of a plot, and had never allowed him to leave him or even to lie down until past noon to-day. The plot appears to have had no existence except on paper, and is probably an invention of the Sultan's doctor and lawyer, to terrify him, and cause him to do something or other which they wish.

Among other fancies the Sultan has lately acquired a sudden taste for farming, and he now wants to find a bailiff who will go partners with him in a certain number of acres: he will not hear of paying him as a servant. A strange and sensible idea for a Sultan with very extravagant ideas on most other points!

To-day we have quite an *embarras* of dinner invitations.

Bulgarian Child's Bracelet.

But we have been engaged for some time past to dine with some old friends, to meet all the ambassadors. Tom has been busy all day on board, but the children went to see the mosques, and the others to look round the bazaars. Mabelle and I have devoted our time to paying farewell visits, for we are to depart to-morrow if fine. One or two of our former intimate friends denied themselves to us, as they now do to everyone, from a feeling of dislike that their altered circumstances should be seen. But how little do they understand the admiration with which one would regard rooms emptied of their splendid ornaments, and the absence of jewels and precious things, when one knows that they have been sold to minister to the relief of the sick and wounded in this dreadful war! The self-sacrifice of the Turkish ladies of the highest rank has been great, and is worthy of all praise and honour, but they are still a little shy and sore about their troubles. Some of them were at home, but they have reduced their establishments considerably, and have fewer servants, carriages, and horses than before. The beautiful ruby and diamond coffee-cups are gone, but their late owners are as charming as ever. One never hears a word of complaint uttered.

Mabelle and I got on board rather late to luncheon, and soon afterwards friends arrived from the bazaars. From that time we had a continuous stream of visitors. When they were gone I went on shore, to have tea with Lady Layard, and met many interesting people. The evening was spent at a delightful dinner party, and it was very late before we got on board the yacht.

Tuesday, December 10*th.*—Still a foul wind and bad weather, which looks as if it may last for a week. Colonel Allen and Colonel Baker, V.C., came to breakfast, and to have a look at the yacht. They told us much that was interesting about the recent campaign, which they both went through until Colonel Baker was taken prisoner by the Russians. He referred in grateful terms to Lady Strangford, who must have been the means of saving his life; and both of them spoke most highly of her self-sacrificing conduct and economical administration of the funds entrusted to her care. The fortification of the lines seems to have proved a wonderful success. All agree that they are perfectly impregnable, being built on rising slopes commanding a vast extent of land, with a river in front, and so constructed that if one work should be taken nine others can fire into it. The authorities are very particular in refusing permission to anybody to visit them. At the same time there is not the slightest doubt that either a Russian disguised as a Turk, or a Turk bought by the Russians, has got it all at his fingers' ends, and that the Russians know just as much about the fortifications as Baker Pasha himself.

After breakfast we started off in caïques across the Golden Horn to look at the bazaars, but did not find much to reward our exertions. It was very rough coming back, and there was some delay about the boat. There seemed to be quite a flotilla of boats alongside, and when we reached the yacht in our modest caïque, we found the Austrian and German ambassadors and their suites were there before us. Musurus Pasha and many others also arrived soon after. Later on I went to call on a friend, and heard more about this pretended plot to frighten the Sultan; but it all seemed trivial enough. Tom met me at the Embassy, where we dined, and saw more of the building than we had hitherto done, as it was lighted up in order that we might see some beautiful copies of old pictures, some choice cabinets, and rare china in the drawing-room. Originally it must have been the most barracklike-looking building imaginable, though the walls and staircase are lined with the choicest marbles, and the present occupants must have had great difficulties to contend with before the house could be made to look as homelike and pretty as it does now. We heard a great deal about the poor refugees and their patient uncomplaining conduct during last winter.

They came in by thousands, but took thankfully what was given them, helped the women and children first, and never squabbled among themselves, perishing with hunger as they were. It must have been heart-breaking work, for, give what you would and do what you could, it was all a mere drop in the ocean. Mrs. Hanson takes a great interest in the refugees, and has quite a number of families close to her at Kandili. She feeds and clothes them, and gives them stuff and silks to embroider, of which they make Turkish towels, which are sold at from 2s. to 12s. each. At Therapia, the other day, Sir Henry Layard had given some of the men work in road-mending, which they were to do in return for their food. Colonel Blunt was riding out one day, when one of their number came and spoke to him, and remarked that on a previous occasion, when on a journey through the country, he had entertained him at his house. Colonel Blunt perfectly recollected the circumstance, and the fact that he had been the owner of a beautiful house and garden and estate, and was the kaimakam, or head man of the district—quite a grand personage. Here he was now mending roads, and grateful for a little rice and flour. Fancy an English deputy-lieutenant, or even a borough mayor, placed in the same situation! And the kaimakam has a much larger tract of country under his control than either of those functionaries.

Wednesday, December 11*th.*—A sudden change of wind and rise of the barometer caused Tom to determine to start without delay. Such a bustle ensued as can only be imagined by those who have gone through a similar ordeal. Everybody here had foretold that the bad weather would last at least another week, and we had therefore made up our minds to remain for that period. Bills had now to be paid, provisions to be got on board, and letters to be sent ashore to put off various engagements.

Several friends, hearing of our sudden decision to start, came off to say good-bye. They told us all the latest *on dits*—amongst others, that it had just been decided that the British Government were to retain Cyprus in perpetuity, and that they would probably also occupy some spot on the mainland, Alexandretta, in the Gulf of Scanderoon, being the most likely place. I believe it would be frightfully unhealthy, though glorious for a sportsman. I have heard that the game-book of a naval officer stationed at Bayas, near Alexandretta, contained the record of no less than two thousand head of game of every sort, killed between the months of November and April; and this without any expense, except for powder and shot.

Mabelle and Phillips, who had been ashore to do the last commissions, came on board about 11.30 a.m. We had got under sail previously, and were standing off towards Skutari. The blue-peter had been hoisted, and soon the last farewells were said, and we were gliding away, all too quickly, past the Golden Horn, the Seraglio Point, and old Stamboul, with its numberless minarets and domes. Hundreds of ships had taken advantage of the fair breeze to start at the same time, and we were all constantly passing and repassing one another, as winds and currents dropped and changed. At one time we were sailing abreast of eight brigs, and for some few minutes no one of the number gained much on his neighbour. The afternoon was warm and damp, with rain, instead of the bitter cold and snow from the Black Sea that had been prophesied to us. The breeze ceased, and the wind gradually veered round by the west to the south. After dinner we resumed our long interrupted games of whist. During the night the wind came strong ahead, and then fell to a calm.

Thursday, December 12*th.*—A calm morning, steam up at 6 a.m. Strong head wind, increasing to a smart gale. Tom decided to take shelter at Lampsaki or Gallipoli, and

Children's Nursery.

finally chose the latter place, as affording the best protection. We had great difficulty, first to get there, and then to pick up an anchorage. We found a spot at last, let go an anchor with 80 fathoms of chain, another with 60 fathoms, and continued steaming up to them till the weather moderated late in the afternoon. The waves ran tremendously high, breaking right over some of the houses in the town. While we were at luncheon, the boarding officer from the 'Flamingo' came alongside in a big steam launch, and offered to take us ashore. We gladly availed ourselves of the opportunity, children and all: it would have been quite impossible for our own boats to reach the shore. We always make a point of getting a run ashore whenever we can, as it makes an enormous difference in the apparent length of the passage, especially when we are likely to have bad weather, and to be constantly obliged to put back, as I fear is only too probable at this time of the year. We were well covered up under the hood, or we should have been drenched, for the launch was very fast, and went through rather than over the waves. Having got within shelter of the little fort, we were able to land in comfort. Phillips went with the captain's steward to try and get fresh provisions, while the rest of us started on a shopping and bargaining expedition. There was not much to buy, but we succeeded in getting some rahatlakoum and some quaint old silver, but we bargained too long for some curious antique cartouche boxes, and lost them. Going off in the steam launch was a far worse job than landing had been, but we managed it pretty well and kept tolerably dry. Just about dusk the 'Téméraire' came steaming in. She had been up in Artaki Bay, practising steam tactics in the Sea of Marmora with the rest of the fleet. We had taken up almost the only available berth, and it was wonderful to see how well with her twin screws she came close round us, turned in her own length, then went back again and turned round once more, like a dog making itself a comfortable bed, till her captain found a place he liked.

Some of the officers dined with us in the evening, and we heard a good deal about the Russians, of whose mode of proceeding they did not seem in every case to have formed a very favourable opinion. A few days ago a Russian officer was invited to breakfast on board an English man-of-war at Bourgas. When he arrived he professed not to understand a word of English, and listened to the conversation that was going on with stolid indifference. Presently the British Vice-Consul came on board, when it transpired that the Russian spoke English much better than French, his mother having been an Englishwoman. A somewhat similar incident had occurred on board another of our ships, where one of the visitors had appeared to be greatly interested in the case of a certain Russian officer who had been taken prisoner by the Turks, and as to whose treatment some complaint had been made. It was afterwards discovered that the visitor was no other than the prisoner himself, who had recently been released on parole by the Turks.

Friday, December 13*th.*—I was awake at 6 a.m. As the wind was much lighter and the glass rather higher, Tom determined to start at once, and would not even let Phillips go ashore, to pick up the provisions he had ordered, though after all we did not start until 8 a.m. Having sent a large mail on board the 'Téméraire' for postage, and received some more papers, we exchanged salutes, and went on our way under steam down the narrow strait of the Dardanelles. As we had to stay at Chanak-Kalesi to leave our firman, some of the party went on shore. Going to the consul's house, we saw a long train of camels which had just come into the town, and went into the stable to examine them. They were handsomer than any of the camels one sees in Africa, their bodies were covered with nice curly woolly hair, and they had not so many unsightly galls and bruises and bare patches.

It was a lovely day, very hot, with a bright sun and light south-westerly wind, rapidly increasing as we got into the open sea, the glass at the same time falling. We made the light on Cape Sigri about 9 p.m., and soon began to roll and pitch in a most unpleasant manner. I went to bed early, but got up about midnight, and we all passed a miserable night. No one on board had ever known so stiff a gale before, except Tom and those who were with him when he crossed the Atlantic in the 'Eothen,' and was caught in a cyclone. It had been smooth till we were well past Cape Sigri, the servants had gone to bed without arranging for a rough night, and things were therefore tumbling about, and the stewards had to be called to put them straight. Phillips, the head steward, who is a man of a decidedly nervous temperament, and who always sleeps half-dressed, ready to jump up at a moment's notice, in case anything alarming should happen in the night, appeared promptly. He looked somewhat scared, and presented the peculiarly dishevelled appearance of a person who has been to bed in his clothes. Upon some reference being made to this point, he remarked that there were too many rocks ahead for him to feel justified in taking his clothes off. The scene in the nursery was one of unparalleled confusion, as all in that department had retired to bed at 8 p.m., when the sea was as smooth as glass. No lee-boards had been put up, and many catastrophes happened in consequence. Fortunately both maids and children took it in a cheery way, and, in spite of their being very sick sometimes, I heard much more laughing than crying proceeding from their part of the vessel. On deck it was almost impossible to speak or even to breathe, the wind was so strong: the clouds looked as though chasing each other wildly through the sky. Providentially it was a clear bright night, or our danger would have been great, surrounded as we were by islands, without any lights on them, in the midst of this raging sea and roaring wind. We hove-to for some time, but when we tried to go round, the 'Sunbeam' declined to obey her helm, and at last we had to wear instead of tacking. The rigging and stays that support the masts had got loose, from much wear and tear, and the masts were aback. We had very little coal or water on board, so that in a really heavy sea the vessel had scarcely sufficient hold of the water for her rudder. At last we rounded and ran before the gale, but when we got under the island of Mitylene the wind had followed us round, and it proved no shelter. Tom was afraid to go further till daylight, and how intensely we longed for the dawn I need hardly say, as we tossed and tumbled about on the waves, the wind howling and the sea roaring.

Saturday, December 14th.—The much longed-for daylight came at last. We ran on into the Gulf of Adramytium, and found shelter and good holding ground in a little bay at about 9.30 a.m. It had been smoother for two or three hours, but it was a great comfort to be really in tranquil water at last in this quiet little bay, which put me in mind of a fiord in Norway, with the green trees growing down to the water's edge, and the high mountains behind. The rain came down in sheets all the morning, but after luncheon we managed to get ashore, though it continued to pour in torrents, and the paths were like watercourses.

The walk, however, did us more good than sitting still on board, thinking how rough it had been, and wondering when the weather would change. Yeni-liman is evidently a port of call for small coasters, the only houses being stores of all sorts of useful things. We met many mules coming down from the interior laden with pigskins full of olive oil. Nothing except eggs, chickens, and vegetables

Braving the Elements.

could be procured, and our want of knowledge of the language added considerably to the difficulty of bargaining.

It seemed set calm and fair when we went on board; but in the middle of the night the wind chopped right round, and it blew so hard from the north-east that we were obliged to get up steam to avoid being driven on shore.

Sunday, December 15*th.*—Under way by 7.15 a.m., with a fair wind, but steam had to be kept up, as the channels were narrow. We proceeded alongside the island of Lesbos till we came in sight of the capital, Mitylene, a large straggling town, or rather three towns joined into one, with a fine mediæval castle. Passing the promontory of Kara Bournou on the mainland, we steamed along the shores of the island of Chios. The pilotage was too intricate in the morning for Tom to be able to read prayers, but we had service in the afternoon at 4 p.m., and about 5 p.m. passed the town of Chios. I wonder if our old passenger, the French Consul, recognised the 'Sunbeam' in her new white dress.

Monday, December 16*th.*—It was really too hot to sleep last night, and the oppression of the thunder in the air made me so restless that I got up at 1 a.m. and spent the remainder of the night on deck. We passed the island of Tenos, and made Syra light on the island of Gaïdaro about 1.45 a.m. At 4.45 a.m. we anchored inside the mole, and then I went to bed.

The town of Syra from the anchorage is very pretty and clean-looking, just like a lot of little toy houses taken out of a child's wooden box and set on three pinnacles of rock, and painted blue, white, red, and green. There are no trees to be seen anywhere, and the rocks look horribly barren and bare. I believe, however, that a large supply of vegetables is exported to Constantinople and other ports; but they must be grown in terraced gardens behind walls, as they are not to be seen. We landed about 11.30 a.m. on a crowded quay. The streets were clean, and everybody seemed active and full of business. We went to call on the vice-consul, who, after attending to our business, kindly sent his man with us to an antiquity shop at the very top of the upper town. Such a climb it was,

up steps and steps and steps, exposed to the sun, and
sheltered from the wind. The proprietor had unfortunately
just been over to Athens, and had disposed of the best part
of his collection; so we found only some pretty old silver
cups and one very good carved cross, with a small bit of
the 'true' cross let into wax at the top. This made it
very precious, and caused the bargain to be a long one
before the difference between the price asked and that

Syra.

offered could be adjusted. We walked down to the Hôtel
de la Ville afterwards, in the square, where they gave us
a very good luncheon and some excellent Greek wine.
Afterwards Mabelle, Muriel, and I mounted donkeys, the
gentlemen walking, and we started for a climb up the hills
at the back of the town, from which there are charming
views over the sea and the adjacent islands. Tenos is not
far distant, with its perched-up white villages, and right

opposite is Delos. Our muleteer took us to a beautifully cultivated garden, irrigated by an old Moorish wheel with earthenware vases bound to it with twisted branches. There were no flowers in bloom, but the gardener gave us oranges and lemons and a bouquet of myrtle, geraniums, and verbena.

We were soon back in the town and glad to get on board and have the pleasure of unpacking some boxes of new books, newspapers, stores, and all sorts of useful things, which have just arrived. Last night has not agreed with either Tom or me, and we are both very sorry for ourselves to-day. To-morrow we have arranged to go to a bay on the other side of the island, where the south-westerly gale breaks in its full force, and the waves are something grand to see.

Tuesday, December 17th.—The wind seemed rather more fair, though the glass was still low. We therefore sent telegrams and letters on shore, and once more made a start for old England under sail. If we had not been so anxious to get back, we should certainly have hesitated, with the glass at only 29·80, to commence the voyage, when we had been told so often that at this time of the year, whatever direction the wind may take, the weather can never be depended upon unless the barometer stands well over 30. Still, though 29·80 may not prognosticate settled weather, it is scarcely low enough to make one fear a really bad gale. We got out of the harbour successfully, and in the course of the day passed Serpho, sailed between Siphanto, Paros, and Antiparos, and at dark had Polykandro right ahead. Paros is a very fertile-looking island, with Mount Elias, 2,280 feet high, rising in its midst; and there is a large long straggling town of white houses, with many monasteries scattered about, visible from the sea. It was originally built at that height on account of the pirates who infested the island. The weather to-day has been cold and unpleasant, the wind so shy that we were obliged to be close-hauled. During the night the wind came on a little freer, and we passed Milo, the glass rather inclined to rise.

Wednesday, December 18*th*, was indeed an eventful day, and if our friends in England could only have seen us, they would have felt much anxiety on our account and have given us much pity. It was terribly rough when I first woke and groped my way on deck in the dark and by 8 a.m. we hove-to in a fearful gale under a trysail and reefed canvas. Three times did we try to get the yacht round under her mizen, but she utterly refused. The stays and rigging that support her masts will have to be seen to as soon as we get into port, or they will be getting us into trouble.

The wind blew harder even than on last Friday, I think, or else we were more fully exposed to its fury. It howled and roared, and really seemed to scream in the rigging, as the sudden blasts rushed wildly by. A tremendous sea was running, and there appeared to be every prospect of the weather getting worse. I therefore tried hard to persuade Tom to run back to Milo, but he was loth to lose twenty miles of the distance we had gained with so much trouble yesterday. The glass kept falling, falling, till at last, about 12.30 p.m., he consented to put the yacht round, and then we had a dusting. Although we shipped only one really big sea just as we were going about, it was quite enough to make everything very wet and uncomfortable. Once round, she rode the waves like a cork, though the water poured over her lee rail—which must be at least ten feet above the level of the sea—like a cascade, and the boats, three or four feet above that again, were frequently full of water, and in imminent danger of being torn, or rather lifted, from their davits. It was indeed an anxious time, and very risky work running before a gale like this, almost under bare poles, close to a lee shore. I cannot recollect ever in my life seeing Tom more anxious. It was a grand sight, though, to see the huge waves tearing alongside of us, threatening every moment to engulf us altogether; rushing along the channels, dashing up the rigging, pouring over the lee rail like a fountain, while still we went rushing along faster and faster before it and with it. Sometimes we seemed to fly before the gale, and sometimes the gale seemed to tear past us. It was a great relief to everybody on board when at last the order was given to jibe. No sooner was it carried out than we were in comparative shelter from the fury of the sea round the point of Milo.

But the strength of the gale still seemed to increase, the wind blew harder than ever. All the morning it had been impossible to light the fires, either for steaming or cooking; but as soon as we had begun to run, and it was possible to do so, fires had been lighted in case steam might be wanted. Very fortunate it was that this had been done, for just as we thought we were safe inside the long harbour of Milo, we found the yacht would not fetch it. Oh! the disappointment of that moment, when we thought all our miseries and dangers were over! We had to wait three long quarters of an hour hove-to at the mouth of the harbour till steam was up. We drifted slowly out to sea and to leeward. All the time there was the certain knowledge that if we once drifted outside a particular spot before steam was ready we should have no choice but to go out to sea again and weather it out as best we could. Never did fires seem so long in burning up. The firemen were urged to use their utmost efforts; the anxiety of the last five or ten minutes was terrible, as we watched the bow of the yacht slowly drifting outwards past that particular rock. At last, not a moment too soon, the joyful sound of the order 'Full speed ahead' was heard. Once more our angel figure-head with outspread wings pointed shorewards to a harbour of refuge, and slowly, very slowly, we steamed up the long harbour against this most fearful gale. It must have been something like a typhoon, I imagine. Of course here we were much sheltered by the shore, and the sea was comparatively smooth.

We passed the town of Castro, near the mouth of the harbour, high perched on a pinnacle of rock, and proceeded up the harbour towards Scala, the capital of the island. Now, as the gulf or natural harbour lies N.W. and S.E., the wind was blowing right on shore at Scala, the usual anchorage; so Tom thought it better to anchor on the opposite side, under shelter of the land and Mount Elias. It was quite dark by this time, and therefore by no means an easy thing to pick up an anchorage in the present state of the weather; but here his piloting talent came out, and he succeeded in finding a capital berth. The difficulty was much increased by the fact that a piece of low land stretching along the shore, with a range of low hills behind, in the shadow of the mountain, makes it almost impossible to judge the exact distance from the shore. I was quite surprised when I saw the next morning what a favourable spot had been secured.

'Let go the anchor' is generally a welcome sound, but to-night it was specially so. As one after another went down, with tens of fathoms of chain, Tom heaved a deep sigh of relief. It had been indeed a trying day for him. Many lives were in his hand—forty-two precious souls. All the way round the world we had had nothing like it, and he really looked ten years older for the trial and responsibility of the day. With two anchors down, seventy-five fathoms of chain on each, and steaming ahead, steering our course, and with a full sea watch on deck, we managed to get through the night pretty comfortably, though between 11 p.m. and 1 a.m. the gale increased in fury; and even in this sheltered place the men could not walk along the deck, but were obliged to crawl from rope to rope under the lee of the bulwarks as best they could. Dinner in tolerable peace after such a day as we had experienced was a great comfort, and we were full of plans for the morrow.

We were at Milo four years ago for a day, and had a charming walk and ride, between walls built of fragments of sculpture and many-coloured marbles, to the quaint little town of Castro, whence there is a most lovely view; then back to the amphitheatre, where there are still remains of fine statuary and splendid marble columns. Anybody with patience, money, and permission to dig, might reap a rich harvest here. There are many antiquities to be picked up among the islanders, and as steamers do not touch here, and there is not a ready sale for curiosities, they are not extravagant in price, and are moreover all genuine. We propose to make to-morrow a somewhat similar expedition to the one we made in 1874, and the children are anxiously looking forward to their donkey ride.

CHAPTER XII.

MILO TO MALEA AND MALTA.

Thus let me live, unseen, unknown,
Thus unlamented let me die;
Steal from the world, and not a stone
Tell where I lie.

Thursday, December 19*th.* — After blowing its very hardest, the wind suddenly lulled and went round at 2.30 a.m. The first thing I heard when I woke at 7 a.m. was that we were to be off in half an hour. This was a great disappointment to us all, both to those who had been here before, and wanted to see the place again, and also to those who were visiting it for the first time. The children were mad at losing their donkey ride, and the steward much upset at not having a chance of getting ashore to procure some fresh provisions. Mabelle and the doctor were specially disappointed, as their expectations had been highly raised by our descriptions last night. I tried hard to persuade Tom to remain even for a few hours, if only just to let us run ashore; but he was determined, and I could not but concur in the wisdom of his decision, considering the constant succession of gales we have had and may expect, the delay they have caused us, and our wish to be in England as soon as possible. He himself was quite recruited by his night's rest, and as fresh as ever again.

We were therefore under way by 7.30 a.m., and had no sooner started than we began to feel the force of the heavy swell. The wind, though fair, was too light to do any good, either in keeping down the sea or in enabling us to sail. We made good way against it under steam, however, and, after making Falconera and Karavi rocks about noon, we passed between Cape Malea on the mainland and the island of Cerigo a little before dusk.

Cape Malea is a fine bold promontory, almost inaccessible from the sea, except on one little spot, where a hermit has built himself a house. Several of our men have been on shore in the neighbourhood of his retreat during various trips up and down the Mediterranean, but have never spoken to him or seen him at close quarters. They all agree, however, in describing him as a very old man with a long grey beard reaching down to his waist. The little plot of land that is not absolutely precipitous near his house is beautifully cultivated in terraces, and he has a small herd of goats and a few fowls. Many steamers and yachts make a point of calling here, to leave him a few biscuits and a little oil. They blow the steam whistle and lower a boat, and the old hermit comes to the shore and brings whatever produce he has to spare (cabbages, milk, fowls, eggs), leaves it on the beach, and retires to a cave close by. The boat's crew land and take the things, leaving in their place whatever they have brought. As soon as they have rowed a little way off, the hermit comes and takes possession of his part of the exchange. He trusts entirely to the generosity of his visitors, and I hope, for the honour of mankind, that he is never cheated. The story goes that the hermit was originally a shipowner of Athens, and always commanded one of his own ships. Three times did he run ashore on this rocky point, on each occasion losing his ship and many of his crew. At last, in despair, he vowed never to speak to anyone again, and to spend the remainder of his life in doing penance for his misfortunes on this solitary cape, with which there is no communication except by sea. We whistled and whistled, but could not induce him to appear, and

Hermit of Malea.

as night was falling, and we were pressed for time, we did not land on the mere chance of seeing him. We steamed quietly on all through the night without any excitement or adventure.

Friday, December 20th.—A fair breeze early, which

soon dropped. The funnel was lowered, but had to be raised shortly afterwards, and we steamed throughout the day against a heavy head swell and a light head wind.

Saturday, December 21st.—At midnight we got a breeze, had the mizen up directly, and stopped steaming at 1 a.m. Fair wind till 6 a.m., head wind all day, close-hauled. There were many discussions as to the best plan of future proceedings, and as to whether we should go to Malta, to pick up our letters and parcels, or keep straight on to Sicily, for which the wind was fairer. Then it became a question whether, after Malta or Sicily, the children and I should be landed at Malaga, Algiers, or Marseilles, to find our way home. The subject has been discussed so frequently, and our plans changed so often, that I feel quite as tired as if I had made the journey at least three times.

Sunday, December 22nd.—A very heavy sea all day. I stayed in bed, and read and wrote until noon. Tom read service at 11.30 a.m., but had a scanty congregation, as the weather was rough and disagreeable. In the afternoon it was rather better, and we had service at 4 p.m. While the service was going on a heavy squall came up, and the congregation was obliged to disperse rapidly, as it increased to a strong gale. We hoped that Malta would have been visible from the cross-trees at sunset; but no, not even at 9 p.m. could the light be seen. It was very rough, and we all turned in early.

I think that at last the battle of eighteen years is accomplished, and that the bad weather we have so continuously experienced since we left Constantinople, comprising five gales in eleven days, has ended by making me a good sailor. For the last two days I have really known what it is to feel absolutely well at sea, even when it is very rough, and have been able to eat my meals in comfort, and even to read and write without feeling that my head belonged to somebody else.

Monday, December 23rd.—At 5 a.m. the sails came down and the funnel had to be raised. We were then off the east end of the island of Malta, and had to plough our way through a heavy swell past Fort Ricasoli and Fort St. Elmo. One or two big rolls more, and we had rounded the point and were floating within the peaceful harbour in perfectly smooth water. Oh! the rest and refreshment of being absolutely still, after so many days of knocking about!

But why are the flags all half-mast high? Can the governor have died, or is it for one of the royal family? None of the dysoe men understood anything about it, and even our old bumboat man could give no better explanation than that it was for 'one of the Queen's little misses.' The question was soon answered, for Mr. Belluti's son came on board almost immediately, and told us the sad news of the death of Princess Alice. What a blow it will be to the Queen and to the nation! for she was beloved by all who had the privilege of knowing her.

The hospital looked white, and Bighi Bay looked blue and bright, as in former days, though we shall miss the warm welcome we have been accustomed to find there. We were hailed by numberless dysoe men, anxious to pilot us in; but we knew our own way by this time, and were soon moored to a buoy in Dockyard Creek, close to the old 'Hibernia.'

By the time breakfast was over, several friends came to

see us, and we all went ashore about 11.30 a.m., and found our old coachman and carriage waiting for us. The children went in it, whilst we walked up the familiar steppy streets. I have always liked Malta from my earliest childhood, and every time I go back to it I like it more and more. Not even the three weary months I passed on a bed of sickness here can take away from its pleasant memories and associations. Everybody is so kind to us, the climate is so genial, and the harbour so bright and gay, that, although there is absolutely nothing to do in the way of sight-seeing, there is always something pleasant going on. I know no more agreeable place at which to spend the winter months. There is a very good opera, nice society, and plenty of gaiety, if you care for it. This time I was more than ever interested in the houses and streets. After our recent visit to Rhodes, one could perceive how true was the statement that the knights brought over their architecture from their favourite island. The Palace, and the Auberges de Bavière, de Provence, and de Castille, &c., are all enlarged reproductions of the original buildings at Rhodes.

The streets are just now full of flowers ready for Christmas, the little kiosks at the corners of the streets are a mass of bouquets for church decoration, and the whole air is perfumed with roses, heliotrope, carnation, and narcissus blossoms. All along the crowded Strada Reale the shop-keepers made efforts to tempt us in and induce us to look at their wares. At the Hôtel d'Angleterre we were warmly welcomed by the master and his family and servants, who gave us a most elaborate luncheon on a gaily decorated table, as a substantial proof of their good feeling After lunch we went for a drive to the recreation ground, the race-course, and to St. Antonio. The flowers and oranges were lovely, and the place is kept in much better order than formerly, and is well guarded by many policemen, but it is not half so pleasant as when one used to wander about at one's own sweet will, unnoticed save by a few civil Maltese gardeners. On our way back I paid some visits, but found nobody at home. We dined at the *table d'hôte* at Dunsford's Hotel, and went afterwards to the opera, where we heard 'Norma' very well performed. We were engaged to a dance at the Gibraltar Palace; but Tom was so tired, after having been up the greater part of the last five nights navigating, that he did not feel equal to it, and as I did not care to go alone, we returned straight on board after leaving the opera.

Tuesday, December 24th.—I woke early, and was arranging plans and writing from 4 a.m. We had decided to spend Christmas Day here, and to leave after the club ball on Thursday. We are both so fond of Malta, and have so many kind friends here, that it is always a pleasure to stay; but Tom has to be home by a certain day, and for some reasons it would be convenient to have the yacht home too. The wind is fair, so that, taking all things into consideration, we have reluctantly decided that we must give up all our pleasant engagements here and be off to-night. The children, servants, and crew are in despair at going to sea on Christmas Eve; but, after our recent experience of gales, it is much more prudent to make sure of the start.

After breakfast we had many visitors, then we went to visit several friends on board other ships, and finally we all started off to buy Christmas presents for the children, servants, and crew. I was tempted with some splendid old Greek lace, of which there are still some good specimens to be found, notwithstanding the calls upon the dealers' resources caused by the rage for collecting. The streets looked even more lovely than they did yesterday, a mass of flowers everywhere, all ready for the churches to-morrow. Instead of holly, ivy, and evergreen, they will be decorated with wreaths of crimson bougainvillæa, tea roses, wild narcissus, heath, broom, orange blossom and fruit. All the shops make their most tempting displays, and many have orange-trees in pots instead of evergreens in the windows.

We went on board about 3 p.m., and held quite a *levée* of old friends and new, who came to see us and the yacht. We were surrounded by boats of all descriptions, containing every imaginable article for sale, animals alive or dead, vegetables and minerals. The children were much interested, Muriel being specially anxious to buy a small family of Guinea pigs, described by their owner as 'the cock Guinea pig, the hen Guinea pig, and the little chicken Guinea pig;' but we thought they would hardly be pleasant fellow-passengers. It was getting dusk by this time, and the fires had been lighted some time before. As the screw began to revolve, the flotilla of boats, with their cargoes of coral, lace, sponges, and miscellanies, had to shove off. We unmoored from our buoy, steamed quickly out from the picturesque Venetian-looking Dockyard Creek into the grand harbour, took a farewell look at the 'Minotaur,' 'Northumberland,' 'Shannon,' and other big ships lying at anchor under the walls of the white oriental-looking town, passed through between the forts, and, quitting this haven of rest, were once more fairly out at sea.

I think we all felt a little sad, not only at leaving Malta and our friends behind after so short a visit, but at the idea that, unless unforeseen circumstances arose, we had just taken our departure from our last halting-place, and that what had been a very pleasant voyage on the whole (though not so full of novelty and adventure as the voyage round the world) was thus fast drawing to a close. The thought that the next time we hear the anchor go down, it will be for the last time during the present cruise, cannot fail to be full of regret to me, and I think to many others on board, notwithstanding the pleasure we all feel in looking forward to seeing once more the friends we have left behind us.

A Quiet Time.

CHAPTER XIII.

FROM MALTA TO MARSEILLES.

*The wind is chill,
But let it whistle as it will
We'll keep our Christmas merry still.*

Wednesday, December 25th.—I woke at 3.50 a.m., and read and wrote till 8 a.m. We had service early, and then spent a long busy morning in arranging all the presents for the children, servants, and crew, and in decorating the cabin. We could not manage any holly, but we had carefully preserved one bough of mistletoe from Artaki Bay, and had brought on board at Malta baskets full of flowers, so that all the pictures, lamps, and even the walls, were wreathed with festoons of bougainvillæa, ivy, and other creeping plants; while in every available corner were placed vases, bowls, and soup-plates, containing flowers. If not exactly 'gay with holly-berries,' so dear to English hearts from their association with yule-tide at home, the general appearance of the cabins was highly satisfactory. In the meantime they had been busy in the kitchen and pantry departments, preparing all sorts of good things for dinner, and pretty things for dessert, in order that the crew and servants might enjoy a more sumptuous repast than usual. A Christmas tree, a snow man, or an ice-cave, for the distribution of presents, was not within the limit of our resources; but we decorated our tables and sideboards with bright shawls and scarves, and wreathed and divided the surface of each with garlands of flowers, placing in every division a pretty Christmas card, bearing the name of the recipient of the present, which was hidden away among the flowers beneath. Mabelle and I took a great deal of pains with this arrangement, which, I think, looked very pretty when completed. Perhaps I ought not to say so; but I am only repeating the opinion expressed by everybody, and what everybody says must be true: therefore it *must* have looked very pretty—Q.E.D. For the men there was plenty of tobacco, besides books and useful things; for the children, toys; and for ourselves, slippers and little remembrances of various kinds, some sent from home to meet us, others recent purchases. The distribution over, one or two speeches were made, and mutual congratulations and good wishes were exchanged. Then the crew and servants retired to enjoy the, to them, all-important event of the day—dinner and dessert. After our own late dinner, we thought of those near and dear to us at home, and drank to the health of 'absent friends.'

All day long the sky had been light and clear, but there had been a heavy roll, which prevented our admiring as much as we could have wished the beautiful west coast of Sicily. At noon we had been off Cape Scalambri, having been much set back by an adverse current. At night I found, to my great disappointment, that all my recent experience had been of no avail, and that I was as ill as if I had never been to sea before in my life. It was certainly very rough, but we were progressing rapidly, which is always a consoling fact, however bad one may feel. During two consecutive watches we ran 50 and 52 knots respectively, or nearly 118 land miles altogether.

Thursday, December 26th.—The morning broke fine and clear. We had a delightful sail all day along the Sicilian coast, which looked charming, with its distant mountains and sloping hills, dotted with houses and villages, and with snow-covered Etna in the background. The scenery of the western side of the island is not, however, so grand as that on the north coast, from Cape Faro to Palermo. I wonder more people do not come yachting to Sicily. It is comparatively near home; it abounds in sheltered harbours, beautiful scenery, and interesting spots. The climate is delightful all the year round, and the flowers and fruit are abundant, lovely, and delicious. Brigands *were* a drawback, and perhaps still are so in the interior; but there are plenty of places near the coast which are perfectly safe, and there could hardly be much danger to a yachting party on this score.

Friday, December 27th.—We were constantly disturbed throughout the night by Kindred or Cook coming to Tom for fresh instructions; so at last I abandoned the idea of sleep as a bad job, and got up and wrote from 1.30 a.m. to 5 a.m. About 8 a.m. the funnel was lowered, and we were able to sail all day, though sometimes close-hauled, and contending with a heavy swell. This latter circumstance was not at all in favour of our packing and preparations for leaving the yacht.

At noon we had run 216 miles, in spite of the still adverse current.

Saturday, December 28th.—A fine morning, but a head wind. At daybreak we were about twenty miles off Toulon, and twenty-five from Marseilles. The funnel was raised, and we steamed among the islands and along the barren rocky coast off the harbour of Marseilles. The scene is rather a grand one, though wild and bleak, and, with the sun shining on the red and yellow pointed rocks and the dark blue sea, it would no doubt have been very fine. To-day, however, it was bitterly cold, with a grey leaden sky and sea, very much as one would expect to find it on the English coast at this time of the year. A pilot came on board and took us through a fleet of fishing boats, past the Château d'If, and into the new harbour of Marseilles. Here we found the 'Sultana' and 'Cuckoo' yachts established, and alongside the latter we dropped our anchor for the last time this cruise.

The rattle of the chain cable, generally so pleasant a sound, as the signal of arrival at a fresh port full of unknown attractions and interest, seems now the knell of past pleasures, announcing the completion of a delightful voyage, and the return to the work-a-day world and the duties and responsibilities of home life.

Michel Venture, who had been with us from Smyrna to Ephesus in 1874, was one of the first arrivals on board to solicit our custom, and was quickly followed by the usual crowd of *proveidors*, washerwomen, &c. We landed and went to the consul's for papers and letters, of both of which we received a large and welcome bundle, our Malta news having been somewhat stale in consequence of our uncertain movements and frequent change of plans. We dined at the *table d'hôte* of the Hôtel de Noailles, where there were not many people, and we had the felicity of sitting opposite to the late Madame Thérèse and her husband. I had never seen her off the stage before, and could not have believed she would have looked so quiet and inconspicuous. She was singing at a theatre quite close to the hotel.

Afterwards we went to the Gymnase, where we saw a very dull little piece to begin with, followed by 'La Périchole,' in which the acting and singing were good.

Sunday, December 29th.—We went to a plain little English church, decorated with much taste for Christmas. In the afternoon we went for a long drive round what they call the Corniche road of Marseilles—a splendid piece of engineering, cut out of the rocks, along the edge of the sea, and commanding beautiful views along the rocky coast. We passed the comfortable Hôtel Roussillon, in Catalan harbour, a spot familiar to the readers of Monte Christo, and then drove along the Prado, a fine promenade, planted with trees, to the *foire de presepio*, which is held near the Château d'Eau for a few days before and after Christmas only. It is like the New Year's fair in Paris. There are hundreds of little wooden booths, built under the shade of the trees, and filled, a few with toys and sweets, but principally with *presepios*, or miniature representations of that place

> In royal David's city, where stood a lowly cattle shed,
> Where a mother laid her Baby, in a manger for His bed.

The models were really very well done, in all sorts of styles and sizes. There was the little wooden shed, with the loft above, full of hay and straw (of a proportionate size), the stable manger with the cattle and asses, and Mary and Joseph sitting in front, sometimes with the Infant Saviour, either between them, receiving the homage of the shepherds and the wise men from the East, or seated in the manger itself. The figures varied in size from the eighth of an inch to five or six inches, and their number from four or five to as many hundreds, while the price of the whole ranged from half a franc to a hundred pounds. Every family in Marseilles could have its little household altar, suited to the length of its purse ; and a representative of every family must, I think, have been present. A large, good-humoured, pushing, bargaining, parcel-carrying crowd it was. One poor woman had lost her child, and was rushing about in a frantic state, shrieking, and literally tearing her hair, and recording its virtues in the most voluble French, till, on finding it again in the arms of a stalwart blouse-dressed peasant, she seized it, put it across her knee, and gave it a real good whipping, just like the heroine of Tom Hood's poem. Our three children were immensely interested in the whole scene, and talked of it for many days afterwards.

Marseilles is greatly altered since we were here some years ago. The new harbours are finished, and as our vessel is at the extreme end of one of the newest of them it was really a long drive to get on board again.

Monday, December 30th.—We were up early, and everybody was hard at work packing, not so much the things we are to take with us overland, as those that are to follow by sea. It is quite decided that the yacht shall be left here for the present, and after a five months' cruise the collections of a family are rather a formidable affair. Such a scene of confusion as the deck presented, covered as it was with deal cases, straw, hay, paper, live and dead objects, dogs, goats, pigeons, canaries, rice-birds, bullfinches, goldfinches, and every conceivable article of attire or ornament, has, I am sure, been rarely witnessed. Of course, all our acquaintances in Marseilles, and some strangers, took this opportunity of coming to see us and the yacht, and a nice impression they must, I fear, have formed of the tidiness of the vessel and its inhabitants.

Having done all I could in the way of packing, I took the children for a drive, to keep them out of the way while all the confusion was going on. We went along the new harbour, crowded with ships of large size from every country in the world, and surrounded by stores and bonded warehouses, containing every imaginable species of merchandise, and were much amused by looking in at the different doors and speculating on the various contents of the buildings. When this harbour was begun, a large new town was laid out close to it, and streets upon streets of magnificent houses were built. Somehow the people never came to live in them, and they are now almost all empty and shut up, or tenanted by the poorest of the poor. Thus, over grand porches, supported on caryatides and surrounded by costly ironwork, miserable rags, hanging out to dry in the sun and air, give the whole suburb quite a mean appearance. Near the port of La Joliette, on the contrary, though the houses are poor and small, everybody seems busy and well-to-do, and there is plenty of life and bustle among the large fleet of coasting schooners and lateen-rigged craft, hailing from almost every part of the Mediterranean seaboard, and perhaps from even farther than that. The Cannebière or *grande rue* of Marseilles leads straight from the port to the most remote part of the town, and always reminds me (though it is not, of course, of so great a length) of the Broadway at New York, with its shops, its houses, its trees, and its motley groups of passers-by from every country in the world. On each side, at right angles, there are fine promenades, with splendid trees, and large and well-occupied houses.

After another visit to the Presepio fair, for the benefit of the children, we drove to the Château d'Eau, a good imitation of the large one at Caserta, with its statues and its fountains. On one side is the Museum of Natural History, on the other the collection of pictures and statues. Behind there are beautiful gardens, containing a mixed zoological and botanical collection.

More visitors came to see us on our return on board, after which we had a busy time in getting our luggage through the Custom House, an undertaking in which Mr. Parr, the consul's clerk, rendered valuable assistance. Then came the moment of our departure, the time for the sad farewells to be said, not only to our gallant little ship, but to the brave crew who have steered and worked her through so many hazards and dangers, and have contributed, in their various capacities, so greatly to our comfort and enjoyment. All old shipmates feel sorrow at parting, and we on board the 'Sunbeam' are rather like one large family, some of the men having been with us for fifteen or sixteen years. I do not think there was a single dry eye among children, guests, owners, crew, and servants, when the last hand had been shaken, and the burgee and ensign had been hauled down, though a melancholy attempt at a cheer was made as we left the ship and were rowed ashore.

Good-bye, dear old 'Sunbeam'! I hope we may soon be on board you again. You have done your work right well, and have borne us and ours bravely over the sea.

The confidence we feel in a favourite hunter, the affection we cherish for a faithful friend, the attachment we bear to a house that contains whatever is nearest and dearest to the heart—all these kindly sympathies and sentiments are bound together in my love for the gallant little bark to which once more I say 'Fare thee well!'

> Farewell!
> The elements be kind to thee and make
> Thy spirits all of comfort.

CHAPTER XIV.

HOME ONCE MORE.

'Tis sweet to hear the watch-dog's honest bark
Bay deep-mouthed welcome as we draw near home :
'Tis sweet to know there is an eye will mark
Our coming, and look brighter when we come.

THE remainder of our journey home presents no features of special interest. We arrived in Paris in due course, and spent a week there very agreeably, visiting many of the old familiar sights and places of interest, which never seem to lose their charm and attraction, even for the oldest and most experienced traveller.

On January 8 we left Paris by the early morning train, and, crossing from Boulogne to Folkestone, reached our own little village once more in the afternoon.

Again the Battle bells rang out a merry peal of gladness at our return; again everybody rushed out to welcome us. At home once again the servants and the animals seemed equally glad to see us back; the former looked the picture of happiness, while the dogs jumped and barked; the horses and ponies neighed and whinnied; the monkeys chattered; the cockatoos and parrots screamed; the birds chirped; the bullfinches piped their little pæan of welcome. Most of the smaller creatures we had brought home from our voyage round the world. From having been so much petted on board ship they are as tame as dogs, and they seem to have the most wonderful memories. Our old Sussex cowman says that even the cows eat their food 'kind of kinder like' when the family are at home. The deer and the ostriches too, the swans and the call ducks, all came running to meet us, as we drove round the place to see them, when they heard the sound of the bells on the ponies.

There is no place like home, after all, and delightful indeed is it to find oneself there again after a long absence, to feel that everybody is glad to see one back, and to recognise, and be recognised by, all one's old friends and favourites. In our own case the pleasure has been greatly increased by the fact that everything has gone on in a satisfactory manner in our absence, and that the confidence reposed in those left in charge has been fully justified by the result.

The soft warm air and bright blue skies of the sunny south possess undoubted charms, for me especially; but old England too, even in mid-winter, when

> A southerly wind and a cloudy sky
> Proclaim a hunting morning,

has its attractions. Very pleasant it was to go out hunting the next day after our arrival, and to gallop once more across the well-known fields and through the big woods of dear old Sussex. It is really a lovely county, and its beauties strike me afresh each time I return to it.

> Green fields of England! wheresoe'er
> Across this watery waste we fare,
> Your image at our hearts we bear,
> Green fields of England, everywhere.

THE LAST PAGE.

The last chapter closed with regrets at leaving the dear old 'Sunbeam.' I finish this one full of joy and thankfulness at our safe return to enjoy the blessings of the land, and of gratitude to our many kind friends for being so glad to see us back again.

The Meet at Battle Abbey.

APPENDIX.

SUMMARY OF VOYAGES,
1874 AND 1878,

Compiled from the Log-Book.

LIST OF OUR PARTY, CREW, AND SERVANTS, &c.

1874.

To complete the story of the homeward voyage, I give the following transcript from Mr. Brassey's log book :—

At 9.30 a.m. on December 24 the 'Sunbeam' steamed out of the harbour of Nice, and remained hove-to until noon, when, having seen my wife and children off at the station, I returned on board, and set out on my long voyage to the Thames.

The crew were employed during the afternoon in securing boats on deck, and making every preparation for the stormy weather which would probably be encountered at this season of the year. At 6 p.m. the 'Sunbeam' was off Hyères. At 8 p.m. we ceased steaming and proceeded under sail. During the day the weather had been calm, and the sea smooth. In the night the wind freshened considerably, working round to the S.W.

At noon on Christmas Day the 'Sunbeam' was distant from Nice 161 miles, in latitude 41.9 N. and longitude 5.33 E. There was a heavy swell from the westward, with a moderate breeze throughout the day, and not a single vessel was seen from sunrise to sunset. The crew were regaled with a Christmas dinner, and the weather caused no interruption to their festive enjoyment.

The following night was fine, and the moon shone brightly. At 2 a.m. on the 26th the mizen topmast was got up on end, and at 6 a.m. the main topmast, and the main and mizen topsails were set.

During the 26th the sea was smooth, with a moderate breeze from the S.W. At noon the distance run was 120 miles ; and as we were approaching the Balearic Isles, crossing the usual track of sailing vessels bound up the Mediterranean, several sail were seen, and in the afternoon we exchanged signals with a German barque. In the night the wind veered from N.W. to E., and we set the square-sail. But the favouring breeze soon died away.

Sunday, the 27th, continued almost calm until noon, when we were in latitude 39.3 N. and longitude 3.47 E. In the preceding twenty-four hours we had made good only fifty miles, the most indifferent day's work since our departure from England. Prayers were read as usual on Sunday in the morning. During the afternoon we experienced a moderate breeze from the W., but the barometer fell to 29·6. Later we encountered a heavy swell, which lifted the dingy out of the tackles, and in the darkness of the night, with all our other boats secured for sea, we were unable to take any steps to recover it. As there was a heavy sea running, and not enough wind to give us steerage-way, I ordered the canvas to be stowed, and the fires to be lighted. At midnight we proceeded under steam. At 6 a.m. we housed topmasts, and set double-reefed staysail and foresail. At 8 a.m. we ceased steaming and lowered the funnel. Notwithstanding the small area of canvas set, there was no perceptible loss of speed after the engines were stopped. At 9.30, after much labour, owing to the sail being full of water from the torrents of rain that had fallen during the night, we took in three reefs in the mizen, and set it.

At noon on the 28th we were in 37.30 N. and 2.47 E., having run 156 miles since noon yesterday. At 1 p.m. we set the double-reefed mainsail. During the afternoon we met numerous vessels, and passed close to an English barque, with foresail and mainsail blown to ribbons. We also passed a large three-masted steamer with the fore topsail blown away from the yard. At 5 p.m. the weather began to moderate.

At 2 a.m. on the 29th we made the light on the Mesa de Roldan, and at 4 a.m. we rounded Cape de Gata. We were now running along the Spanish coast, with a fresh and favourable breeze and a smooth sea. At 8 a.m. we set the square-sail and mizen topsail. At 9 a.m. set the fore topsail and the main topsail. The weather was lovely, the sky cloudless, the sun bright and genial. We were surrounded with shipping. At noon we found the day's run to be 188 miles, and we were in 36.18 N., 2.42 W. At 11.15 p.m. we were becalmed, and as I was anxious to leave Gibraltar to-morrow evening I lowered canvas and got up steam.

At 6 a.m. on December 30 we rounded Europa Point, and at 6.45 a.m. we brought up off the New Mole. The morning was occupied in taking in water and provisions. I lunched with the

Marilliers, and at 4 p.m. returned on board, weighed anchor, and steamed out into the straits. The weather was splendid, sea perfectly calm, and not a breath stirring.

At 8 a.m. on the 31st, off Cape St. Mary, we ceased steaming, and set all sail, including topsails. The wind continued light until noon, when we set square-sail and topmast staysails. In the afternoon the wind died away. During the night it was dead calm, and at 4 a.m. we proceeded under steam.

At 9.30 a.m. on New Year's Day we rounded Cape St. Vincent. The weather continued calm throughout the day, the barometer standing at 30.4. Our crew were able to devote their energies to beating carpets, and other occupations more commonly adapted to a sheltered harbour than the exposed North Atlantic in the winter season. Our run from Gibraltar to noon on December 31 was 146 miles, position at noon 36.43 N., 7.53 W.

January 1 the run was 90 miles, position 37.28 N., 9.7 W. At 8 a.m. January 2 we were off the Tagus, and at 1 p.m. we passed the Burlings. The weather continued calm during the night, but at 8 a.m. on January 3 a moderate breeze sprang up from the S.S.W. We ceased steaming, and set the square-sail and jib-headed fore topsail. Our run at noon was 190 miles, our position 40.34 N., 10.4 W.

During the ensuing twenty-four hours we made steady progress before a moderate running breeze, and at noon on the 3rd we had made good 105 miles, and were in 42.25 N. and 9.55 W. In the afternoon the wind worked round to the S.W., and we set foresail, mainsail, and main topsail. At 4 p.m. Cape Finisterre was distant ten miles on the starboard beam. The wind tacked round to the southward, and increased very much during the day watches. At 6 p.m. we stowed all fore-and-aft canvas.

At 1 a.m. on the 4th, we sighted the light on Cape Villano. During the night we continued bowling along at from ten to eleven knots an hour, under square canvas, over a moderate sea, before half a gale from the southward. At noon we had made a fine run of 228 miles, position 45.55 N. and 7.40 W. In the afternoon the sun broke through the clouds, producing glorious effects of light over the tumbling sea of the Bay of Biscay. In order to give Ushant a wide berth we hauled out more to the westward, bringing the wind on the quarter. We set the double-reefed mizen and reefed mainsail and foresail, and took in our square canvas. At 11 p.m., the wind moderating, we shook out reefs in the lower canvas, and in the middle watch set the mizen topsail.

At 4 a.m. on the 5th, we got the fore topmast on end, and set the square-sail and fore topsail. At 8 a.m. we set the main topsail. At noon the run was 205 miles, and the position in 49.0 N. and 5.49 W. We were now in the chops of the Channel, and altered our course to E.N.E. The sea was smooth, the wind fresh and 'fair as fair could be,' and every sail set, including square-sail, studding-sail, and main and mizen topsails. The 'Sunbeam' was on her very best point of sailing, with the wind on the quarter. At 9 p.m. we sighted the Start, visible only from the cross-trees. At 4.30 a.m. on the 6th, St. Catherine's was abeam, distant thirteen miles. At 6.30 a.m. we passed the Owers. At 9 a.m. we rounded Beachy Head, and at noon we hove-to off Hastings, having run the great distance of 286 miles in the previous twenty-four hours. I landed, saw my mother, heard that my wife and children were all well, spending the day at Sedlescombe, and at 5.30 p.m. resumed the voyage to the Thames under sail.

We brought up in the Downs off Walmer at 11 p.m. It was a dangerous manœuvre, as the tide was carrying us down very rapidly on other vessels at anchor, and we had but little room to round to before letting go. However, all's well that ends well. We weighed at daybreak on the 7th, and proceeded under steam through the Downs, and, rounding the well-known promontory of the North Foreland, proceeded up the Thames to Gravesend, where, as we were too late to go into dock to-day, we dropped anchor until to-morrow.

I landed at 1.30 p.m., thankful to have been so mercifully preserved from the disasters of the sea through a long voyage of 13,000 miles.[1]

[1] This distance includes a voyage to Norway and the Arctic Circle, made by the 'Sunbeam' just previous to the cruise in the Mediterranean.

1874.

LIST OF THE MEMBERS OF OUR PARTY, CREW, AND SERVANTS, IN 1874.

(Portsmouth, September 13.)

THOMAS BRASSEY, M.P., Owner and Captain
ANNIE BRASSEY
G. EVELYN ROBINSON
HON. A. Y. BINGHAM
HERBERT SWIFT, left at Gibraltar September 21
THOMAS ALLNUTT BRASSEY ('Tab'), left at Gibraltar September 21
MABELLE ANNIE BRASSEY, left at Gibraltar September 21
MURIEL AGNES BRASSEY ('Muñie')
VANDELEUR CRAKE, arrived at Constantinople November 7; left at Messina December 12

FRANCES HOME, Nurse
EMMA WILLIAMS, Maid
SOPHIA FISHER, Children's Maid; left Gibraltar September 21
THOMAS HARRIS, Chief Steward
FREDERICK PARSONS, Saloon Steward
HENRY BALLARD, Bedroom Steward
GEORGE SOULE, Mess-room Boy
WILLIAM CARTRIDGE, Cabin Cook
EBENEZER SOUTHGATE, Cabin Cook's Boy
THOMAS POWELL, Forecastle Cook
WALLACE C. HOWLEN, Forecastle Cook's Boy

ISAIAH POWELL, First Mate
HENRY KINDRED, Second Mate
WILLIAM CHECK, Carpenter
CHARLES COOK, Signalman
BENJAMIN WALFORD, Coxswain of the 'Gleam,' Cutter
JOHN FALE, Coxswain of the 'Glance,' Cutter
WILLIAM PERCIVAL, Coxswain of the 'Ray,' Light Gig
JOSEPH WADE, Coxswain of the 'Mote,' Dingy
JOHN WALFORD, Store-room Man
JAMES C. ALLEN, A.B.
JESSE CRANFIELD, A.B.
HENRY PARKER, A.B.
SAMUEL WADE, A.B.
WILLIAM SIBBORN, A.B.
GEORGE CLARK, A.B.
JAMES HARRIS, A.B.
EDGAR JONES, A.B.
THOMAS JAY, A.B.
ROBERT ROWBOTHAM, Engineer
ADAM RUSSELL, Second Engineer (left at Constantinople)
GEORGE SALISBURY, Fireman
T. KIRKHAM, Fireman

1874.

SUMMARY OF THE VOYAGE OF THE YACHT 'SUNBEAM'

from England to Tangier, Gibraltar, Palermo, Messina, Piræus, Constantinople, Moudania, Smyrna, Milo, Zante, Corfu, Naples, Nice, and Gravesend, September 4, 1874, to January 7, 1875.

Date	Lat.	Long.	Distance run, Sail and Steam	Remarks
1874	° N ′	° E ′	Knots	
September 4	51 10	1 18	57	Started from Brightlingsea
5	50 54	1 0	41	Off Dungeness
6	—	—	16	Arrived at Hastings
7	50 40	WEST 0 50	100	Left Hastings
8	—	—	94	Off Ryde
9	50 43	1 10	10	Arrived at Ryde
10 and 11	—	—	—	At Ryde
12	—	—	—	Left Ryde for Portsmouth Harbour
13	50 35	1 48	47	Off St. Albans Head
14	48 9	5 36	231	Off Chaussée de Sein
15	46 37	6 44	112	In the Bay of Biscay
16	43 45	9 2	197	,, ,,
17	40 53	9 48	183	Off Cape Finisterre
18	37 0	9 0	244	Off Cape St. Vincent
19	35 50	5 48	170	Off Tangier
20	—	—	—	At Tangier
21	36 5	5 30	18	Left Tangier
22 to 29	—	—	—	At Gibraltar
30	36 10	4 40	25	Left Gibraltar
October 1	36 39	0 30	225	Off Marbella
2	37 16	WEST 3 48	206	Off Algiers
3	37 40	6 38	137	Off North Coast of Africa
4	38 14	10 9	198	,, ,, ,,
5	38 8	13 15	171	Arrived at Palermo
6	—	—	—	At Palermo
7	38 10	13 35	16	Left Palermo
8	8 11	15 34	110	Off Messina
9	37 49	16 25	56	Left Messina
10	37 5	20 43	223	
11	36 55	23 23	169	Off the Morea
12	37 58	23 43	74	Arrived at Piræus
13	—	—	—	At Piræus

E E

1874. *Summary of Voyage*—continued.

Date	Lat. ° N ′	Long. ° E ′	Distance run, Sail and Steam Knots	Remarks
1874 October 14	38 2	24 10	69	Off Cape Marathon
15	38 28	23 35	66	Off Euripo
16	39 3	23 45	111	Off Scopelo
17	39 18	25 50	166	In the Dardanelles
18	41 0	29 0	214	Off Stamboul. Seraglio Point
19 to 21	—	—	15	At Constantinople
22 to 25	41 12	29 0	12	At Therapia
26	—	—	25	Returned to Constantinople
27 to Nov. 1	—	—	—	At Constantinople
November 2	40 50	29 0	11	Off Prince's Islands
3	—	—	39	Off Moudania
4	—	—	—	At Moudania
5	40 38	28 45	20	Off Silevri
6	40 54	28 50	64	Off Cape Stephano
7	—	—	10	Returned to Constantinople
8 to 16	—	—	—	At Constantinople
17	40 20	26 35	138	Left Constantinople
18	39 56	26 5	54	In the Dardanelles
19	38 25	27 6	147	Arrived at Smyrna
20 to 22	—	—	—	At Smyrna
23	—	—	6	Left Smyrna
24	38 22	26 10	93	Off Port Castro
25	37 5	24 35	124	Off Nikaria
26	36 42	24 30	53	At Milo
27	36 25	23 0	111	Off Cape Malea
28	37 27	21 17	161	In Gulf of Arkadia
29	37 47	20 54	36	Off Zante
30	—	—	—	At Zante
December 1	38 10	20 29	45	Off Argostoli
2	38 23	20 42	42	Off Cape Dekalia
3	38 48	20 30	48	Off Santa Maura
4	39 37	19 56	59	Off Corfu
5	39 43	20 0	8	In Butrinto Bay
6	39 37	19 56	8	Returned to Corfu
7	38 42	18 33	107	To Cape Spartivento, 128 miles
8	37 23	16 11	130	,, ,, 45 ,,
9	38 11	15 34	138	Off Messina
10	39 38	14 55	157	Driven back

1874. *Summary of Voyage*—continued.

Date	Lat.	Long.	Distance run, Sail and Steam	Remarks
1874	° N ′	° E ′	Knots	
December 11	38 12	15 33	126	Driven back to Messina
12 and 13	—	—	—	At Messina
14	38 15	15 40	7	Left Messina
15	40 23	13 33	177	Off Stromboli
16	40 50	14 16	40	Arrived at Naples
17 and 18	—	—	—	At Naples
19	41 27	12 28	95	Off Porto d'Anzio
20	42 41	9 26	187	Arrived at Bastia
21 and 22	—	—	—	At Bastia
23	43 40	7 18	141	Arrived at Nice
24	—	—	—	At Nice
25	41 26	5 33	155	Left Nice
26	39 26	4 44	121	
27	39 3	3 47	50	Off Balearic Islands
28	37 30	1 0	155	
		WEST		
29	36 18	3 0	185	Off Cape de Gata
30	36 6	5 20	105	Off Europa Point
31	36 43	7 53	146	Off Cape St. Mary
1875				
January 1	37 25	9 7	84	Rounded Cape St. Vincent
2	40 34	10 4	180	Off the Tagus
3	42 25	9 55	99	
4	45 55	7 40	218	Cape Finisterre E 10 miles
5	49 0	5 49	194	
6	50 51	0 35	278	Off Hastings
7	—	—	112	Arrived at Gravesend

Total distance run . 8,472 knots

1878.

LIST OF THE MEMBERS OF OUR PARTY, CREW, AND SERVANTS, IN 1878.

(Cowes, September 20, 1878.)

THOMAS BRASSEY, M.P., Owner and Captain
ANNIE BRASSEY
MABELLE ANNIE BRASSEY
MURIEL AGNES BRASSEY
MARIE ADELAIDE BRASSEY
THE HON. A. Y. BINGHAM
JAMES B. HOFFMEISTER

EMMA ADAMS, Nurse
HARRIET HOWE, Maid
ISABELLE BERTHOLET, Children's Maid
ALEXANDER PHILLIPS, Chief Steward
WILLIAM PULLIN, Deck-house Steward
HENRY PRATT, Saloon Steward
WILLIAM PHILLIPS, Bed-room Steward
JAMES STOKES, Mess-room Boy
EBENEZER SOUTHGATE, Cook
JOSEPH SOUTHGATE, Cook's Mate
ÆNEAS TURFF, Forecastle Cook

HENRY KINDRED, First Mate
CHARLES COOK, Second Mate
JOHN WALFORD, Storekeeper
JOHN FALE, Quartermaster
WILLIAM HUSK, Carpenter

HENRY PARKER, Sail Room (charge of)
HENRY CRANMER, Coxswain, 'Glance'
WILLIAM MOULTON, Coxswain, 'Ray'
CHARLES BONNER, Coxswain, 'Gleam' (died at Cyprus)
FREDERICK WILSON, Coxswain, 'Mote'
BENJAMIN WALFORD, Coxswain, 'Flash'
HENRY DOWMAN, Lamp Trimmer
WILLIAM PITTUCK, A.B.
JAMES STURMER, A.B.
ROBERT HATCH, A.B.
DAVID APPLEBY, A.B.
HENRY WARREN, A.B.
GEORGE COLBERT, A.B.
THOMAS KIRKHAM, Chief Engineer
GEORGE SALISBURY, Second Engineer

COURSES D'ORAN.

(*See p. 213.*)

[In case anybody cares to see the difference between an English and an African race meeting, I append a copy of the card of the races which took place at Oran on the day of our arrival.]

PROGRAMME OFFICIEL.

LUNDI 14 OCTOBRE 1878.—DEUXIÈME JOURNÉE.

PREMIÈRE COURSE, A 2 HEURES PRÉCISES.

Prix du Conseil général : 1,000 francs.

COURSE MIXTE ENTRE EUROPÉENS ET INDIGÈNES, POUR POULAINS ET POULICHES NÉS EN 1874 ET 1875.

Distance, 2,400 mètres (2 tours) 3'50". Poids, 60 kilos.—Les pouliches portent 2 kilos en moins.—Entrée : 75 francs.

NOMS DES PROPRIÉTAIRES DES CHEVAUX	NOMS DES CHEVAUX	SEXE	ÂGE	TAILLE	ROBE	NOMS DES JOCKEYS	COULEUR
Seban	Barbare	C. E.	4 ans	1 47	Bai foncé	Kalech	C. et I. rouges
Laurent Solano	Lièvre	C. E.	4 ans	1 48	Alezan	Mohamed	C. et T. noires
Boulfred	Escargot	C. E.	3 ans	1 50	Gris rouanné	Piat	C. rose, T. verte
Saint-Romain	Paupaul	C. E.	4 ans	1 50	Gris foncé	Hamida	C. et T. jaunes
Deliot	Draham	C. E.	4 ans	1 52	Gris pommelé	Jean Fischer	C. verte, T. noire
Joseph Torregrossa	Tonnerre	C. E.	3 ans	1 50	Noir	Abd-el-Kader	C. et T. noires
Cabolo	Tentateur	C. E.	4 ans	1 48	Gris clair	Ahmed	C. rose, T. bleue
Dartagnan	Miloud	C. E.	3 ans	1 55	Bai	Dartagnan	C. et T. rouges

DEUXIÈME COURSE, A 2 HEURES 1/2.

Grand Prix offert par le Conseil général et la Société : 5,000 francs.

Dont 500 fr. au second de la belle.

COURSE MIXTE ENTRE EUROPÉENS ET INDIGÈNES (EN PARTIE LIÉE).

Pour chevaux et juments de 3 ans et au-dessus.

Distance, 3,600 *mètres* (3 *tours*) 5'25" *pour chacune des deux premières épreuves et* 2,400 *mètres* (2 *tours*) *pour la belle si elle a lieu.*
Poids pour chevaux de 3 *et* 4 *ans*, 60 *kilos* ; *pour chevaux de cinq ans et au-dessus* : 63 *kilos.*—*Les juments et pouliches portent*
2 *kilos en moins.*—*Entrée* : 200 *francs.*

Nota.—Le prix sera réduit à 3,000 fr. s'il y a moins de cinq chevaux engagés.

A. Caniciu	Espoir	C. E.	5 ans	1 49	Gris	Mohamed	C. et T. noires.
Joseph Torregrossa . . .	Cartoufa	C. E.	5 ans	1 50	Bai	Abdelkader	C. et T. noires.
A. Solano	Lièvre	C. E.	4 ans	1 48	Alezan	Mohamed-Fartas	C. et T. noires.
Boulfred	Insouciant	C. E.	6 ans	1 55	Noir	Piat	C. rose et T. verte
Hamed-ben-Taieb . . .	Balek-Balek	C. E.	6 ans	1 48	Bai	Taieb	Costume indigène
Agha, Ghanem-ould-el-Bachir	Malbrouk	C. E.	7 ans	1 50	Bai avec balzane	Hamida	C. et T. jaunes.

TROISIÈME COURSE, A 3 HEURES.

Prix du Conseil général : 1,000 francs.

COURSE AU TROT MONTÉ POUR CHEVAUX DE RACE ARABE

Distance, 3,600 *mètres* (3 *tours*). *Poids*, 65 *kilos.*—*La tenue de jockey et de rigueur.*—*Entrée* : 100 *francs.*

Grondonna . . .	Moustique	C. E.	9 ans	1 30	Blanc	E. Moralès	C. et T. roses
Pitcairn . . .	Oméga	C. E.	9 ans	1 45	Bai foncé	Cenac	—
Spiteri . . .	Jupiter	C. E.	6 ans	1 31	Gris rouanné	Philippe	C. et T. roses
Brun	Kaddour	C. E.	7 ans	1 54	Gris pommelé	Paul	C. rouge et T. bleue

QUATRIÈME COURSE, A 3 HEURES 1/2.

DEUXIÈME MANCHE DE LA DEUXIÈME COURSE.

CINQUIÈME COURSE, A 4 HEURES.

Prix de la Chambre de commerce et des Communes mixtes : 750 francs.

COURSE DE CAVALIERS INDIGÈNES (FELLAHS).

Distance, 2,400 mètres (2 tours) 3'50" pour chevaux et juments de 3 ans et au-dessus. Poids libre.—Entrée : 25 francs.

PREMIER PELOTON.

NOMS DES PROPRIÉTAIRES DES CHEVAUX	NOMS DES CHEVAUX	SEXE	ÂGE	TAILLE	ROBE	NOMS DES JOCKEYS	COULEUR
Caïd-bou-Médine	Messaoud	C. E.	5 ans	1 45	Blanc	Mohamed-Fartas	Costume indigène
Galem-bou-Djeffal	El-Horri	C. E.	8 ans	1 54	Bai	Hadj-Mohamed	"
Mohamed-ould-Cadi	L'Aigle	C. E.	10 ans	1 53	Gris truité	Taïeb-bou-Djema	"
El-Hamiani-bel-Arbi	Goumeri	C. E.	4 ans	1 49	Gris	Bouziam	"
Mohamed-ben-Hamidi	Gazelle	C. E.	4 ans	1 45	Gris de fer	Ben-Hamidi	"
Mohamed-ould-Saïd	Sultan	C. E.	7 ans	1 45	Alezan	Hamed	"
Taar-ould-el-Habil	L'Inconnu	C. E.	5 ans	1 54	Alezan rouanné	Son propriétaire	"
Setenafi	Hari	C. E.	6 ans	1 42	Noir	Belgid	"

DEUXIÈME PELOTON.

NOMS DES PROPRIÉTAIRES DES CHEVAUX	NOMS DES CHEVAUX	SEXE	ÂGE	TAILLE	ROBE	NOMS DES JOCKEYS	COULEUR
Larbi-ben-Chenafi-de-Douair	Sultan	C. E.	7 ans	1 52	Gris	Kauldour-ben-Gaïd	Costume indigène
Abd-el-Kader-ould-Mazouzi	Mica	C. E.	8 ans	1 54	Alezan doré	Son propriétaire	"
Kadda-bou-Jaffar	Tessalah	C. E.	6 ans	1 40	Gris clair	Id.	"
Messaoud-ould-el-Bachir	Djerray	C. E.	7 ans	1 53	Bai	Ali	"
Mohamed-bel-Bachir	Lakdar	C. E.	8 ans	1 50	Gris	Son propriétaire	"
Miloud-ben-Zmerti	Clotaire	C. E.	6 ans	1 48	Rouge	Mohamed-ben-Zmerti	"
Bou-Guedra	Hamari	C. E.	7 ans	1 40	Bai	Taïeb	"
Abd-el-Kader-ben-Aouda	Zereg	C. E.	5 ans	1 40	Gris	Saffi	"
Yaya-ben-Moktar	Brahmi	C. E.	9 ans	1 41	Bai	Taïeb-bou-Djema	"

SIXIÈME COURSE, A 4 HEURES 1/2.

Prix du Conseil municipal d'Oran : 1,000 francs.

COURSE D'OBSTACLE, EUROPÉENS ET INDIGÈNES, POUR CHEVAUX ET JUMENTS DE 3 ANS ET AU-DESSUS.

Distance, 2,400 mètres (2 tours), 6 haies. Poids libre. — Entrée : 75 francs.

Le prix sera réduit à 500 francs, s'il y a moins de 5 chevaux engagés.

Zin-ould-Ancur		Bad-Alah	C. E.	7 ans	Rouan	A. Fischer	C. et T. noires
Deliot		Draham	C. E.	4 ans	1 55 Gris pommelé	Jean Fischer	C. verte, T. noire
A. Canicio		Sardine	C. E.	3 ans	1 52 Gris de fer	Mohamed-Farta-	C. noire, T. noire
Grondonna		Trompeur	C. E.	6 ans	1 52 Bai foncé	F. Moralès	C. rose, T. rose
De Saint-Maur		Chergui	C. E.	6 ans	1 44 Gris rouanné	Abd-el-Kader	C. T. noire et raie cerise
Cénac		Phénomène	C. E.	7 ans	1 52 Gris de fer	Cénac	C. bleue, T. noire
Seban		Barbare	C. E.	4 ans	1 48 Bai foncé	Kalech	C. rouge, T. rouge
Cabolo		Tentateur	C. E.	4 ans	1 47 Gris blanc	Hamed	
Abd-el-Kader-bou-Ellouch		Ben-Alame	C. E.	6 ans	1 48 Gris clair	Abd-el-Kader-Bouziul	Costume indigène
					1 50		

A 5 HEURES.

DÉFILÉ DES CAVALIERS INDIGÈNES.

TEMPERATURE OF CYPRUS.

So much has been said and written as to the climate of Cyprus, that I think the following register of temperatures, very accurately kept by a friend, may not be without interest to my readers.

CHIFLIK CAMP.—BELL TENT.

July	23	4 p.m.	105°			10.30 p.m.	73°	
,,	24	4 p.m.	103	7 p.m.	83°	11 a.m.	99	11 p.m. 75°
,,	25	5 a.m.	67	9.15 a.m.	94			
,,	26	5 a.m.	68	8.30 a.m.	103			
,,	30	11.30 a.m.	100	10 p.m.	75			
August	5	8.30 a.m.	90	—	—	12 midnight	74	
,,	6	9 a.m.	90					
,,	8	10 p.m.	68					
,,	9	8 a.m.	93	2 p.m.	96	10.30 p.m.	73	
,,	10	8 a.m.	94					
,,	11	10.30 p.m.	71					
,,	12	8 a.m.	85	2 p.m.	91			

NIKOSIA.—IN A HOUSE.

August	17	9 a.m.	83°	1 p.m.	89°	11.30 p.m.	87°
,,	18	11 a.m.	83	2 p.m.	89	8 p.m.	85
,,	19	5 a.m.	90	9 p.m.	83		
,,	20	6.45 a.m.	83	9 a.m.	85		
,,	21	9 a.m.	85				

APPENDIX.

Date		Time	Temp	Time	Temp	Time	Temp	Time	Temp	Time	Temp
August	22	6.30 a.m.	78	10 a.m.	84	4 p.m.	88			10 p.m.	84°
,,	23	6 a.m.	78	9.30 a.m.	85	8 p.m.	85	7 p.m.	85°		
,,	24	6.30 a.m.	81	11.30 a.m.	85						
,,	25	2.30 a.m.	82	3 p.m.	90						
,,	26	5 p.m.	89								
,,	28	9 a.m.	81	4 p.m.	87	9 p.m.	81				
,,	29	6 a.m.	78	9.30 p.m.	85						
,,	31	5 p.m.	89	9 p.m.	85						
September	1	7 p.m.	80								
,,	2	6 a.m.	79	7 p.m.	87	8.30 p.m.	85				
,,	4	5.30 a.m.	77								
,,	6	6 a.m.	80								
,,	8	1.30 p.m.	83								
,,	9	9 a.m.	82	7.30 p.m.	82						
,,	10	8 a.m.	80	7.30 p.m.	79						
,,	11	2 p.m.	82	8 p.m.	80						
,,	12	1 p.m.	82	7.30 p.m.	80						
,,	13	7.30 p.m.	80								
,,	14	3 p.m.	83	7.30 p.m.	80	10 p.m.	79				
,,	15	11.30 a.m.	81	7.30 p.m.	80						
,,	16	5 p.m.	81	7.30 p.m.	80	10 p.m.	78				
,,	17	8 a.m.	76								
,,	18	2.30 p.m.	81								
,,	25	11 a.m.	75								

428   APPENDIX.

MATHIATI.—INDIAN PAL TENT.

Date		Time	Temp.	Time	Temp.	Time	Temp.	Time	Temp.
October	14	6.30 a.m.	56°	9.30 a.m.	74°	12.30 p.m.	84°		
,,	15	6.30 a.m.	58	1 p.m.	82	10 p.m.	58		
,,	16	7 a.m.	59	12 noon	86	1.45 p.m.	88		
,,	17	6.30 a.m.	52	9.30 a.m.	77	12 noon	90		
,,	18	6.30 a.m.	58						
,,	19	9 a.m.	78	11 a.m.	87				
,,	20	9.30 a.m.	78					9.30 p.m.	62°
,,	27	7 a.m.	56	9.30 a.m.	78	1 p.m.	82	5 p.m.	67
,,	28	6 a.m.	52	1 p.m.	79	5 p.m.	70	10 p.m.	58
,,	29	6 a.m.	52	2 p.m.	82				
,,	30	6 a.m.	50	1 p.m.	82	10 p.m.	58		
November	1	6.30 a.m.	54						
,,	2	6 a.m.	58						
,,	5	1 p.m.	79	10 p.m.	60				
,,	6	7 a.m.	57	7 a.m.	55				
,,	7	12 noon	85						
,,	8	10 p.m.	58						
,,	9	7 a.m.	58	1 p.m.	86	10 p.m.	57		
,,	10	1 p.m.	81					9.30 p.m.	63°
,,	11	6 a.m.	60						
,,	12	6 a.m.	48						

MATHIATI.—WOODEN HUT.

Date	Time	Temp	Time	Temp	Time	Temp
November 17	2 p.m.	82°	10 p.m.	63°		
,, 18	7 a.m.	55	2 p.m.	79	10 p.m.	61°
,, 19	7 a.m.	54	2 p.m.	79	9.30 p.m.	62
,, 20	6.30 a.m.	48	2 p.m.	82	10 p.m.	60
,, 21	6 a.m.	53	2 p.m.	85		
,, 22	7 a.m.	53	2 p.m.	82	10 p.m.	62
,, 23	7 a.m.	52	3 p.m.	81	10 p.m.	61
,, 25	7 a.m.	57	2 p.m.	75	10 p.m.	78
,, 26	7 a.m.	52	2 p.m.	77	10 p.m.	61
,, 27	7.30 a.m.	51	2 p.m.	77	10 p.m.	56
,, 28	7 a.m.	54	2 p.m.	68	9 p.m.	61
,, 29	6.30 a.m.	58	2 p.m.	74	10 p.m.	59
,, 30	7 a.m.	54	12 midnight	59		
December 1	8 a.m.	54	9.30 p.m.	59		
,, 2	8 a.m.	60	2 p.m.	66	10 p.m.	58
,, 3	6 a.m.	48	2.30 p.m.	69	9 p.m.	55
,, 4	8 a.m.	47	2.30 p.m.	69		
,, 5	7.30 a.m.	49	2 p.m.	71		

NOTE A, p. 253.

The gardens of the Temple of Venus, at Paphos, are thus described by Ali Bey :—'I went to visit Inoschipos Aphroditis, or the famed Garden of Venus. It is a plain upon the sea-coast, which may be about two miles long, and slopes gradually towards the sea-shore. The upper part is surrounded by a perpendicular height of horizontal layers of calcareous rock, which forms the prevailing feature of the country, and gives the appearance of a cavern to the garden ; for on whatever side you enter you must descend a ravine ; and when the wind blows strongly (which it did when I was there) upon the high land, it is perfectly. serene in the garden. At different parts in the rock, several streams of pure and limpid water gush out, and it may be perceived that there were many others formerly in various places. As the water comes from above, it may have been easily distributed in various parts of the garden, on account of its descent. The rocky heights form several windings, which diversify the picture, and facilitate the division of the garden into several compartments, in which there are several grottoes or habitations, hewn out of the rock.

'The principal descent appears to me to have been a sort of staircase, also hewn ; it exists at the side of the present village. The vault is fallen in, and leaves the passage encumbered with ruins, which confirms me in my opinion that the garden was entered by a grotto similar to that I have mentioned.

' Perhaps the candidate was detained here to undergo his probation, or to participate in the mysteries of initiation. In this case, when he was restored to light in the garden, he thought himself transported into the celestial regions. It is certain that this rock is considerably undermined, for it may be observed that in several places there are many openings and fallings in ; and, according to this hypothesis, who could describe the obscure labyrinth which those who were to be initiated had to traverse before they entered into the garden?'

NOTE B, p. 301.

The following is a description given by the same traveller, Ali Bey, of his reception and treatment by the then Archbishop of Cyprus, in 1800, from which it will be seen that matters have not changed greatly since that time :—'Having finished my visit to the Serail, I repaired to the archbishop's palace, and found at the entrance the Archimandrite and the steward, with twenty or thirty domestics to receive me. At the foot of the staircase a multitude of priests took me up and carried me to the first gallery, where the "In partibus" received me, with another lot of priests. In the second gallery I found the archbishop. The venerable old man, although his legs were exceedingly swelled, had got himself transported by the Bishop of Paphos, and five or six more, who supported him, to meet me. I made some friendly reproaches for the trouble he had taken on my account; then, giving him my hand, we entered into his room. An Italian physician, called Buononi, settled at Nikosia, who had adopted the dress, manners, and customs of the Greeks, served me as interpreter. He is a man of pleasant humour, well-informed, very arch, and quite free from prejudice. The venerable archbishop related to me the vexatious treatment he had suffered the last year from the rebel Turks of the island. I strove to comfort his heart, still sore from past evils. We talked long together on the subject, and after the wonted honours of coffee, perfumes, and scented water, we parted, with sentiments of cordial affection.

'I afterwards visited, in his dwelling, the steward, where we met the Bishop of Paphos and his colleagues "in partibus;" and what was my surprise when, on coming out, I found again the venerable archbishop in the gallery, who had made them conduct him hither to bid me a last farewell. I cannot express how much I was affected at this kindness from the respectable old man. I tried to chide him for it, but the words died away on my lips. In this manner I concluded my visits of etiquette.'

NOTE C.

By an oversight, two days were omitted from page 111 in printing my 1874 journal, viz. November 13 and 14. Unfortunately the portion thus omitted contains the description of the following incidents, which are specially referred to in the 1878 journal.

(1) *Visit of Turkish Ladies to the 'Sunbeam.'*

Friday, November 13.—To-day Madame Hilmeh, granddaughter of Fuad Pasha, came off to pay me a visit and see the yacht. She wore the very thinnest of yashmaks and a lovely blue silk feridjee, trimmed with Brussels lace, which, when removed, disclosed a lovely pale salmon-coloured dress, with a Pompadour peplum, trimmed with a good deal of light blue, and a bonnet to match, with salmon-coloured feathers. She bowed and spoke to all the gentlemen on board, and had quite a long chat with Tom in the deck-house in French; but then she is one of the most eager for emancipation among the Turkish ladies. Her husband and her father, Khanil Bey, are liberal-minded men, and the former even talks of realising all his worldly goods and settling in Paris, that his wife may enjoy herself a little more. She was delighted with the yacht, and was very anxious that we should get up steam and carry her off to England, leaving her husband and children to follow by land; but the difficulties in the way of her getting leave to quit the country would be enormous. Some years hence, if a revolution occurs in the manners and customs of Turkish ladies, it will be rather interesting to look back on the visits of the first four ladies who had courage to obtain permission to break what, for ages, have been the civil and religious laws of their country, and pay their first visit to a European. We are rather amused to hear that the Sultan is getting quite jealous of the yacht, and thinks it attracts more attention than anything not belonging to him ought to do. Having heard of the visits of the other Princesses and ladies, the Imperial Princesses are anxious to come on board also, and that would be a still more terrible infringement of etiquette. His admiration of the yacht, however, has made him extremely kind to us, and has procured us permission to see Beylerbey and Tcheragan in the most agreeable manner, and under the pleasantest circumstances.

(2) *Visit to the Palace of Tcheragan.*

Saturday, November 14.—We were called early, and started at 9 a.m. for the palace of Tcheragan, Mr. Foster and Mr. Wrench accompanying us; for it is so difficult to get permission to see the palaces, that, though these gentlemen have been here for years, they have never thought it worth while to take all the trouble necessary for a resident to do so. We found the servants all ready to receive us, and, entering a large hall, went up a magnificent staircase into another large hall of exquisite proportions and beautifully decorated. This was surrounded with suites of rooms on the same plan as Beylerbey, only much larger and handsomer. All the rooms were splendidly furnished. A great deal of the furniture is by Turkish workmen. Some cabinets, wooden, marqueterie, and others, inlaid with mother-of-pearl and lapis lazuli, were about the most beautiful I had ever seen. The doors, too, were all inlaid with mother-of-pearl, and had solid silver handles. The chairs were handsomely carved and gilt, the divans were covered with the richest stuffs. One or two of the rooms were hung with stiff gold brocade, another with Damascus work, all hand-woven, with threads of gold and solid bullion tassels. The bath itself and all the adjacent rooms are perfectly lovely in shape, and are decorated with the purest white marble, carved and traced with an infinitude of patterns. The cushions were all white and gold brocade—no colour. Downstairs there were more splendid rooms, and a magnificent hall, with black and white marble columns. But how am I to go on describing palaces where everything is alike beautiful, and each room and hall more gorgeous and larger than the last? We went to the gardens, which were full of flowers, and to a very pretty kiosk, and then stepped into our boat again, after feeing the civil servants, who looked far too great swells to think of backshish, but who nevertheless accepted it with gratitude.

1878.

SUMMARY OF THE VOYAGE OF THE YACHT 'SUNBEAM' from Portsmouth to Brest, Vigo, Cadiz, Gibraltar, Oran, Cagliari, Naples, Messina, Cyprus, Rhodes, Gallipoli, Constantinople, Yeni Liman, Syra, Milo, Malta, and Marseilles, September 20 to December 29, 1878.

Date	Lat. ° N ′	Long. ° W ′	Distance run Sail (Knots)	Distance run Steam (Knots)	Remarks
1878 Sept. 20	50 0	3 7	95	—	Off Start Point
21	48 19	4 45	—	132	Off Cape St. Matthieu
22	—	—	—	—	At Brest
23	48 16	4 40	—	57	Left Brest
24	45 19	7 50	221	—	Bay of Biscay
25	43 1	9 28	111	63	Off Cape Finisterre
26	42 13	8 40	—	72	Arrived at Vigo
27 and 28	—	—	—	—	At Vigo
29	41 14	9 6	42	39	Sailed from Vigo
30	39 20	9 30	120	—	Off Cape Peniche
Oct. 1	37 0	8 46	172	—	Off Cape Sagres
2	36 56	7 18	81	—	Off mouth of Guadiana
3	36 30	6 12	—	60	Arrived at Cadiz
4 to 7	—	—	—	—	At Cadiz
8	36 6	5 20	80	—	Cadiz to Gibraltar
9 and 10	—	—	—	—	At Gibraltar
11	—	—	6	—	Left Gibraltar
12	36 17	EAST 4 29	60	—	Off Malaga
13	36 31	WEST 2 5	84	37	Cape de Gata N 16 miles
14	36 13	1 20	108	—	Off Cape Falcon
15	35 43	0 28	6	25	Arrived at Oran
16	36 30	EAST 0 15	34	32	Left Oran. Off Mostaghanem
17	37 34	3 38	129	32	Off Cape Bengut
18	38 17	6 38	168	—	Cape Spartivento E 90 miles
19	39 12	9 7	45	71	Arrived at Cagliari
20	—	—	—	—	At Cagliari
	—	—	—	—	Left Cagliari, and becalmed all day
22	39 6	9 43	51	—	Off Cape Carbonara
23	39 59	12 25	145	—	

1878. Summary of Voyage—continued.

Date	Lat. ° N ′	Long. ° E ′	Distance run Sail Knots	Distance run Steam Knots	Remarks
1878 Oct. 24	40 50	14 15	90	—	Arrived at Naples
25 to 30	—	—	—	—	At Naples
31	40 30	14 19	25	—	Left Naples. Hove-to off Capri
Nov. 1	38 56	15 16	114	—	Off Stromboli
2	38 11	15 33	71	34	Arrived at Messina
3	37 10	18 16	135	28	
4	35 52	22 46	234	—	Off Cerigo
5	35 31	26 39	193	—	Off Naxos
6	34 55	29 53	164	—	
7	34 43	32 28	27	122	At Port Papho
8	34 38	33 2	—	40	Arrived at Limasol
9	34 36	33 39	—	45	Arrived at Larnaka
10 to 12	—	—	—	—	At Larnaka
13	34 56	33 52	—	—	Left Larnaka 11.30 a.m. Off Cape Pila
14	35 20	33 19	—	171	Off Kyrenia
15	35 8	32 47	—	40	In Morfu Bay
17	35 36	31 24	11	69	Rhodes WNW 160 miles
18	35 54	31 19	16	—	Off Cape Khelidonia
19	36 27	28 19	—	153	Arrived at Rhodes
20	36 28	28 1	3	10	Left Rhodes
21	37 40	25 57	7	149	Off Nikaria
22	38 59	25 39	98	—	Off Mitylene
23	40 1	26 10	87	—	In the Dardanelles
24	40 24	26 41	19	17	Off Gallipoli
25	40 28	27 0	30	—	Left Gallipoli. Off the lines of Boulair
26	40 23	27 33	98	—	Arrived at Artaki Bay
27 to 30	—	—	—	—	In Artáki Bay
Dec. 1	41 0	29 0	80	10	Arrived at Constantinople
to 11	—	—	—	—	At Constantinople
12	40 24	26 40	105	20	Left Constantinople. Arrived at Gallipoli
13	40 7	26 23	—	23	Off Chanak
14	39 20	26 22	82	64	At Yeni Liman
15	38 48	26 37	—	39	
16	37 28	24 55	—	135	At Syra
17	37 10	25 0	25	—	Between Syra and Paros

1878. *Summary of Voyage*—continued.

Date		Lat.	Long.	Distance run		Remarks
				Sail	Steam	
		° N ′	° W ′	Knots	Knots	
1878 Dec.	18	36 26	24 29	106	—	Off Milo
	19	36 35	23 46	38	45	Off Karavi
	20	36 6	20 12	—	176	⎫
	21	36 7	16 32	63	117	⎬ To Malta
	22	36 9	15 23	95	—	⎭
	23	35 53	14 30	80	18	Arrived at Valetta
	24	—	—	—	—	At Malta
	25	37 25	12 54	—	147	Off Cape Granitola
	26	38 24	9 7	161	53	Off Cape Spartivento
	27	41 8	6 21	60	146	
	28	43 2	5 21	107	24	Off Ciolat
	29	—	—	-	—	Arrived at Marseilles

		Knots
Total distance run	⎰ Sail	4,182
	⎱ Steam	2,515
		6,697

POSTSCRIPT.

Many people have remarked that in my last book I did not give any idea of the cost of such an expedition as the one therein described. To do this with absolute correctness would be rather difficult, as the items come under so many different heads, and so much depends on the administration, and on the tastes of the party. Pilots we employ very rarely,—never, in fact, except when compelled to do so. Their fees, moreover, are not so high as is generally supposed. Harbour and port dues are not an expensive item to a yacht flying the flags of any of the Royal Yacht Clubs. Yachts can now be bought at almost any price, ranging from 10*l.* per ton. An able seaman, with his clothes, costs about 30*s.* a week. Wages now average 26*s.*, with a shilling or two more for men performing extra duties, such as coxswains, quartermasters, storekeepers, or sailkeepers. The men all find themselves in provisions. Cooks get from 30*s.* to 2*l.*, stewards the same, the rates varying according to the size of the yacht and the responsibility of their position. Skippers and engineers receive from 3*l.* to 4*l.* a week. The owner usually provides for this latter class, besides giving them a certain allowance for clothes.

Living is not more expensive afloat than on shore. Taking one place with another, some things are dearer here, cheaper there, and thus the average is maintained throughout.

Steaming we find, on the whole, much cheaper than sailing, as the consumption of coal is not nearly so costly as the wear and tear of sails and ropes, especially when they flap about in a calm. Of course, on board a yacht, as everywhere else, expenses depend very much on the disposition of the owner and the way in which he manages his affairs. Having determined the size of the yacht and the number of his guests, staff, and crew, he can easily calculate his approximate expense, always remembering that alterations on board, however trifling, long land journeys, hotel bills, and shopping on shore, add largely to the cost of the voyage.

The 'Sunbeam' was designed by Mr. St. Clare Byrne, of Liverpool, and, as first launched, may be technically defined as a composite three-masted screw schooner. Topsail yards were added to her foremast, and several other slight alterations made for her voyage round the world. The engines, by Messrs. Laird, are of 70 nominal or 350 indicated horse-power, and developed a speed of 10.13 knots on the measured mile. The bunkers contain 80 tons of coal. The average daily consumption is 4 tons, and the speed ten knots in fine weather under steam. Under sail she has done fifteen, frequently twelve, and for many days together on a long voyage kept up an average of nine. The principal dimensions of the hull are :—Length for tonnage, 157 ft. ; beam, extreme, 27 ft. 6 in. ; displacement tonnage, 531 tons ; area of midship section, 202 square feet.

INDEX.

AAR

A ARIF Pasha, 86, 107, 109
    Abdul Aziz, Sultan, 67-71 ; his nephews, 71 ; his fancy for the yacht, 78 ; his message of thanks, 86 ; sketches by, 88, 113
Abdul Hamid II., Sultan, 336; description of, 348 ; his character, 350 ; his farming partnership scheme, 368
Acropolis of Athens, 40, 41
Adramytium, gulf of, 377
Adrianople, excursion to, 354, 356 ; havoc wrought in, 358 ; festive scene at, 360
Ægean, rough night in the, 376
Ægina, island of, 37
Africa, north coast of, 27, 216
Ajaccio, 167
Alcazar, the, 197
Alexandretta, wonderful sport at, 372
Alexandria Troas, 49
Algeciras, 24
Algiers, 26
Ali Bey, 105
Ali Bey, the traveller, cited, 265
Allix, Colonel, 369 (*misprinted* Allen)
Almeria, 210
Amalfi, 238
Anacapri, excursion to, 245
Anchor, ship's chain fished up by, 93 ; dragging of, 120
Andoe, Captain, 15
Anemones, sea, 24
Antiparos, island of, 381
Apostoli, 44

BAR

Aqueducts, Turkish, 75, 122
Arab riders, 9 ; races, 213
Arbutus bushes, 331
Archimandrite of Cyprus, 268, 299
Archipelago, 48 ; commerce of the, 125
Argalasti, 48
Argos, 36
Argostoli harbour, 134
Armenian women, 80
Armenians, money-making habits of, 275
Arta, gulf of, 138
Artaki Bay, 323 ; sports at, 329, 332
Asp, a real, 302
Athens, excursion to, 39
Athienu, 263, 281
Athos, Mount, monastery on, 48
Atlas mountains, 16, 216
Ayasolook, 121
Azimuth compass carried overboard, 7
Azizieh, Princess, 78, 97 ; presents from, 112 ; her visit to the yacht, 348

B ABIES, French, 180
    Bagtcheh Keui, 75
Bairam, 103 ; Kourban, 345, 360
Baker Pasha, 345, 369 ; his fortifications, 351, 369
Balbus, house of, 229
Balukli, miraculous fishes of, 106
Bantams, 91
Barb, pugnacious, 17

BAS

Bastia, 166
Bathing at Gibraltar, 24
Battle, welcome back to, 405
Bayona Islands, 182
Bazaars, 53, 57, 92, 101, 116, 342, 344, 345
Beccaficos, 259
Beikos, 73
Belgrade, forest of, 75
Belo Poulo island, 36
Besika Bay, 49, 314
Beylerbey, palace at, 63; visit to, 107
Biddulph, Colonel, 271
Bighi Bay, 391
Bigliotti, Mr., 117
Bill of fare, Constantinople, 95
Bill of health left behind, 8, 166, 193
Birds blown on board, 217
Biscay, Bay of, 6, 181
Bishop, Mr., 3
Black Sea, 76
Blunt, Colonel, and the poor Turk, 371
Boar-hunt in Morocco, 19
Boarding by night in a gale, 4
Bolton, Captain, 287
Bonchurch, 3, 179
Bonitas, 206
Bonner left ill at Larnaka, 282; his pigeon, 317, 320; his death, 337
Boolgoorloo, view from, 63
Boom, main, accident to, 6
Bordighera, 170
Bosphorus, up the, 64
Boulair, 318
Bowsprit snapped, 93
Boyer, Madame, 97
Brackenbury, Colonel, 267
Brassey, the late Mr., 55
Brest, 179
Briar-root pipes, 168
Bride, Moorish, 13
Brigand, history of a Syrian, 285
Brigands, 28, 44, 47, 150, 398; capture of, 238
Brine, Captain Lindesay, 331
Broussa, excursion to, 91

CAT

Buffavento, 290
Building, Turkish superstition concerning, 108, 336
Buoys, Spanish fishermen's, 190
Butrinto river, 140
Byron, Lord, scene of his adventure with robbers, 44; his house at Melaxata, 136

CAASBA, the, 12
Cadiz, 193, 201; pigeon caught at, 317
Café à la turque, 11
Cafidje, the Sultan's, 351
Cagliari, 218; streets of, 220
Caïques, 52, 62, 63; the Sultan's, 84
Calais, 172
Calvert, Consul, 361
Camels, 116, 121, 375
Camp, a model, 291
Campimento, 25
Cannebière, the, 402
Capes: Agate (de Gata), 210; Blanco, 256; Falcon, 211; Finisterre, 6, 182; Gallo, 27; Gatto, 256; Hydra, 36; Kormakiti, 294; Malea, 129, 388; Matapan, 36, 129; Monda, 136; Ortegal, 6; Peniche, 191; Sacratif, 207; Sagres, 191; St. Mary, 8; St Vincent, 8; St. Vito, 27; Scalambra, 397; Seakeas, 133, 136; Sigri, 49 376; Skinari, 133; Spartel, 8; Spartivento, 151, 217, 247; Sunium, 43; Tenez, 26; Zeogari, 256
Capri, 242, 245
Caralis, the ancient, 228
Carob trees, 292
Carpets, Turkey, 118
Castellamare, Bay of, 27; visits to the dockyard at, 235, 239
Castles of Roumelia and Anatolia, 315
Castro, 127, 384
Cats, wild, of Cyprus, 256; lavender-coloured, 327

Cathedrals: Cadiz, 194; Cagliari, 222; Monreale, 28; Vigo, 185; Seville, 195
Cavias, beauty of its inhabitants, 227
Cemeteries, Turkish, 81; at Gibraltar, 203; Sardinian, 227
Cephalonia, 135
Cerigo island, 36
Cerigotto, island of, 248
Cesnola, excavations of, 256; his work cited, 280
Ceuta, 22, 207
Chalcis, ancient, 45
Chanak-Kalesi, 49, 115, 315, 375
Chaos, village so called, 302
Chaussée de Sein, 6
Chicken-pox, 181
Child, a lost, 401
Children sent home from Gibraltar, 14
Chinese midshipman on board the 'Minotaur,' 252
Chios, island of, 49, 123, 379, 313
Chlebowski, Mr., 88, 101; present from, 113
Christmas, preparations for, at Malta, 392, 394; keeping of, on board, 396
Chumleyjah, 63
Church, Greek, interior of a, 268, 300
Circello, Mount, 165
Citium, site of, 259
Cloaks, Turkish ladies', 84
Cockatoo, honour paid to a, 352
Collision in Portsmouth harbour, 177; narrow escapes of, 120, 208
Commanderia, the, 257
Companion smashed in, 7
Conca d'oro, Palermo, 28
Constantinople, 51, 334, 364; walls of, 105; altered condition of, 339; change of ministry in, 346, 348
Contract work in Turkey, 110, 356
Convent, Carthusian, 160, 234; Greek, 298
Coral, black, 246
Coral shops, Messina, 33; Naples, 159
Corcubion, 182

Corfu, 139; dress of women in, 145
Corsica, 166
Cortazzi, Mr., 115
Coruña harbour, 181
Cowes, 5
Crabs, peculiar, 195
Crake, Mr., 95, 154
Crete, coast of, 248
Cross, the 'true,' 380
Cyclamens, 302
Cyclades, among the, 381
Cyclopean masonry, 119, 127
Cypresses in graveyards, 81
Cypriote women, 297
Cyprus, coast of, 250, 256; shape of, 288; climate of, 252; fertility of, 254, 258; temperature of, 268, 271, 274, 277, 296; prevalence of fever in, 278; antiquities smuggled from, 282; cheapness of provisions in, 291; women of, 297; health of our party in, 304; British possession of, 305; hasty occupation of, 325
Cyzicus, 329, 330

Dali, 279
Damos, Bay of, 136
Daniel, Mr., 331
Dardanelles, 375; entering by night, 50; by day, 315
De Lancey, Captain, 295
Delessert, M., cited, 225
Delis, 44
Delos, 381
Deluge through porthole, 140
Derelict toy ship, 187
Dervishes, dancing, 77; howling, 81
Devil's current, 105
Diamonds, Paphian, 255
Diana's bath, 117; temple, 121
Dining scene, 181
Dixon, Mr. Hepworth, 253
Djamil Pasha, 365
Dogs, Constantinople, 53, 56, 58, 59; dying from fever in Cyprus, 305

DOL

Dolmabagtcheh, 67, 84. 367
Donkey, dead, 263
Dormer, Colonel, 267
Dresses, secondhand, market for, 53
Dressing-table, diamond and ruby, 61
Drokho, 44
Duranta, shrub so called, 151

EAGLE, 121
　Earthquakes at Euripo, 47; Rhodes, 308
Eclipse, solar, 35
Elias, Mount, 381
Elliot, Sir Henry and Lady, 72
Embassy, Austrian, 353; English, 65, 107, 370
Encampment, our, in Morocco, 17
Engineer of the 'Violet,' 94
Ephesus, 121
Episcopi, 256
Etna, Mount, 34, 151, 398
Euripo, 44
Evil eye, Jewish charms against the, 21; Sultan's dread of the, 108

FAIR, Spanish, 188
　Falconera, island of, 388
Falconer's shipwreck, place of, 44
Famagousta, 283
Farming by the Sultan, 368
Feast of Tabernacles, 21
Fergusson, Mr., referred to, 337
Fernando, San, 201
Ferns, 187
Fête, Arab, 213
Fever 3,000 feet above sea level, 293
Fever-haunt, a sportsman's, 287
Fire, Sultan's dread of, 69
Fire-engines, Turkish, 64
Fish-market at Vigo, 184, 188
Fisheries off Bayona islands, 182, 189
Fitzroy, Captain, torpedo experiments of, 331
Fleet, Turkish, 109; French, 215

HAS

Fleet hounds, the, 314
Flying-fish, 27, 206
Fog, a night of, 189
Foster, Mr., 55, 80
French, Empress of the, her visit to Constantinople, 61, 63, 108, 109
Friday, starting on, 1, 2, 178
Fruit amidst drought, 38
Fuad Pasha, reforms of, 99
Fundukli, 77, 334
Furin, village of, 262

GADAKIRA Bay, 48
　Gaïdaro, island of, 379
Galita island, 27
Gallipoli, 115, 316, 373
Gamecocks, Turkish, 91
Garousta, 144
Genoese castle at Smyrna, 119
Giant's mountain, 73
Giaour, the kiss of a, 109
Gibraltar, 14, 202
Gifford, Lord, 267, 268
Gluttony, a Sultan's, 70
Golden Horn, 52, 86, 110, 334
Grampuses, 114
Grapes, 'fragola,' 244
Greaves, Colonel, 267
Greci, church of the, 154
Greeks, costume of, 37, 145; curiosity of, 128, 271
Grenfell, Captain, 239
Grotto of the Nymphs, 137; stalactite, 168
Guadalquivir, mouth of the, 192
Guinea pigs, family of, 394
Guy Fawkes at sea, 249

HALIL Pasha, 99
　Hammick, Commander, 331
Hanson, Mrs., 371
Harems, reform of, 68, 99, 349; visits to, 78, 96; furniture of, 87, 108
Hastings, 2

HAW

Hawks, 17, 141
Hay, Lord John, 251
Herbert, Mr., 267, 290, 277, 295, 303
Hermit of Malea, 388
Herodotus, referred to, 132
Hilmeh, Madame, 79; present from, 112
Hobart Pasha, 342
Holbech, Lieutenant, 290, 291
Holiday at Seville, 201
Holland, Commander, 331
Honey from Mount Hymettus, 42
Horaghe, Sardinian, 227
Hornby, Admiral, 324, 328, 329, 333, 349; his impression of Cyprus, 324
Horses, Arab, 9, 17, 67, 348
Hurricane off Milo, 382
Huts, soldiers', in Cyprus, 270, 292

ICARUS, legend of, 312
Idalium, the ancient, 279
Indian troops in Cyprus, 261
Inns, curious, 18, 311
Ionian islands, government of, 133. 144
Ioos, island of, 48
Ipsara, island of, 49, 314
Irrigation, Athenian, 41; Moorish, 214
Ischia, island of, 158
Italian innkeeper at Artaki, his adventures, 327
Ithaca, 136
Izachastra, village of, 297
Izzet Bey, 99, 102, 344, 365

JANISSARIES, museum of the, 60
Japanese midshipman on board the 'Minotaur,' 251
Jelly-fish, 7
Jewellery, Sardinian, 221
Jewels, cheap, 342
Jews of Tetuan, 18, 21
Joshua's tomb, 73
Jupiter Olympius, temple of, 41

LIS

KAIMAKAM, misfortunes of a, 371
Kaloyera rocks, 313
Kampos, village of, 297
Kandili, 64, 105
Kara Bournou, 379
Karamania, mountains of, 307
Karavastasia, 294, 303
Karavi, island of, 388
Kattirdji-Janni, a Syrian brigand, 285
Khabyles, disturbances among the, 12
Khaireddin Pasha, 367
Khania, 248
Khedive, the, 98; his fleecing, 64
Khilid-Bahri, 315
Kiasim, Madame Ikbal, 99, 344; her visits to the yacht, 102, 348; present from, 112
Kikko, convent of, 298
Koran, Turkish lady's view of the, 99
Koulleli-Bourgas, 363
Kourban Bairam, 345, 360
Ktima, 253, 254
Kyrenia, 290
Kythræa, excursion to, 273

LACE, old Greek, 394
Lamp, peculiar Moorish, 23
La Pais, convent of, 293
Lapps and Arabs, 10
Larnaka, 260, 281
Layard, Sir Henry and Lady, 346, 369
Lefka, excursion to, 302; Mudir of, 303
Lemon, enormous, 143
Levant, Flower of the, 333
'Levant Herald,' editor of the, 365
Lilford, Lord, natural history collection of, 301
Lilies, peculiar, 151
Lilli Bourgas, 356
Liman, island of, 333
Limasol, 257
Lipari islands, 32, 158
Lisbon, rock of, 6

MAC

M'CALMONT, Captain, 290, 295, 303; his adventures with the Turkish army, 302
M'Crae, Captain, 14
Madona, island of, 139
Maidenhair fern, 132, 275
Malta, 391
Man-of-war, Spanish, 12; Turkish, 87
Mansell, Captain, 46
Mansourah, 214
Marathon, 44
Marbella, 207
Maritimo island, 27
Maritza, river, 357
Market-boats, Spanish, 185
Marmora, Sea of, 51, 333; rough day in, 93; perils of navigation in, 114
Marseilles, 399; parting from the yacht at, 403
Mars-el-Kibir, 215
Mashleck, 65, 88
Mastic, cultivation of, 123
Mastic liqueur, 297
Mathiati, camp at, 277
Melaxata, 136
Messina, town of, 32, 153, 247; strait of, 34
Meteors, 35
Millis, orange gardens of, 225
Milo, island of, 126, 383
Minerals ejected from Vesuvius, 242; of Cyprus, 281
Minerva, temple of, on Cape Sunium, 43
Missolonghi, 91
Mithags, Sardinian, 224
Mitylene, island of, 49, 314, 377; town of, 379
Mohammed's wet-nurse, 262
Monaco, 171
Monastery, absurdly strict, 48
Monreale, excursion to, 28
Monte Carlo, 171
Montpensier, palace of the Duke of, 200
Moorish costumes, 10; café, 11; music, 11, 13; wedding, 12

OLI

Morfu, 294
Morocco, camping in, 17
Mosaic decoration, 28, 29, 60
Mosques, Turkish: Ahmedyeh, 60, 338; Ali Pasha, 358; Eyoob, 106; Pigeon, 57, 101, 343; St. Sophia, 59, 337; Selim II., 359; Sulieman-yeh, 60
Mosquitoes, 198
Moudania, 90, 93
Mouflons, 302
Murad V., 71; his imprisonment, 351
Murillo, pictures of, 196, 197
Murray, Captain, 317
Music, Moori-h, 11, 13; Turkish, 52; Sardinian, 228
Mustapha Fazil, 98
Myrtles, 22, 48

NAPIER, Lord and Lady, 205
Napier, Mr., 331
Naples, 158, 233, 239; bay of, 232
Naumachia, 329
Nauplia, gulf of, 36
Navarino, 36
Navigation laws, breach of, 80
Naxos, island of, 249
Nazli, Princess, 78, 98; self-sacrifice of, 339; her visits to the yacht, 102, 348; her travels, 349
Needles, the, 5
Negropont, island of, 44
Nice, 170; return by land from, 171
Nicopolis, ruins of, 138
Night alarms, 31, 35, 208
Nikaria, 312
Nikosia, 264; the Monastery Camp at, 267; buildings of, 271
Nisida, island of, 239
Noel, Lieutenant, 284, 288

OLDENBURG, Grand Duke of, 82
Olive-gathering in Cephalonia, 135; at Artaki, 326

Olympus, Mount, 334
Opera at Argostoli, 136; Messina, 155; Naples, 159, 160; Malta, 393
Oran, 212
Orange gardens of Chios, 123, 313; Millis, 225; Kyrenia, 291
Oranges, mandarine, 151
Orios, channel of, 44
Oros Stavro, convent of, 262
Owl, adventure of the, 313, 322

PADISHAH, prayer for the, 320
Pæstum, 239
Pal tents, 272
Palermo, 27
Panaria, 32
Paphos, 253
Paris, 171, 405
Paros, island of, 139, 381
Parr, Mr., 403
Partridges, decoy, 200
Passengers, uninvited, 124
Patmos, 313
Paus, Señor Antonio, 23
Peacocks, the Sultan's, 86, 112, 335
Pedæus, river, 273
Pellegrino, Monte, excursion to, 29
Pelleki, drive to, 139
Pentadactylon mountain, 269, 275, 290
Pentelicus, Mount, 44
Pera, 52; the great fire at, 66
Pheasants, wild, 84
Phœnician antiquities, 223
Phosphorescence of the sea, 7, 34
Pianosa, 166
Pigeon, adventure of the, 317, 320
Pilate's house, 198
Pilot-fish, 207
Pilots, navigating without, 37, 50
Pindus, Mount, 48
Piræus, harbour of, 37
Pisani, Count, 73
Pitch wells, 132
Plates, Rhodian, 309
Point St. Matthieu, 180

Pompeii, relics from, 160; excavations at, 235
Ponies, pugnacious, 294
Porpoises, 7, 206
Porters, Constantinople, 346
Porto d'Anzio, 165
Portraits, sailors', 240
Portsmouth harbour, 5, 175; collision in, 177
Portugal, coast of, 8
Portuguese men-of-war, 7
Posilippo, 159, 239
Presepio fair, 400
Prévésa, 138
Preziosi, Mr., 101
Prisoners, Turkish, removed from Nikosia to Kyrenia, 273; at Rhodes, 310
Procida, island of, 158
Promotion, Turkish, 80
Puercas rocks, 202
Pulpits, singular, 269, 301

QUARANTINE at Spanish ports, 193, 207
Queen, native garments made in Cyprus for the, 276

RACES at Oran, 213
Railway, Turkish, 355
Ramazan, fast of, 53, 57, 80
Raouf Pasha, arrest of, 365
Redondela, trip to, 186
Refugees, Turkish, 336, 338, 339, 371; proposed importation of, into Cyprus, 325; sufferings of, on board the 'Asia,' 352; desperate railway ride of, 363
Resina, excursion to, 162
Rhadmis, ruins of, 44
Rhodes, 308; climate of, 312
Road-making in Cyprus, 279
Rodriguez, Señor, 23
Roomili Hissar, 64; 'devil's current' at, 105

Rosalie, St., shrine of, 29
Rosalio, San, feast of, 201
Rose-water sprinkling, 297
Roses, green, 132, 147
Roumania, Prince and Princess of, 2; proposed visit to, 74; puzzling telegram from, 76; letter of explanation from, 89
Round towers, 218
Rowing, Turkish, 85
Run aground, 322
Russian soldier, attempted theft by, 356
Russians, outrage at British consulate by, 361; artifices of, 374
Rustem Pasha, 106
Ryde, 3, 5

SABBATH, a Sultan's view of the, 114
Sahara, whirlwind from the, 216
Sailors' hospital, Cadiz, 201
St. Alban's Head, 5
St. Hilarion, 290
St. John the Evangelist's cavern, 312
St. John, Knights of, 309; Grand Hospital of the, at Rhodes, 310; their buildings in Malta, 392
St. Julian, Mount, 27
St. Luke, signature of, 301
St. Paul, scene of his scourging, 254
Salamis, island of, 37
Salerno, 238
Salinas or salt-pans, 195
Salt trade, Sardinian, 218, 230
Salto di Tiberio, 244
Sandown, 3, 179
San Martino, convent of, 160, 234
San Salvador mountain, 139
San Stefano, 354
Santa Maura, island of, 138
Sardinia, 218; people of, 221; costume of, 221, 222; seldom visited by yachts, 225
Scala, 384
Sculpture used as ballast, 331

Scylla, rock of, 32
Scyros, island of, 49
Sea, luminosity of, 7, 34; blue colour of, 36; shop on the, 210
Sedan chairs, 107
Seismometer, the, 242
Selemlek, the, 99
Seraglio, Constantinople, 61; Adrianople, 358
Seraglio Point, 52, 94, 333
Serenade, birthday, 202
Serpho, 381
Serpieri, Enrico, monument to, 227
Sevanza island, 27
Seville, excursion to, 194
Seymour, Captain, 317, 320
Sheep for the sacrifice, 346
Sherry, unadulterated, 195
Ships spoken or alluded to: Achilles, 323; Africaine, 16; Alaska, 129, 132; Alexandra, 323, 326, 328, 349; Antelope, 75, 349; Asia, 352; Assistance, 177; Australia, 24; Black Prince, 273, 274; Captain, 182; Cuckoo, 399; Curlew, 205; Cygnet, 323; Dandolo, 233; Dos Hermanos, 23; Duilio, 233; Eothen, 376; Eurydice, 176; Excellent, 5; Flamingo, 374; Foxhound, 283, 288; Glen Eagle, 283; Helicon, 26, 323; Hibernia, 391; Himalaya, 233, 235; Humber, 260, 291; Invincible, 323; Ione, 159; Iron Duke, 189; Italia, 233, 235, 239; Khedive, 14; La Gallicionère, 179; La Plata, 158; Lancashire Witch, 204; Minotaur, 251, 253, 394; Monarch, 323, 329; Muffa, 115; Nave de Tolosa, 12; Northumberland, 394; Osmanlieh, 87; Pallas, 314; Prince Pajowski, 37; Raleigh, 260, 304; Research, 314; Salamis, 323; Sarah Smart, 89; Shannon, 394; Sultana, 399; Swiftsure, 16; Téméraire, 317, 374; Thunderer, 314, 321, 323, 331; Torch, 37; Vanguard, 189; Violet,

SHO

94, 162; Vittorio Emanuele, 218, 231; Zantha, 159
Shooting in Morocco, perils of, 20
Shot across our bow, 49
Siamese coinage, 204
Sicily, coast of, 27, 32, 398; as a cruising ground for yachts, 150, 398
Sidler-Tchiflik station, refugees at, 363
Silevri, bay of, 94
Silk of Cyprus, 276; manufactory of, at Broussa, 91
Sirocco, a, 217
Skutari, 63; English cemetery at, 82
Slaves, Turkish, 79, 97, 102, 349
Sleeper, rousing a, 289
Smyrna, 116; fever of, 130
Snake on board, 118
Snake-charmers, 10
Snakes, rarity of, in Cyprus, 272
Snow in Corsica, 167
Solaro, Mount, 245
Soldiers, Russian, 360; Turkish, 318
Solent, the, 5, 175
'Son of a Slave,' 109
Sorrento, 243
Sowajees, street horses of Constantinople, 56, 334
Spanish workwomen, 199; worshippers, 201
Sponge, Kyrenian, 270
Sport in Albania, 142; at Alexandretta, 372; at Artaki, 330; in Corsica, 168; in Cyprus, 279, 295, 303; in Morocco, 17, 19
Stafford House Committee, scene of their labours, 355, 359
Stamboul, 52, 105; bazaars of, 53
Stars, shooting, 35
Start Point, 5
Stiletto, use of the, 168
Stock, Mr., case of, 361
Strabo, referred to, 308
Strangford, Lady, 338, 369; her hospital at Adrianople, 359
Stromboli, 32, 246; eruption of, 152
Suda Bay, 248

TIM

Sultan attending mosque, 66, 84, 103, 347; working for the, 113; plot to frighten the, 367, 370
Sultan Valideh, 68, 350; why not veiled, 104; kissed by the French Empress, 109
Sultanas, 71
Sultans, tombs of the, 56
Summer, remarkable Turkish, 336
Sunday, luck of starting on, 5
Sweet Waters of Asia, 65; of Europe, 65, 86, 112, 335; Valley of, 88
Sycamino, 44
Syra, island of, 125; town of, 379

TALANTA, channel of, 44
'Tancred,' cited, 340
Tangier, 8; trip from Gibraltar to, 16
Taormina, ruins at, 156
Tarantella dance, 244
Tariff of one pound each item, 189
Tchekmedje, lines of, 345
Tcheragan, palace of, 87
Tchergatasch, 362
Tchorlou railway station, 355, 364
Telemachus, café of, 137
Telika, vehicle so called, 357
Tenedos, 49, 314
Tenos, 379, 380; our passengers to, 125
Tetuan, excursion to, 18
Tharras, 227
Theatres, ancient Greek, 127, 156
Theatres at Argostoli, 136; Cagliari, 228; Constantinople, 79; Messina, 155; Naples, 159
Therapia, 65
Thérèse, Madame, 399
Theseus, temple of, 39; scene of his legendary dip, 49
Thessaly, mountains of, 138
Thieves, a village of, 207
Thousand and One Columns, 56, 338
Thynne, Mr., 317
Tiles, remarkable, 198, 359
Time, Turkish, 72

Timepieces, a mania for, 54
Tlemcen, 214
Tobacco manufactory, 199
Toilette in a Greek convent, 299
Tophaneh, 52 ; scene at, 104
Torpedo experiments, 331
Tortoise on deck, 333
Trafalgar Bay, 202
Trikhiri, channel of, 48
Troödos, Mount, 300
Troy, plain of, 49
Truefitt's establishment in Cyprus, 252
Tryon, Captain, 323, 328
Tunja, river, 357
Turk, wayside lunch with a, 330
Turkey, succession in, 56, 71, 98 ; condition of women in, 68, 79, 99 ; marriage of princesses in, 72 ; time of day in, 72
Turkeys of Cyprus, 275
Turkish ladies, bowstringing of, 350 ; self-sacrifice of, 369 ; first visits ever paid to a European by, 102, 348 ; ministers, 80
Turks, manners of the, 281
Turtles, 27

ULYSSES, grotto of, 137 ; ship of, 146
Unseaworthy ship, 94 ; her wreck, 162
Ushant, 6

VAROSHIA, 287
Vathi, 136
Vendetta, the, 168
Venetian remains, 45 ; cannon, 188
Venus, statue of, found in Milo, 127 ; temple of, at Paphos, 253
Vesuvius, 163 ; eruption of, 240, 242, 245 ; ascent of, 241

Viaduct, remarkable railway, 186
Vietri, 237
Vigo, 182 ; unwholesome water of, 203
Vine-growing, 195
Virgin Mary, St. Luke's portrait of, 301
Volo, gulf of, 48
Voting at the bayonet's point, 133
Vyner, Mr., scene of his murder, 44

WARREN, Colonel, 258
Warships, Italian, 233
Watchmen, Spanish, 183
Waterspouts, 150
Whales, 7
White, Colonel, 281, 337
Whittaker, Mr., 364, 365
Wight, Isle of, 3, 178
Williams, Sir Fenwick, 24, 26
Williamson, Mr. and Mrs., 337
Wine, Greek, 42 ; manufacture of, in Cyprus, 257, 300
Wolseley, Sir Garnet, 267, 277, 293 ; invitation to camp from, 260 ; meeting with, 295
Wood, Captain, 267
Wood, Mr., excavations of, 121
Woodcocks, 142

XERES, 195

YASHMAK, law of the, 104
Yeni-liman, 378
Yildiz kiosk, 336

ZANTE, 35, 129
Zoophytes, luminous, 7

www.ingramcontent.com/pod-product-compliance
Lightning Source LLC
Chambersburg PA
CBHW051843300426
44117CB00006B/257